Disabled Chilc

Disabled Children's Childhood Studies

Critical Approaches in a Global Context

Edited by

Tillie Curran
University of the West of England, UK

and

Katherine Runswick-Cole
Manchester Metropolitan University, UK

First published 2013 by
PALGRAVE MACMILLAN

Palgrave Macmillan in the UK is an imprint of Macmillan Publishers Limited,
registered in England, company number 785998, of Houndmills, Basingstoke,
Hampshire RG21 6XS.

Palgrave Macmillan in the US is a division of St Martin's Press LLC,
175 Fifth Avenue, New York, NY 10010.

Palgrave Macmillan is the global academic imprint of the above companies
and has companies and representatives throughout the world.

Palgrave® and Macmillan® are registered trademarks in the United States,
the United Kingdom, Europe and other countries.

ISBN 978-1-349-43555-5   ISBN 978-1-137-00822-0 (eBook)
DOI 10.1057/9781137008220

A catalogue record for this book is available from the British Library.

A catalog record for this book is available from the Library of Congress.

Typeset by MPS Limited, Chennai, India.

For my children Joe, Fin and Bonnie,
In loving memory of my sister, Claire Cykowska

Tillie Curran

For my children William and Imogen,
In loving memory of my father, Adrian Runswick

Katherine Runswick-Cole

Contents

Preface

The purpose of the book

This book is about 'disabled children's childhood studies'. Its primary purpose is to centre our attention on the experiences of disabled children and young people and to develop theories about their childhoods. As editors, we have enjoyed reading the chapters in this book. They have demanded us to think differently about disabled children's childhood studies. We hope that you will also enjoy these chapters and that they will inspire you to think and, perhaps, act in productive ways that recognize the potential of disabled children's childhood studies to act as a lens that enables us to think positively and productively about all children's lives.

The background and approach

The process and identity relations involved in bringing this book to publication have been influential from its origin. The idea for an edited collection of studies came about through the editors' engagement with a series of conferences called Child, Youth, Family & Disability (2008 – present). The conferences were held by The Research Institute for Health and Social Change at Manchester Metropolitan University (MMU) and were organized by Katherine Runswick-Cole, Dan Goodley, Anat Greenstein, Pat Humphries, Rebecca Lawthom, China Mills, Damian Milton, Amanda Morgan and Jenny Slater with the support of other colleagues and students at MMU. The editors made contact there and met several of the authors in Manchester as well as at other inter/national conferences about disability and childhood. The Child, Youth, Family & Disability conferences draw together academics, disabled children and their families, and professionals to talk about the issues that affect their lives. Professionals are welcomed at the conference and their presence is, of course, valued, but the aim is that they do not lead or dominate the discussions – that role is taken by children, young people and families.

The editors and authors continue to play an active part in the above productive networks, and the approach taken in this book reflects the above relationships. We review and reflect on our learning arising from the writing process and the aims of the book in the concluding chapter.

The audience

The book is intended for undergraduate and postgraduate students, researchers and academics in disability studies, childhood studies, social work, health, social care and education. It will also be of interest to practitioners and policy-makers in those fields as well as parents/carers of disabled children and their families. By exploring the richness and potentials of disabled children's lives, we aim to inspire early career and experienced professionals in health, education and social care to think creatively about disabled children's lives. The discussion of the global context alongside examples of local research studies will challenge readers internationally to examine their own cultural assumptions and to bring a community development dimension to their thinking.

The aims of the book

Disabled children's childhood studies are very different from studies of child development or children's impairments. The book has the following three aims.

The first aim is to discuss and to develop the future agenda for disabled children's childhood studies. In order to address this aim, the book begins with first-hand accounts that are presented as Part I, *Voices for Creative theory, Policy and Practice*. These voices highlight the dynamic links between concepts, research and professional practices and childhoods that are explored in Part II, *Contemporary Inquiries* and Part III, *Contemporary Theories*. Disabled children provide stories about their lives, including their likes and dislikes, people and things that are important to them. Disabled adults provide reflections on their childhood and how those are part of their full adult lives. Family members of disabled children write about how living with a disabled child changes and challenges their beliefs and values, and leads them to question what it means to be a disabled child and, in turn, to question and to challenge the assumptions of others, including other parents/carers, family members, strangers and professionals working with their family. These stories are not simply about individual lives, rather they reveal the wider social, structural and cultural factors that shape disabled people's lives (Runswick-Cole & Goodley, 2012).

The second aim is to show how disabled children's childhood studies contribute to methodology and theory in this area, and more widely to the fields of childhood, disability and professional studies. Chapters in Part II, *Contemporary Inquiries*, discuss authors' choice of methods and the complex ethical issues involved when working with and listening to disabled children and young people. In Part III, *Contemporary Theories*, the chapters present contemporary theories that draw on such studies. A wide range of theories from critical disability studies, critical psychology and sociology are applied, and contemporary concerns around issues including resilience, embodiment and governance are extended.

The third aim of the book is to reflect on North/South global relations, the imposition of Western concepts of disability and childhood, and developments that engage with postcolonial theory. Each author considers their location and global political links so that the book offers an analytical approach to understanding global relations in relation to disabled children's childhoods. This includes how concepts of disability and childhoods historically and currently *globalize*; how inequalities felt by disabled children, young people and their families are global productions; and how global relations are also relations of resistance. This book is a product of global relations and networks, and authors here do not wish to make universal claims but intend a self-conscious, knowing partiality – that is to say, we know our voices will be limited and we intend to show the ways in which they are limited. We outline each chapter in a commentary for each part of the book and return to theses aims in the concluding chapter.

Tillie Curran and Katherine Runswick-Cole

Acknowledgements

We would like to thank: Dan Goodley, mentor and friend, for hearing our book idea and suggesting we do it; Andrew James, at Palgrave, for trusting that we would do it; and, most of all, the contributors for making this a profoundly enjoyable project.

With thanks to John Hooper and Jonathan Runswick-Cole for their love and support.

Notes on Contributors

The contributors to the book come from a diverse range of backgrounds and experiences. The authors are disabled children and family members sharing their experience; disabled and non-disabled researchers listening to disabled children; educator/trainers working towards changing practice; early career researchers and established academics theorizing disability and childhood. The authors reflect on disability in both the global North and global South and the points of intersection between them, and there are chapters that focus on Guatemala, Africa, Iceland and England.

David Abbott is a Reader in Social Policy at the Norah Fry Research Centre in the School for Policy Studies at the University of Bristol, UK. He has worked there since 1999 on a range of research projects relating to disabled children, young people and their families on topics including: residential schools and colleges, transition to adulthood, the experience of living with long-term conditions, the use of direct payments and other forms of personal budgets, access to childcare and the impact/benefits of multi-agency working.

Tsitsi Chataika is a lecturer in Special Educational Needs at the University of Zimbabwe. Her research interests include disability and gender mainstreaming in development processes, postcolonial theory and inclusive education. Her recent projects and publications address access to education in Africa; postcolonialism, disability and development; and social inclusion of persons with disabilities in poverty-reduction policies and instruments in Malawi and Uganda. She recently developed a gender and disability mainstreaming training manual, which will be used by various stakeholders in Africa and beyond.

Harriet Cooper is a doctoral candidate in the Department of English and Humanities at Birkbeck, University of London. Her research explores the figure of the disabled child in contemporary culture. Drawing on both her personal experience of growing up with a physical impairment, and on a wide range of cultural objects and texts, Harriet's work seeks to understand how the disabled child gets 'made' by culture, with a particular focus on the impact of gazes and discourses.

Tillie Curran is a senior lecturer in social work at the University of the West of England, and is interested in how social workers listen and respond creatively to disabled children and their families and use research. Her research focus is on the specific ways that discourses, support and relations between people can limit or generate energy to refocus, as shown by disabled children's childhood studies and the involvement of disabled children and adults in research and education as experts by experience.

Linda Derbyshire is an Honorary Research Fellow at Manchester Metropolitan University, UK, and the mother of a disabled young person. She has presented talks at Manchester Metropolitan University, the University of Leeds, Bradford College and Sheffield Hallam University, in the UK, focusing on inclusion.

Dan Goodley is Professor of Disability Studies and Education, School of Education at the University of Sheffield, UK. His research seeks to theorize and challenge disablism, and he has a particular interest in de-psychologizing teaching and practice. His recent publication offers an interdisciplinary introduction to disability studies. He is the Dad to two girls and is a Nottingham Forest Fan.

Shaun Grech is Research Fellow at the Research Institute for Health and Social Change, Manchester Metropolitan University, UK. He is Editor-in-chief of the international journal, *Disability and the Global South* (DGS). His research and publications cover disability and poverty in the Global South; colonialism and coloniality; decolonizing methodologies; intersectionalities; and interactions between theory and practice as a project of decolonizing pedagogy and praxis. He is an activist and has extensive field-level experience combining ethnographic work with practice with disabled people in extreme poverty in Guatemala.

Freyja Haraldsdóttir was born in 1986. She has a BA degree in social pedagogy from the University of Iceland and is now working towards a postgraduate diploma in equality studies from the same university. Freyja has worked in play schools and an elementary school, done public speaking at all education levels on the human rights of disabled people and was also a member of the Icelandic Constitutional Council. Freyja has done disability research and is the managing directress of the first and only personal assistance and independent living cooperative in Iceland. Freyja is now also taking her first steps in national politics and was recently elected to parliament as a part of a new political party in Iceland.

Rebecca Lawthom is Professor of Community Psychology, Department of Psychology at Manchester Metropolitan University, UK. She is a community psychologist and feminist, and has published in this area.

She is currently chair of the Psychology of Women section of the British Psychological Society. She is the mother to two girls and is proudly Welsh.

Judith McKenzie is a lecturer in Disability Studies at the University of Cape Town, South Africa. She has worked in rural areas of South Africa, particularly in the areas of inclusive education and family life. Her recent research relates to the development of sexuality among children with disabilities, and the role of parents and service providers in sexuality education of young disabled people. Her publications include articles about sexuality and disability, rights and ethics of care and intellectual disability in Africa, and the implications for research and service development.

Katherine Runswick-Cole is Senior Research Fellow in Disability Studies and Psychology at Manchester Metropolitan University, UK. Her research focuses on the lives of disabled children, young people and their families. Her work is influenced by her own family's experiences of disablism. She has published extensively in the area.

Sonali Shah is Lord Kelvin Research Fellow at Strathclyde Centre for Disability Research at Glasgow University. Her research adopts different qualitative methodologies to examine the impact of public policy and practices on private lives of disabled people over historical time and in a national and international context. This includes an interplay of biography and historical policy analysis, and also performative methods to transmit social-scientific disability research to school-age audiences. She is the author of *Career Success of Disabled High-flyers* and *Young Disabled People: Aspirations, Choices and Constraints*. She teaches about disability issues across different level programmes, including social policy, education, psychology and medicine.

Jo Skitteral is Head of Learning and Development for SeeAbility, a national charity that works for disabled adults across the South of England. She brings the experiences as a disabled woman, social worker and having been a disability equality trainer.

Jenny Slater is a lecturer in Education and Disability Studies at Sheffield Hallam University, UK. Her doctoral work with young disabled people drew on critical disability studies frameworks to consider the cultural constructions of 'youth' and 'disability'. Jenny is also interested in how youth and disability 'play out' with other intersectional identities, particularly as they relate to gender and sexuality.

Billie Tyrie talks about life with her sister, Stevie. Her presentation formed a part of the fourth Child, Youth, Family & Disability Conference

xvi   *Notes on Contributors*

held at the Research Institute of Health and Social Change at Manchester Metropolitan University in May 2012.

Stevie Tyrie is five years old and lives with her family in a city suburb in the north-west of the country. Stevie originally told her story as part of a research project that one of the editors of this book, Katherine, was carrying out at the Research Institute for Health and Social Change at Manchester Metropolitan University with Scope, the UK disability charity. The *Resilience in the lives of disabled people across the life-course* project was carried out between September 2011 and September 2012 in England.

Part I
Voices for Creative Theory, Policy and Practice

The chapters in Part I provide the 'call for the book' from disabled children, their families and disabled adults reflecting on their childhoods. The authors have all been involved in thinking about and shaping the agendas for disabled children.

In Chapter 1, Stevie Tyrie tells us about her life, the things she likes, the things she doesn't. She tells us what a 'bad' day would be for her but also what would make the day better, and she tells us what she thinks people around her need to know about her. Stevie's story is given a context by Katherine, who explains how Stevie's story was created with Stevie and her family. The chapter also reflects more widely on resilience in the lives of disabled children.

In Chapter 2, Billie Tyrie, Stevie's sister, tells us her story. The story is based on a presentation given by Billie at the Child, Youth, Family and Disability Conference at Manchester Metropolitan University in May 2012. Billie tells us more than about her relationship with her sister as she also offers some considered advice for people working with disabled children.

Chapter 3, Freyja Haraldsdóttir tells us about growing up in the shadow of the 'norm'. Freyja describes how she negotiated, with the support of her parents, her identity as a disabled young woman. Her story clearly illustrates the barriers she faced and the power of adults over disabled children's lives and their failure to listen. She urges us to recognize that disabled children are 'simply children'.

Chapter 4, Jo Skitteral reflects on her experiences as a disabled child and the impact they have had on her life as an adult. She challenges us to think 'outside the problem box' of disability and to throw some 'pebbles into the pond' in the hope that the ripples will challenge people

1

to think again more positively and creatively about the lives of disabled children.

In Chapter 5, Linda Derbyshire describes her experiences as a mother of a disabled young woman. She picks up on the challenge to rethink disabled children's childhoods as she explains how she has fought to make sure that expectations for her daughter Hannah were high. Using the very powerful metaphor of the mug and the teacup, she explains how she has fought other people's low expectations of Hannah, and other disabled children, and demanded that she should never be given a mug, always a teacup and saucer.

1
My Story

*Stevie and Cath, Colin and Billie Tyrie with scribing,
introduction and reflection section by Katherine Runswick-Cole*

Introduction

This chapter is Stevie's story about her life as a disabled child in
England. Stevie is five years old and lives with her family in a city suburb in the North-West of the country. Stevie originally told her story as
part of a research project that one of the editors of this book, Katherine,
was carrying out at the Research Institute for Health and Social Change
at Manchester Metropolitan University with Scope, the UK disability
charity, called *Resilience in the lives of disabled people across the life-course*
carried out between September 2011 and July 2012 in England. The
project had a number of aims:

- to explore what resilience means to disabled people at different
  stages across the life course;
- to explore how resilience, or a lack of it, has affected disabled people's ability to negotiate challenges and make the most of opportunities in their lives;
- to understand what works in building resilience among different
  groups of disabled people;
- to develop a toolkit for use by Scope's policy and services functions
  that outlines what Scope means by resilience, what does or doesn't
  work in supporting people to become resilient, and what we can do
  to build resilience in disabled people throughout the life course.

These aims were explored through four phases of the research project:
a literature review; a life story phase; a focus group phase; and a
Community of Practice phase (Lave & Wenger, 1991) in which disabled
people and researchers worked together to produce a toolkit for use by

Scope in their service delivery. Full details of the project, recruitment, methods, findings and outputs from the project, including research reports, can be found in Runswick-Cole and Goodley (2013).

Stevie participated in the life story phase of the research. We adopted a narrative approach to the interviews. Life story methods have been used extensively in research with disabled people and their allies (Booth & Booth, 1998; Goodley, Lawthom, Clough & Moore, 2004; Goodley & Runswick-Cole, 2011; Runswick-Cole, 2007). The approach to life story research taken by the research team was underpinned by the belief that disabled people are experts in their own lives and that it is possible for all disabled people (who want to), including children, to participate in research (Goodley & Runswick-Cole, 2012). Crucially, here, disabled people are not seen as simply subjects of research but as active participants in the research process. And so, the participants were invited to talk about aspects of their lives that addressed the resilience research project aims, but they were also encouraged to share aspects of their lives that were important to them (Runswick-Cole & Goodley, 2013).

Life stories are rich and thick accounts of people's lived experiences offering unique insights into personal worlds (Goodley et al., 2004), but they also move beyond individual narratives, giving access to the contemporary social, political, policy, service, community and familial contexts in which the stories were framed. Stories are never simply about individual lives; they also reveal the wider social, structural and cultural factors that shape disabled people's lives (Runswick-Cole & Goodley, 2013).

Participants in the project were recruited from throughout the North-West region of England and from a range of urban and rural locations between November 2011 and March 2012. Information about the research was disseminated via a range of organizations including: disability-specific support organizations, pan-disability organizations, parents' groups, carers' groups, disability mailing lists and by word-of-mouth. Stevie's parents heard about the project through a voluntary organization, and they talked to Stevie and to Billie about the family being involved in participating.

The research team took seriously the imperative to listen sensitively to children (Morris, 2003). We aimed to respond to their different communication styles in the interviews. We drew on the principles of the Mosaic Approach (Clark, McQuali & Moss, 2003), and used pictures, tours and drawings to support the interview process. Some children, including Stevie, chose to be interviewed with their parents/carers/ siblings. Where this is what the children wanted, we adopted what we termed a 'distributed methodology' (Runswick-Cole & Goodley, 2013). A 'distributed methodology' meant that we aimed to combine ethically, sensitively and carefully the perspectives of the child with those of significant others in their lives.

We were cautious about adopting such an approach, not least because we are aware of research that has prioritized the views of children's proxies over the views of disabled children themselves. So we sought to address the potential dangers here of adults' and siblings' stories dominating disabled children's accounts. While we acknowledged these dangers, we hoped that the richness of narratives was further enhanced through the bringing in of disparate, distributed but interconnected voices.

From ethical approval to voice

Katherine met members of the Tyrie family a total of four times. Each time Katherine met with Stevie, she was constantly checking that Stevie was continuing to give her assent to the interview (Cocks, 2006). This involved watching Stevie closely to see if she was tired or fed up, checking with her and with her family that she was happy to continue, and that the interviews were conducted in a way in which the questions were clear to her and at a pace that she was happy with.

Stevie and her family decided that they were happy to tell the story using their names and as co-authors of the story, but the names of other people mentioned in the story have been changed to protect their anonymity. As a research team, we saw ethics as an active process rather than something that is signed off at the start of the research project (Cocks, 2006). As co-authors of this chapter the family are shaping the research process and are involved in creating the opportunity for the an approach that aims to give *ethical voice*.

Stevie's story (told by Stevie Tyrie with Cath, Colin and Billie Tyrie)

My name is Stevie, I am five years old and I got a special school. I was born a bit too early and I like crawling and using my buggy. I live with my mum, dad and my sister, Billie, who is eight.

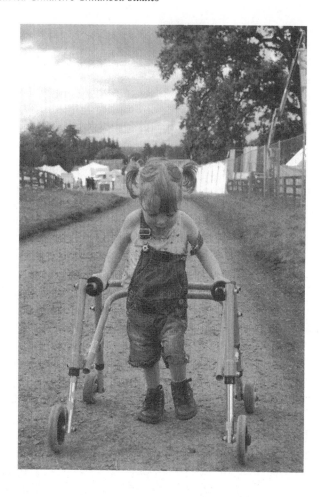

I love my mum and my dad and my sister very much. I have a best friend called Dan and I really like Dean, the head teacher at my school, Lily, my teaching assistant, Louise, my dinner lady and Mary the lady from [the voluntary organization] who takes me out.

People say that I am funny and kind and loving and good at listening. I like being tickled. I like playing with my sister – we play teachers. I like sitting on my sister's lap. I like being read to and I like singing, but I don't like it when other people join in. I like *Charlie and Lola*, *The Little Princess*, chocolate, bananas, *Pig goes pop!* and turning my light on and off.

I also like being in the garden, digging in the mud, getting messy and growing things.

And I like going to eat fish and chips at the furniture store's cafe.

I like learning about colours and numbers and matching games. I like stories and I like dressing up and pretending to be a princess, or a fairy, a nurse or Frankenstein or a dentist. I want to be a dentist when I grow up.

I don't like the noise of hand driers. I don't like busy places with lots of people. And I don't like the sound of the toilet flushing. I don't like the squeak of balloons or the sound of them popping and I don't like bumble bees, or wasps or flies because they buzz. And I don't like mashed potato.

I also don't like it if someone pushes me in my wheelchair by someone who hasn't asked me if they can and I don't like being tipped out of my wheelchair!

A bad day for me would mean I had to get up early and eat all my breakfast. I would have to get dressed and wear my splints. I wouldn't be able to wash my hands or to get muddy. I would have to go to crowded places where people flushed toilets and used hand driers. And then I would have to go to a place where a balloon would pop and be taken out for tea at a place I didn't know.

But, my day would be made better if I could watch a favourite DVD and have a cuddle.

If you want to support me, you can learn about all the things I like and don't like, like toilets and hand driers. You can be quiet and cuddly. You must listen to me and get down to my level if you want to talk to me. Don't talk for too long and sometimes you might need to explain things to me a bit more. You need to tell me what is going to happen and prepare me for new things, showing me a picture can help. And don't forget my biscuit at bedtime!

So, to remind you of the things that are important to me and for me:

- My mum, my dad and my sister
- My friends and people at school
- That you know about things I like and don't like
- That you are calm, quiet and kind to me
- That you listen to me
- That you help me to do the things I enjoy.

Reflections on Stevie's story

Stevie's story stands for itself; it paints a vivid picture of one disabled child's likes/dislikes, favourite pastimes and least favourite things. And yet, although this is the story of the life of one disabled child in England, it reveals themes that are, perhaps, important for all dis/abled children: family; school; friends; music; food; toys; play; shopping; learning; being listened to; and having choices

Stevie's story teaches us that resilience is not something that a disabled child simply has or doesn't have. Resilience is a process and not an end point. Stevie's resilience is negotiated in her relationships with other people and with the environment (Runswick-Cole & Goodley, 2013). Stevie feels resilient when she has her family around her, supportive friends and teachers, mud, singing and *Charlie and Lola* (a children's television programme).

This understanding of resilience is different from 'common sense' understandings of resilience in childhood that focus on an individual children's ability to 'bounce back' or to 'do well' in spite of difficult circumstances (Masten, 2001). It is also a view of resilience that challenges that assumption that to be resilient a child must conform to developmental and societal norms. Stevie's story reveals that to be a resilient disabled child does not always mean doing what non-disabled children do.

Stevie's resilience is revealed in her story. Her likes and dislikes are clearly articulated, and the important people and things in her life are shared. And yet Stevie's story also touches on threats to her resilience, including: her growing awareness that her body is perceived 'differently' from other children's bodies; people who help, but don't ask; and difficult environments, including those with noisy hand driers and crowds. Sadly, these threats illustrate the disabling attitudes and barriers that disabled children meet in childhood.

Reflections on research methods

Stevie reminds us of the importance of listening to disabled children in research, in professional practice and in the home. Stevie's story allows us to reflect on our aim to give *ethical voice* through the use of a 'distributed' story. The research team strived to present Stevie's story carefully and sensitively in collaboration with her and her family. We have already described how we attempted to avoid adults' and siblings' accounts dominating the voice of the disabled child. However, we were also aware, as Clark et al. (2003) remind us, that the more imaginative the methods we use in listening to children, the greater the danger that we are invading children's private worlds for our own purposes as adult researchers (Clark et al., 2003). This is a particularly sensitive issue for

a group of children who already experience heightened levels of surveillance from the professions (including teachers, social workers, psychologists, doctors – among others) (Goodley & Runswick-Cole, 2012).
We sought to address this issue by working with Stevie and her family to
make sure that they were happy with how the story was shared.
Stevie's story teaches us much about the life of a disabled child in
England, but it also teaches us about the wider challenges and opportunities that working with disabled children in research can bring.

References

Booth, T. & Booth, W. (1998) *Growing up with parents who have learning difficulties* (London: Routledge).
Clark, A., McQuail, S. & Moss, P. (2003) *Exploring the field of listening to and consulting with young children*, RB 445 (London: DfES).
Cocks, A. (2006) 'The ethical maze: Finding an inclusive path to gaining children's agreement to research participation', *Childhood*, 26, 13, 247–266.
Goodley, D. & Runswick-Cole, K. (2011) 'The violence of disablism', *Journal of Sociology of Health and Illness*, 33, 4, 602–617.
Goodley, D. & Runswick-Cole, K. (2012) 'Decolonizing methodologies: Disabled children as research managers and participant ethnographers', in S. Grech & A. Azzopardi (eds) (2012) *Communities: A Reader* (Rotterdam: Sense Publishers).
Goodley, D., Lawthom, R., Clough, P. & Moore, M. (2004) *Researching life stories: Method, theory and analyses in a biographical age* (London/New York: Routledge Falmer).
Lave, J. & Wenger, E. (1991) *Situated Learning: Legitimate peripheral participation* (Cambridge: Cambridge University Press).
Masten, A.S. (2001) 'Ordinary magic: Resilience processes in development', *American Psychologist*, 56, 3, 227–238.
Morris, J. (2003) 'Including all children: Finding out about the experiences of children with communication and/or cognitive impairments', *Children & Society*, 17, 337–348.
Runswick-Cole, K. (2007) '"The Tribunal was the most stressful thing: More stressful than my son's diagnosis or behaviour": The experiences of families who go to the Special Educational Needs and Disability Tribunal (SENDIST)', *Disability & Society*, 22, 3, 315–328.
Runswick-Cole, K. & Goodley, D. (2013) *Life Story Report: Resilience in the lives of disabled people across the life course* (London: Scope). Online at: http://disability-resilience.posterous.com [accessed 7 January 2013].

2
My Sister Stevie

Billie Tyrie

Introduction written by Katherine Runswick-Cole

This is chapter is based upon a presentation given by Billie talking about life with her sister, Stevie. The presentation formed a part of the fourth Child, Youth, Family and Disability Conference held at the Research Institute of Health and Social Change at Manchester Metropolitan University in May 2012. The aim of the conference is to bring together disabled children, young people, their families, allies, practitioners and academics to share their perspectives and to celebrate disabled children's lives. Billie took up this theme in her chapter and challenges us to think differently about disabled children.

My sister Stevie

My name is Billie and I am eight years old. I have a little sister, Stevie, who is five. Stevie has cerebral palsy, or, as I used to say when I was little, 'terrible palsy'! Stevie can't walk and she understands the world a little bit differently from most of us.

Here are some good points about being Stevie's sister.

- Stevie is funny and cheers me up
- Stevie is sweet
- Stevie plays with me
- Stevie listens to me
- Stevie is pleased to see me (most of the time!)
- And likes nearly everyone she meets (as long as they don't wind her up!).

Here are some bad points about being Stevie's
sister. She ...

- screams and shouts
- throws things at me
- doesn't listen
- gets frustrated
- is VERY bossy
- sometimes hurts me
- is REPETITIVE (a lot)
- and snores (very loudly!).

I used to think that our family was the same as every other family and
they all had a disabled child.

It took a while to figure out that not EVERYONE has one!

I am writing this chapter because I want to point out that disabled
children are different. ... Sometimes they look a bit different. ... And
sometimes they think a bit differently. ... BUT disabled children have
the same feelings, likes, dislikes, hopes and dreams as other children.

People often don't understand this and it makes me very sad. Sometimes
when people meet my sister they stare or point, they laugh or shout
names, they look scared and ignore her or even run away!

But one day, when we went to the aquarium, my mum, my dad and I were sitting down a little way away from Stevie. Stevie was looking at the fish in the tank and a little girl came over and started talking to her. She asked Stevie's name and told Stevie that she was called Ella. Stevie and Ella talked about the fish and which ones they liked best. Stevie told Ella all about being born too early and explained why she was in a wheelchair. Ella told her Stevie she would be her friend. When we got home Stevie said it was the best day ever!

It would really make me and Stevie so happy if people treated Stevie like this little girl did.

So here are some of the ways that might help people to do that. Together we can ...

Listen to disabled children and learn from them.	Hold disability days using wheelchairs, blindfolds and ear muffs.	Have a special buddy system where children get to know disabled children.
Invite teachers to disability days in special schools.	Ask disabled children to talk about their lives in schools.	Hold self-portrait art competitions
Hold story competitions about disabled children.	Include disabled children more in clubs.	Celebrate disability history month – everywhere!
	Treat disabled children with respect!	

3
Simply Children

Freyja Haraldsdóttir

Clueless

I was born 27th of June 1986. Three weeks later my parents took me home from the hospital, completely clueless about what the future would hold for us, I am their first child. With only dramatic and terrifying information from the doctors about my *'severe'* impairment and that my life was a ticking time bomb, my parents were supposed to be confident and help themselves in their new role as parents of a disabled (said to be dying) little girl. Even though all this was terrifying for them, and my family as a whole, they soon decided that my impairment was not going to control our lives. They tried to push away the constant reminder from health professionals that my life wouldn't be very long; I wasn't sick and didn't seem to be interested in anything else other than being a part of this world. They wanted me to be able to live life to the fullest and experience the same things as my peers would. They were soon eager not to over-protect me; they let other people babysit me, took me overseas, with them to work in their flower shop and to anywhere they would have taken me if I hadn't been physically impaired.

When I became a bit older and started talking and asking questions (which was way too early from my parents' point of view) they decided that it was not their place to force upon me the fact that I had an impairment or because of it I should behave in some particular way. I therefore had great intentions and dreams. I told everyone who wanted to hear that I was going to play soccer, learn to dance, have children, work in a shop and get my driver's licence when I turned seventeen. If I was asked why I couldn't walk I replied without hesitation, 'well, I will walk when I grow up'. Even though my parents knew that some of these expectations were very unrealistic, they wanted me to find out my limitations myself. Even though it would hurt, I should be the one to find out when I was ready and if I needed to. As they often said, 'we didn't have a clue about what you would be able to do, so who were we to tell you?' I didn't realize about my impairment, or at least found it as normal as having glasses, blonde hair or brown eyes. I even thought that breaking a bone a few times a month was what everyone did.

But not everyone agreed. As soon as my family needed to be in contact with professionals like physiotherapists, occupational therapists, psychologists, doctors and teachers on a daily basis because of therapy, the diagnostic period and analyzing of my impairment, it was clear that they thought my parents were out of their minds raising me as a child – not a physical impairment.

The great burden

I was a really happy child. I loved having a lot of things to do and being around many people. One of my favourite things was to go with my parents to work where I could boss them around and talk to the customers of the flower shop like it was my own. I did not hate being the centre of attention and therefore did not hesitate telling jokes and putting up all kinds of shows at birthday parties and family gatherings with my cousins. I was of course often in pain from bone fractures, but when I look back I don't remember much of it – my parents worked very hard to not to make a fuss of it or be to dramatic even though they of course comforted me when I was feeling frustrated and tired from all the physical pain.

What shadowed our family's otherwise great life together was usually communicating (or struggling) with the professionals and the service system as a whole. It began for real when my parents wanted me to go to an inclusive play school, not a special one for disabled children. They went to one meeting after another listening to teachers explain that being there would be too dangerous for me, that I would only feel vulnerable and other children would be uncomfortable with me around. A year went by until I was finally accepted to my nearest play school; it was like my parents were trying to get their three-year-old daughter into Oxford University. We had to spend a lot of time at the Icelandic Diagnostic and Counselling Centre for disabled children. The main goal from their point of view seemed to revolve around making me as 'normal' as possible. The physiotherapy was all about being able to sit up and hold my head from the ground while lying on my stomach. It didn't matter that it hurt like hell to sit up right, broke bones in my back and lifting my head was pointless because I didn't like lying on my stomach all the time with my face to the floor. The shape of my wheelchair seat was supposed to force my legs into positions that would make them straight (and normal), even though it resulted in me not being able to use my wheelchair when I had a broken bone or was tired in my body, which was often. I even went through surgery where all the bones in my arms and legs were broken up so it was possible to straighten them. I was in hospital for many weeks because of all the pain (morphine didn't even do the trick), it took me half a year to learn to do things I could to before my hands were made straight and a year to become just as bent as before the surgery because of all the new fractures. All this was for making the freak-looking child a bit more like the cute non-disabled ones showed in on TV ads.

Because of how painful this was I was so afraid to go to physiotherapy that I couldn't sleep at night and woke up with nightmares; I tried to lie about being sick (which I sometimes was from stress) and threw tantrums before leaving from home, in the car and in the car park at the centre. To protest even harder I stopped speaking in situations where I didn't feel safe or felt humiliated – which was usually with the professionals. My parents knew why this was happening because I only did this in particular situations, I often begged them to stop the physiotherapist from hurting me and told them that I hated to answer the 'childish questions' from the psychologist. I simply was trying to refuse these situations. My parents tried to discuss this with the professionals, but they wouldn't listen and diagnosed me instead with selective mutism (which is a anxiety disorder that makes children stop to speak in particular situations for no obvious reasons), and of course judged me as both too demanding and misbehaving.

At every meeting with professionals, the problems and difficulties always seemed to outweigh the positive factors, and there never seemed to be anything good to say about my existence. In a file from the from the Icelandic Diagnostic and Counselling Centre for disabled children about me a doctor wrote:

> The prognosis for such children is that they continue to be equally fragile. They can hardly be touched without risk of a fracture, and thus all the care and handling of these children is one of the most difficult tasks faced by health professionals dealing with disabled children – not to mention the great burden placed on the parents of a child who is in such a bad shape.

My parents became absolutely defeated by the negativity they encountered there. This did not fit very well with my parents' decision about me being raised as a child and not a physical impairment. As time went by they found it almost intolerable to have to meet with innumerable doctors, psychologists, physiotherapists and occupational therapists.

We were constantly being reminded of abnormality, negativity, defects and helplessness. There was rarely any consciousness of what we were like, our talents, progress or ability. I was disabled, and my progress was measured in baby steps. My inabilities outweighed my abilities. They said I had to be able to do more and that often I did not try hard enough. Opportunities simply to enjoy life on our own terms, and rejoice in being alive, were rare. And at regular intervals we were taken back to be reminded that I was disabled, that I wasn't normal. And that not to be normal was awful. The more often they met these people the harder it was for them to believe in themselves and in me. Therefore it was more difficult for me to be happy.

Being like *this*

It came a time when my parents decided they had had enough and slowly lessened the times going to the Diagnostic and Counselling Centre. The professionals, even though some of them were helpful, took more from our family than they gave, and seemed to push me further and further towards social exclusion rather than inclusion. A psychiatrist suggested that my parents should apply for me as soon as possible to live in a group home for children since I had already become such a burden, and also saw nothing more obvious that I would go to a special school or a school with a special unit for disabled students. My parents couldn't stomach more and decided to follow their heart and hope for the best.

When I started at my neighbourhood school I first remember realizing that I was maybe a bit different from my peers. I had good assistance at school and made friends fast, was a quick learner and enjoyed school hours a lot. Very soon I became aware that this *difference* had a name: *disabled*. All of a sudden children were staring at me in the hallway, asking questions, giving remarks on how I looked and wondering if they should dare talk to me or not.

One boy in my class came up to me one day and whispered 'I have a crush on you ... even though you are like this'. My first reaction was disgust because I DID NOT WANT A BOY TO HAVE A CRUSH ON ME, but then the 'even though you are like this' part hit me. What was he saying? What did being 'like this' mean? Did it mean I was different? Did it mean I was not good enough for most boys? And the 'even though' part also confused me; would it be better if I could walk, stand up and look like the other girls? I had never got that message before. What would I then be *like*?

I also started feeling that others sometimes expected different things from me. It confused me because, though I was starting to understand that I was disabled, it was hard for me to see why it mattered. Also, it seemed like I soon let it control me, both what I did, said and thought. For example, when I was playing dolls with my friends when I was little I was always the father. Somehow it became a matter of fact that I couldn't be the mom because she had to dress the baby, feed it, put it to bed, give it a bath and hold it. But the dad, he just went to work, watched television and told off the kids when they were misbehaving for their mother. That I could do. Very soon I didn't expect any other role and offered to be the dad to prevent embarrassing moments – moments of children glancing at each other thinking: 'how is *she* going to *hold* the baby?' I secretly played the mother when I was playing on my own. I used to have small dolls that I could hold and remember wishing that real babies could also be so small. I needed mom to help me dress it, but I thought that would be fine, she wouldn't mind dressing my babies when I was a grown up. Obviously, since I knew no babies were so small in real life, I decided I was not fit to be a mother. I really wanted to, but that was *my* secret.

Although this realization of difference came mostly from communicating with the children the school, staff increasingly made me feel different. I soon felt that many adults, both parents of other children and teachers, were surprised that I was in school and able to learn. Therefore I became quite obsessed with getting good grades. I wanted to show everyone that I was just as good as the others, preferably better. I also felt that everyone expected me to be well behaved and innocent. One of my biggest dreams became going to the principal's office for misbehaving, probably because I always got away with much more then my peers. I was never stopped by the teacher no matter how much I talked while the teacher was talking and laughed while I was supposed to be studying. As I realized this I started challenging them by being rude, turning up late and not doing what I was supposed to. But it didn't work – the teachers didn't see it and my dream of going to the principal's office did not come true.

The asexual closet

When I became near my teenage years I started to be more self-conscious about my label. I found it difficult to find fashionable clothes and to participate in the activities my peers did. Everything started to revolve around how you looked, how your body was changing and who you had a crush on.

Since I didn't find many cool clothes and my body didn't seem to follow the rules of the 'one and only girl body' I felt out of place talking to and about boys. I decided that since I wasn't 'normal' enough I better just not think about them or get my hopes up. It didn't help that my friends did not expect me to talk about boys, and if I did they became uncomfortable. In teaching nothing whatsoever brought out people's diversity, and when learning about the body and sexuality it was always the Barbie and Ken kinds of bodies. Different bodies were not to be discussed. I, for example, was so devoted to not getting my hopes up, that when I was asked by a classmate to go with him to a dance, I was certain that he was only asking to make fun of me – so I said no, loud and clearly. It turned out I was wrong; he was not making a joke. I did that all by myself.

These feelings kept growing inside me, and when I was about fifteen years old I was disgusted by myself. No matter how hard I tried to be 'normal' I just felt like a failure. I became terrified of not being accepted as a human being and as a woman. I did not feel like one, and to make me feel better I just hid in my asexual closet, pretending not to care.

At family gatherings I often felt the worst. Relatives asked my cousins, who were at similar age, about their future plans, whether they had a boyfriend, if they were going overseas and what they were planning on doing after college. I wasn't asked a thing. I remember being astonished this one time when a distant relative asked me if I was seeing someone and what plans I had after graduation. I almost fell out of my chair of surprise. But it felt good, being cross-questioned, just this once.

At this very same time I felt that having to rely on my parents and friends for all the assistance I needed started to become more disabling. I was not able to participate in the social life of my friends, I didn't want my parents there, and felt that my needs were starting to be a barrier in the relationship with my friends who were also teenagers and busy with their own lives. I became scared about what would happen to me when my family and friends couldn't assist me any more, and if I would be able to study at the university, live independently, have a family and a career. The service system, that I needed to use more and more, was designed by the professionals and was often more limiting than enabling. What the service system also did was to keep me out of all discussions concerning myself as long as they possibly could, despite the fact that I had very strong opinions about how I wanted my services to function from an early age. But I felt that it was none of my business. So there I was, the girl who didn't recognize her impairment from an early age, hating my body, terrified of the future, obsessed on my abnormalities and kept the doors of the asexual closet closed as my life was at stake for it.

Coming out

Years have passed and things have changed. Today I have personal assistance, rent my own apartment, have finished an undergraduate university degree, work as a managing directress at the first and only personal assistance cooperative in Iceland, participate in disability research and have run for parliament. On 28 April 2013, I became the deputy parliamentarian in my constituency for my party. This means that I deputize for the member of parliament in his absence. I haven't started a family but I am confident that I will. It is a decision I have made and will stick to it. It is not my little secret any more. Obviously, I wouldn't be doing any of this if I still felt like ten years ago, hiding in my asexual closet. This change didn't happen by itself. I had to work very hard to build up the courage to feel more secure in all aspects of life and start to peek out of the closet – to see what was there.

When I was eighteen years old I went with my family to a conference in the United States for people with Osteogenesis imperfecta. I had mixed feelings towards it since I barely knew a disabled person and didn't want to be categorized among them, but it turned out to be the best thing I had ever experienced. I met people in similar situations who were doing the things I was afraid I couldn't do. They were working on the open labour market, going to university, moving away from their parents, getting married and starting families. This was possible for many of them because they had user-controlled personal assistance with direct payment. I came home with so many questions answered, real role models to look up to and remind me where I was heading. I also applied for personal assistance around the clock that was fully accepted after a great struggle seven years later. Through that I came across human rights activists and got to know the independent living movement. Now working towards independence for disabled people in Iceland is my job.

In this time I have also got to know disability studies and gender studies. I first read about disability studies in my college years when I was preparing an essay on disability. Within thousands of articles about medical definitions on impairments there was a PowerPoint presentation on the social model of disability. Even though it wasn't a detailed piece I was so relieved reading something that focused on disability as a consequence of social barriers, like discrimination, physical environment, attitudes, lack of assistance, and so on. Since I had usually blamed myself and my abnormalities for everything that went wrong in my life, getting to know disability studies was a way to understand myself all over again, be aware of society's responsibilities and focus more on my rights as a human being. Gender studies I got to know more in university not so long ago, and I got a similar feeling. Feeling that I didn't have to blame myself for not being good enough.

I have come to realize that the most disabling factors in my life are the structures of society, the oppression of stereotypes, the power of the majority who decides who is good enough or who is fit for what. In a way it set me free from taking the blame and hiding in the closet as a human being and a woman. I now try to challenge many of these preconceived ideas about 'being like this' by not living the stereotype and start conversations that make non-disabled people (e.g. relatives) and even some disabled people uncomfortable. I make a political decision every morning, for instance, to dress up and put make up on because that way I am imposing my gender upon many people who look at me as asexual.

By doing this I am not only challenging others, but most importantly, also myself. I still get the tense eye glances when talking about having children or being in a relationship. I still go through days where I just can't stand what I see in the mirror and believe I will never be good enough. It still crosses my mind, when a male human being pays me attention, that he is either making fun of me or feeling sorry for me. I still get scared when thinking about what attitudes I will face when I will take my future son or daughter to their first day at school.

So, in a way, I'm still in the closet. But I have opened the closet, peeked out and will hopefully soon step out of it and shut the doors behind me. Because even though my body is not to blame for me not being treated as a person and a woman, I'm responsible for treating myself like one.

Simply children

When I was little my mother was very often asked if she was raising me as a disabled or a non-disabled child, which she found quite amusing. 'I am just raising a child' she always replied, half laughing. I think no matter what it has been the most important factor in my life. My parents refused to impose my impairment on me and gave me freedom to develop my identity without a consistent reminder that I was not able or something less. It would probably have hurt me more having someone telling me all the time to not get my hopes up about the future since I would probably never have one. For that reason I did not realize that I was disabled until later. I got to be a real person, not the girl in the wheelchair watching my life go by without having anything to do with it. I am thankful that my parents went through with it despite being forced in some ways by professionals to *disable* me by diagnosing them as parents in denial. I remember this was not an easy task for them to follow their heart and stop listening to the professionals that society seems to teach them to believe in no matter what. Also I am thankful that my parents never treated me as a burden on them or my younger brothers, but instead pointed out that the burden was the structure of society and lack of support, understanding, access and assistance.

As I have explained, the messages were mixed from home and from outer surroundings. When I started to feel different and blaming myself for it, my parents always kept on reminding me that my impairment didn't matter, my right should be the same as any other person and that I should not expect anything less than my non-disabled friends at school. I often did not believe them because other messages became so loud about me being 'like this' that should define my future and myself. I am convinced that even though I found my parents speaking nonsense when I was a teenager and was sure they were only saying encouraging things to make me feel better, it trickled in to my thoughts and somehow rooted somewhere in the back of my mind. My parents are still the ones who encourage me the most. Not always directly but just by being there and saying things that remind me that I am not the reason for society's problems.

A few years ago I was discussing to my parents that I wanted to move overseas to keep on studying, my father sighed and said with a smirk on his face, 'And how long will this take? You know; when on earth are you going to have time to have children? I was hoping to become a grandfather soon.' I remember being a bit surprised because I am not used to people talking about or pressuring me to start a family. But it put a smile on my face because it reminded me how my parents talked to me when I was little. There was never a question of me having a great future, because they saw me simply as a child and therefore a human being, capable of anything. Nothing more. Nothing less.

I believe the society's reaction to our impairments is what disables us the most. These reactions seem to come alive from the moment we are 'suspected' to have an impairment. Therefore suppression, exclusion and marginalization becomes scaringly normal and mundane in our lives. It is important to challenge these disabling reactions, both so parents have the courage to stand up for their children and so disabled children will not be violated the right to be human beings – not impairments. Simply children.

4

Transitions? An Invitation to Think Outside Y/our Problem Box, get Fire in Your Belly and Put Pebbles in the Pond

Jo Skitteral

Introduction

This chapter is written in the form of a particular process that I have developed through my own life and my current role in learning and development across the South of England. I bring the experiences as a disabled woman, social worker and having been a disability equality trainer. The process begins with questions. These are questions that I have found to be the basis for learning, questions that uproot expectations and invite us to think outside our 'problem box'. These questions are followed by two further steps around 'putting fire in your belly' to be creative, and then being active by 'putting pebbles in ponds' for further development on into the future. This is an invitation to try something new and to keep reflecting and being creative. The process finishes with a final question concerning 'how we know what we think we know?' This is about recognizing that there are various perspectives and asking how do we check out what we think we know and, especially, how do we know what a disabled child wants or might want once having the opportunities for trying things out and making real choices?

This chapter is an invitation to think outside the 'problem box', the 'problem box' that is often the starting point in statements made about disabled children and continues to be used throughout their lives. The chapter is about disabled children's childhoods. It is about disabled children whose childhoods and adulthoods are hugely influenced by the ways in which people behave towards them individually and as part of organizations etc. That is to say, the chapter is not about the experiences disabled adults have who have not been disabled children, and this distinction will be clear as the focus on disabled children's childhood unfolds below.

The process is illustrated with instances drawn from personal and professional life. For ethical reasons sources are not made recognizable. In the case of my own experience, what has been included has been shared with my family and they are happy for me to share my experiences.

I begin with some questions:

Why is having a disabled child always perceived as bad?

Why is diagnosis important? Why is it linked to 'bad news', 'good news' and benefits, services and everything else?

As soon as a baby is born, what is the first thing said by parents – is she or he healthy? This is especially the case if there were no 'concerns' picked up in pregnancy. We are still negative about disability in society. We are not ready to celebrate and value our disabled babies. This gives all of us, disabled people and non-disabled people, a strong message that, as the chapter will show, ripples out at many points throughout all our lives and is invariably vividly remembered and recalled very immediately. This question of our welcome is the starting point of our childhood and life.

Is my body 'bad'?

The emotive use of such language then goes on to be bad bits – 'bad legs', a 'bad back', as my doctors said. At two years old my Dr 'M', as I called him, tested my reflexes by holding me down and running his thumb up my bare foot. My mother was told I would not do anything, not walk – but at two, I walked naked down the hospital corridor to show them!

My early memories of the hospital have the smell of it, watching the TV hospital shows brings that back each time. When in the hospital with people who do not know me, it's still hard to feel in control. 'Oh', one doctor recently said, ' I did not think I would see you alive again.' I'm still practising what I will say to him. He makes a statement, but I always respond and I will be going back to say to him 'you have said this before'. I need to explain reality to him. 'I drive, life is risky, is my life riskier than yours – you fell off your bike!' The doctors say these things without stopping to take the time to think – they don't have to think about the consequence of what they are saying – they are 'experts'. I take time to work out what I need to say in response that will be a reality check for the doctor and be a pebble in the pond for their further thinking. His ease of making such comments comes from shared privilege where he does not have to think.

I know my doctor more now and he is getting an understanding ... pebbles I've given him. Here I am again being my doctor's doctor. I had to learn this skill because if I didn't I would accept that negative approach and it would limit every situation I am in. Although people do this type of 'protecting', the actual reality is that disabled children are often left with adult responsibility. They are living adult lives and are expected to function in an adult world and are not protected as a non-disabled child might be as a 'child' might be. So how is it that disabled children's adulthood is seen in a problem box and yet disabled children often take adult roles and responsibilities and, paradoxically, are kept outside of their own 'transitions' to adulthood? And in my work life I speak my mind, put my head above the parapet, ask questions – however challenging it might be ...

And when disabled children die where is the 'protection'?

In special schools disabled children are seen to be protected, if not 'over-protected'. In some special schools more than others, disabled children will have their own or their peers' experience of young people diagnosed as having limited life expectancy, serious health conditions or death. In my own experience in the 1980s no-one ever spoke to us children about that – the notion is disabled children are not psychologically the same as non-disabled children, we are not so affected by death, it's not as significant, it happens more often so will have less impact. A friend might be 'missing', and there was nothing said. It seems to me looking back that the bereavement process was gone through by adults – it was seen as an event for staff and parents but not for us children. I knew where one young person had gone, that they had died. I spoke to my mother, but us children did not have that conversation between ourselves. This was a fairly common form of 'under-protection'. The death of children, our peers, was treated as if we were psychologically different and would not experience grief. It also said subtly that it did not matter. All traces were removed – there was no attempt to remember them. Once a parent donated a pool table, and the child's death was remembered like that. I remember all the children who died – only one child who was in my school is alive today.

In my working life with disabled people, it's about not repeating the above history. When a person has died, I use my experiences and am supporting staff to make sure we tell each individual who knew them in a way that they can understand that the person has died and is not coming back or is 'on holiday'. It is about finding the ways to say this to individuals who use various forms of communication. Without the organization embracing this approach we would be continuing the practice each time that a person's death is made as if it were invisible and had not occurred. Sometimes there are celebrations of people's lives arranged by families and staff together that might include memorial gifts such as garden trees but this is part of sharing real memories of the person. This carries on with close friends and training is provided for staff. For me friends are very, very important. It's the aftermath. It makes me very aware of places like hospitals and intensive care. It also makes me aware that the people I work with experience multiple losses and often do not have friends. They have people work with them and then leave again and again, and have to start again and again. It can be 10 support workers in a day, seven times a day and so on and the staff group employed as temporary and at the most a year or two – those are the paid staff and then there's volunteers, managers and so on.

Upbringing

Upbringing, what part does upbringing play for a disabled child to find out about these people's roles and the limits? Without ordinary and confident upbringing in this complex set of relations, the processes of developing one's *grounded* identity towards adulthood are not supported. How do non-disabled parents gain the expertise of disabled people to provide this kind of upbringing? Training non-disabled parents I have provided has been appreciated as empowering, supportive, confidence-building to be parents, and, to do that when faced with many professionals – fire in their bellies. Seeing me working and being the provider of support was sometimes a first experience of contact with a disabled person – a pebble in the pond to start the process off from where they are.

What about transitions?

'Transitions' is a term used in policy in England to refer to going through key phases in life. For non-disabled children this generally means moving, for example, from primary to secondary school or on to college, having a family as so on. These are seen as developmental stages of growing up and also seen as rites of passage significant in gaining adult status. For disabled children there are many more 'transitions' characterized by meetings to make decisions about where the disabled child will go – who and where will accept them. This is one of the many differences disabled children face. Decisions are made that have ramifications for their future. Being excluded from major decisions can also have an impact on expectations and decision-making later. What are the opportunities disabled children have to grow up? To learn, to know what is OK to say, to play, to make mistakes, to be creative?

Disabled children do therapy, they don't play. They can't get messy, they are fragile, angels, are in wheelchairs, and play spaces are not accessible. Disabled children with complex needs are not encouraged to use their hands. Lack of early opportunities is also about career opportunities. Lack of aspirations? It was stated that my best destiny was to be a receptionist where they would not see my disability, or next best to be in day services – the usual plan. I wasn't having any of that either – I had fighting spirit from my mother: 'fight your own battles' she said, and she showed me how – she gave me the tools! My short-stature friends wanted to be actors!

In my work life I worked with a very young disabled child who was only secure in the arms of an adult and not on the floor with other children running about as he was unable to see. I took him things for him to play with using his hands – cornflour squeaks, butterscotch mousse tasted good. Although he did learn dexterity etc. it was about messy fun, and his mother enjoyed him having this time and didn't mind how messy he was when she came to pick him up. He then spent the afternoon having a relaxing massage, some positive touch enabled him to process when he has learned.

My career has been and continues to be based on my having to do *extra* work – without positive expectations and being continuously disadvantaged disabled people generally do more in jobs when they are in them. I went to mainstream college, and we were seen as 'a group' of disabled students put with the same tutor though we had very different learning needs, and so I became a tutor too, supporting peers rather than being a student. It's a theme throughout – opportunities seen as too risky, capabilities not recognized and paradoxically expected to do more with less support.

Who am I really?

Identity – well, you don't have one, do you? Disabled children, not disabled girls and boys. We were all the same, and this was inside and outside of school – where are the separate gender public toilets? Our identity was not informed by different surroundings as it would be for girls and boys. This is not the same for disabled adults who have not been disabled children. Their socialization and whole childhood would be different in forming identity. Our peer group was a given, we did not choose 'best friends'. I was a friend and often their carer – more adult roles in school. Many people may not have a best friend but would know of the concept. We did not.

In my work many of the people living in the various settings provided do not have close relationships they have chosen and formed themselves. Some would say they are friends with support workers. They don't necessarily know about two-way friendship. These are the aftermaths as above. We look at 'person-centred' plans. This can include making connections through, for instance, leisure interests in the wider community – that is very much an individual practice by those with fire in their bellies – staff, for instance, doing more than they are expected to. It's about growing up, forums, relationships – relationships where people are. Having a family.

Grown up! What relationship? Having a baby!

Staff in my work school, college and work experience anticipate the 'worst' when they see two disabled young people starting a relationship – they get the 'sex talk' when they were about to try a cup of tea together! Little snips from TV say things but do not make links between, for instance, names of genitalia and sexual relationships in the fullest sense. So I hear a young disabled person say they have a girlfriend and are 'dating'. He says I don't want children and she does, but he has snippets, words that are shared, but an understanding of 'relationship' as a concept is not there. So there is knowing how to talk about their bodies, but how without informal peer group and without disabled children, teenagers and adults being there in books, films and in information given out by professionals – what are the words? Talk is also about keeping safe – good touch, unwanted touch. Do we get used to personal care? No. How is it to be seen by others and be unconscious without people protecting privacy? I had by then a lot of experience of us disabled children being viewed as conscious or unconscious. Many experiences of people commenting on my body freely, even peeking while I was unconscious and then telling me what I was like! Again it's about the opportunities to be grounded, to know and choose and refuse.

So in my training role I remind staff to acknowledge what has been overheard even if they do not appear to have heard it, otherwise history is repeated. I still get told I must have done something bad in a previous life by a passing shopper. Also a student when I'm training says the same thing, and again it is said freely! I respond – I always do – 'so what does that mean about me?' 'Oh not you', the student replies – 'so who am

I then?' I ask. So it is about me or I am the exception, and it's about those 'other' disabled people. I am being put somewhere by others, dressed up as nice if I am the exception, but still I am being put there – again with ease. I respond – I can advocate.

Family? Babies? No expectations in childhood. So it's a shock – let's go back to the 'bad news' at the start of this chapter! Some people are expected to have a family and a baby – an assumption that they are heterosexual. Some have no expectations said to them throughout childhood, no sexuality. So the next section of the chapter considers how we know what we think we know.

How do we know what we think we know?

The examples above and the process of questioning, setting up creative fires in bellies and from that putting pebbles in ponds for longer-term learning rely on this final question. As you can see, many people have things to say about us. So how do we know what we think we know? The freely said 'truths' said by others about us does not start with this question. So to find out how we know, we first need to identify what we think we know, and that's about self-awareness and the will to do that thinking. Then it's about checking out with the disabled child and young person what they know and think about a situation or issue. And then working out what they are saying and what the process is that they have available to learn and form their opinions and make decisions. It's about direct conversations, being together, speaking with disabled children and young people, getting to know disabled children, it is best to meet at lunchtime – before or after a meal, is it best to meet in school? Things have moved on due to the stepping-stones people have put down. We generally know if you have the will to find out what we think. And we choose if we want to tell you – some things are private (we are not public property).

Developing my own expectations is the thing. I was included and excluded in education. Partly this meant mainstream and segregated school, and partly it was within each place – the worry of being crushed, three years without a proper seat, low qualifications, having to catch up. Disability equality education became the way I met disabled adults and heard songs and poems about individuals' experiences, began to learn about or history and learnt skills in offering workshops. We were not educated about our history at school, and yet as you can see the above messages have a history and are alive in the present. At university none of the case studies had a person who had my socialization, and the literature had texts about disabled people who were service users, not disabled professionals. I was again expected to be teacher by the teacher, and he isolated me from the peer group. Being expected to 'leave my disability behind me' and also being expected to 'warn people ahead of my arrival' were just some more contradictory statements. Determined to think outside the box given to me – the 'suggested reading' (how would I pass 'reflection') once more twice the amount of work to do, and I did well, framing my research with relevant literature – this was self-directed learning. The literature like various networks and organizations include very different perspectives, and it was not a case of being 'in' those groups either. Those who had a non-disabled child's education and childhood are very different; who are the trainers and who are the academics and why?

I now see how being part of the organizations I have encountered is where I can make a difference. I make films with disabled adults, so we hear what they say and it's documented, our meetings are also videoed. This is how I think I know what I know.

A colleague said the other day, 'I keep dropping pebbles in ponds now'!

Out of our problem boxes!!! We as disabled people and parents of disabled children need to give the pebbles to the people who make negative and problem statements readily without thought; its not our stuff and its important to give it back as anger is not good for us.

There isn't a day that goes by that I don't draw on my experience – I'm always doing the extra. I do my own grounding. It's also about having the career support that others have now in a leadership role, but is it going to be any more relevant than the earlier programmes of study I have done? I 'over-process', constantly analyze, reflect and ground myself, and I have a form of continuous resilience making. There are disabled leader training opportunities – will I be supported to take them up? I'll let you know.

It was not until I wrote this that I realized I have been back to each of these places, school, workplaces and all – physically I have revisited the place and in different roles. Anybody who has contact with disabled children and young people, think outside your box, so that they can have their own dreams, wishes, desires, support; do not put the lid on the box.

5
A Mug or a Teacup and Saucer?

Linda Derbyshire

This is a story about a mug, a teacup and a saucer. When I was asked to talk about my life as the mother of a disabled child in England, I spent ages wondering what I could say. I could spend hours telling you about the fights I have had with education and health services over the years, or I could tell you about the prejudice and bullying we have all had to face because of Hannah's additional needs. Or maybe I could tell you about the heartache, the worry, the stress and frustration we have experienced. But it occurred to me that many of the readers of this book will already know those stories for themselves whether as professionals working with disabled children and their families or as parents and carers of disabled children or as disabled young people themselves.

So I would like to talk about a cup, a saucer and a mug! So let me explain how that cup, saucer and a mug became the motivation behind my family's special needs journey.

It stems from a time in my teens long before my daughter Hannah was born, in actual fact, it goes back when I was only 8 years old. I had a friend called David; we played together as part of a group, both in and out of school. David was funny, good fun, very happy, well liked and was very much an important part of our friendship group. The thing was, David had learning difficulties, not that it meant anything to us. He was just who he was; we accepted his character and personality as readily as he accepted ours. We all had a very happy childhood and then the time came for us to go to secondary school.

At that time, the schools in our area were single-sex so the lads went off with a good support group of other lads from our primary school and the girls went off to theirs. We all found comfort in having familiar faces around us in this big new school, and friendship groups formed in primary remained strong.

I say all of us, but there was one wasn't given that opportunity, and I am sure you will have guessed by now that that person was David. He was sent, on his own, to the local special needs school. I remember at the time talking to my mum and saying that it wasn't fair that he couldn't go to the same school as his best friend Nick as they were both very close, and inseparable. And I knew how miserable I would have felt if I had moved away from my friends. Soon after the move we would all go round and ask David to play out with us, but he wouldn't come any more, and eventually we moved on through secondary school and lost touch.

When I was a teenager, I worked for an agency that found people temporary jobs, and a position came up at a local company that employed people with disabilities, both physical and learning. Other girls had been asked to go, but they said they were too scared to work in a place with what they described as 'those weirdos'. I had no problem with going, and received a warm welcome from day one from many of the workforce and enjoyed my time there. However, there were things I saw and experienced that ultimately had a huge impact on me. Firstly, I came into contact with David again. I couldn't believe the change in him. He no longer laughed, his eyes didn't sparkle, he wasn't sociable, he didn't even have the confidence to come up to say hello. He followed me around at a distance, and it made me feel really sad at the time, when I tried to approach him he looked uncomfortable and would walk away.

Now looking back with my daughter Hannah's circumstances in mind, I feel that the decision made for David at that time had a huge negative impact on his life, and I have always been mindful of David, and his experiences when decisions have had to be made in regards to Hannah. I want to be able to look my daughter in the eye when she is older and say 'I might not have always got it right, but I really did try my very best'.

David was put on the special needs merry-go-round. He went from special needs school to special needs workplace, his social life was around special needs people, the people he socialized with who did not have a disability were family, carers or other educational or health professionals. No matter how hard he tried he couldn't get out of that merry-go-round – he had been handed his mug for life, nobody ever offered him a teacup.

Now where did the analogy of the mug and the teacup come from? Whilst I was working at the same company as David, the management had a practice at that time whereby the employees with learning difficulties would have their breaks and lunches in the staff canteen.

However, the employees with physical or no disabilities would take their breaks and lunch in a separate room, and were waited on by those with learning difficulties. The ones in their own private dining area would be served their tea in teacups on saucers whereas the canteen served its tea in mugs.

Eleven years after I worked for this company Hannah was born, and two and a half years after this Hannah was finally recognized as having learning difficulties. I remember the first thing I did was hold her and made her a promise, and that was 'NOBODY WOULD EVER HAND HER A MUG', but I never imagined the hard work, determination, tears, frustration and sheer bloody mindedness we have had to endure to keep hold of that teacup and saucer.

We have always maintained that Hannah was not born into some parallel special needs universe, and that she is a member of our society, and she has to learn to live within it, unlike David who was forced into remaining within a special needs environment, and now can find no way out of it. Unfortunately, many people on hearing she has learning difficulties see and treat Hannah as a young lady whose cup is half empty, whereas we, on the other hand, have always seen Hannah's cup as half full. She has the potential to do anything she likes, but unfortunately we constantly find that because people's expectations of her are low. Their low expectations, in fact, create more of a problem to us than Hannah's particular needs. In other words, the mug is always handed to her before a teacup, for no other reason than she is labelled as 'special needs', or as 'having a learning difficulty', even by people who have not even met her.

From a very early age we have experienced many occasions where the mug has been offered. Sometimes in cruel actions and words, by people who are ignorant and openly bigoted, but funnily enough these are the easier situations to cope with. I have always found it difficult to deal with those people whose intentions have been kindness, but it always comes with a sting in the tail. My earliest memory of this was taking Hannah on a children's train ride, when she was three years old. I handed the man the right money and he gave me 50p back, but when I asked why he smiled at me kindly and said, 'Don't worry, I never charge for retards'.

Another occasion where people were trying to help but, in fact, were handing her a mug was when she was aged about ten and at primary school. Hannah asked me if she could meet me at the car rather than at the school gates, just like the rest of her friends were doing at that age. So we talked it through, I told her where the car would be and I had every confidence she could do it. So the next day, I informed the teaching assistant what I was doing through the notebook we had to communicate between home and school. I got to the school at two-thirty, half an hour before school finished, so that I could be sure to park the car exactly where I told her it would be. I waited and waited until all the children had gone, and feeling panicked, I went in to school to be told that, although Hannah had come out, the other parents kept bringing her back into school as soon as she walked through the gates!!!

They had no idea what Hannah's abilities or limitations were, only that she had the 'special needs' label, they were, in effect, handing her a mug. I realized then that it wasn't Hannah's additional needs that would be detrimental to her, but other people's ill-informed and low expectations of her. It was really a case of dealing with their insecurities and fears. I do understand those fears, I have them myself, and I have to work very hard not to put that burden onto Hannah's shoulders, because I have learnt over the years, that given the chance, Hannah is a very capable young woman, and very often it is others holding her back, not her abilities.

It has always been our number one priority with Hannah that her confidence and self-esteem remains high, and we encourage this with everyone she meets. I believe having these qualities will be the tools that will help her to achieve any ambitions or goals she may have through life. Hannah may always need extra help, support and guidance, but I will always encourage her to accept nothing less from anyone than a teacup and saucer.

In order to stop people handing Hannah the mug we have become very imaginative and, dare I say it, a little manipulative over the years! For example, when Hannah was five, there had been a few parties where everyone in her class had been invited except Hannah. We arranged a party the following month for Halloween and we invited every child in the class. They all came because at that age no parent wants to see their child left out. We put a huge amount of effort into the party to make it extra special, and the children had a wonderful time. After that, Hannah was always invited to parties. Partly, I think because the parents who came to drop their children off got to know John, my husband and me, but also because they could see that Hannah was playing just like their children and that their fears were ill-founded. Also what was born out of hurt and rejection became a wonderful, positive, encyclopaedia of memories. In fact over the years, the parties have become legendary and, despite being sixteen, the young people still talk about them. It was one occasion where we successfully side-stepped that mug and had taken the cup and saucer, and Hannah was given the opportunity of inclusion.

I have come to realize that there are things that can be done to challenge the mug. Very often it takes only little steps to side-step that mug, sometimes, however, it takes the effort required to climb Mount Everest. We do have those rare and fantastic times when the teacup and saucer is offered, and no effort is required by us at all. The results are always wonderful, and each time it feels that you have just been given a huge lottery win. Recently for Hannah this has been experienced in the success she has had in her work experience in a clothes shop and as a waitress. Here she was given jobs to do and was expected to do them, she had been given support and guidance, but everyone reports back that once she is shown they are more than happy to let her get on with it. And, in doing so, Hannah has proved that she is no mug girl and no one has tried to hand her one. The successes she has achieved have been beyond expectations. In the reference she was given for the work experience she has done in the clothes shop, the manager said:

> over the two weeks Hannah began to show initiative and to take responsibility for her own workload, including knowing when to have breaks, when to tidy, when to talk to customers and when to ask for help and assistance from other team members. Throughout the entire time, Hannah was fun, friendly, incredibly well presented and professional. She bought an unending amount of laughter and happiness into the store for customers and staff alike. She was a pure joy as such I would have no qualms either employing Hannah in the future or recommending her for employment.

Last year, we purchased a static caravan on a holiday campsite not far from where we live. I have to say this is the best thing we've ever done. Not only has this given the opportunity to be independent and to make many new friends, but she also takes friends from school, and they all have their chance to go to the disco on their own, watch shows, go bowling, enjoy sporting activities and hang out like any other teenager.

Of course, there have been some tough times, and you often wonder if you've made the right decisions, especially over our choice of not sending Hannah to a special needs school, as we were put under quite a lot of pressure to do so. But when we see Hannah making new friends, having the confidence to try new things and to make a success of them, we are so glad we stuck to what we believe in.

But often, I find myself asking WHY? Why do we have to face so many challenges, not just Hannah as an individual but also John and I as a whole family? Is it because of the historical nature of how people with special needs have been treated in the past, this awful legacy of excluding and alienating those perceived as being 'different'? Is it so tightly embedded in our minds and personalities that even the most kind, caring, compassionate and intelligent of people fall foul of treating people with additional needs as an underclass in the way that so many people do, even unconsciously?

I feel like my life was enhanced by David being a part of my childhood, and knowing him and the life he has been forced to lead has helped me greatly with regards to decisions made with Hannah. I hope that in years to come, Hannah and people like her can be an inspiration to the young people around them, who themselves may go on to have children of their own with additional needs, or choose to work in an environment with young people with disabilities. I want them to realize there are no boundaries, that with the right support, encouragement and confidence their children can reach for the stars, because they once knew a girl at school, called Hannah, who had tried to do just that and at times succeeded.

Being around young people in school with additional needs will educate and inform future generations that historical limitations are just that history!! And the ignorance carried from the past can finally be put to rest. Inclusion must be in everyone's consciousness for it to filter into everybody's lives, and it must start with the government, educators and industry. There is such a long way to go, but we ourselves have seen an improvement since Hannah joined the education system.

I can count on less than one hand how many times I have cried over Hannah's disabilities, but I have lost count of the number of times I have cried because of others' insistence to hand her that mug. They come from all walks of life – educational, medical, the person in the street, even family and friends. But nobody deserves to be handed a mug, everyone who works with disabled children and young people should make it their goal to see they all get that teacup and saucer.

Part II
Contemporary Inquiries

Part II responds to the call of the book, so clearly articulated in Part I, for adults to listen to disabled children. The chapters in Part II set out the current research context for disabled children's childhood studies. The authors in this section are all academics working with disabled children, young people and their families in research. Authors share their experiences of the research process as well as offering analyses of the lived experience of the participants in the research in a range of contexts, ever mindful of the need to listen to disabled children and their families.

In Chapter 6, David Abbott offers a reflective account of doing 'real-world' research with disabled children. His thoughtful and sensitive account exposes the details of his interactions with disabled children, young people and their families as he carried out a study with young people with Duchenne Muscular Dystrophy, a life-limiting condition. The chapter reveals the challenges of carrying out research at the intersections between childhood, youth, parenting, disability and life-limiting conditions.

In Chapter 7, Sonali Shah reflects on inclusive education in the context of international legislation and treaties. The chapter then moves focus to discuss the policy context in education and the lived experiences of people with physical experiences of disability growing up in post-war England and their reflections on their experiences of segregation and inclusion. Sonali urges us not only to focus on individual biographies but also on the institutions, policies, environments and relationships that have shaped these stories. Finally, she asks us to consider how macro-level policies can better connect with the micro-level lives of disabled children and young people.

In Chapter 8, Shaun Grech shifts our attention to disability, childhood and poverty in the global South, in the context of his ethnographic research in rural Guatemala. Shaun sets out the global contexts in which disabled people live, which have often been marginalized within (British) Disability Studies. He describes how global North concerns about disability and childhood have been imposed on the global South in ways that have failed to attend to local contexts and cultures. He concludes the chapter by calling for a genuinely 'global' disabled children's childhood studies.

In Chapter 9, Katherine Runswick-Cole turns our attention to the lives of disabled children, young people and their parents. Drawing on a research project carried out in England with disabled children, young people and their carers (2008–11), Katherine employs the work of Hochschild (1993) to explore emotional labour in families' lives. Katherine reveals the impact of the 'omnipresent ableist gaze' (Campbell, 2009) in families' lives and asks how this impacts of the lives of disabled children and their mothers, in particular.

6

Who Says What, Where, Why and How? Doing Real-World Research with Disabled Children, Young People and Family Members

David Abbott

Introduction

There is an increasing body of social science research and writing that explores the lives of disabled children, young people, their families and allies. Much of this in recent years has been linked to work funded by government or services with an evaluative and applied focus – although there have been some important exceptions that have taken a more holistic approach to understanding the lives of disabled children and young people (for example, Connors & Stalker, 2003; Goodley & Runswick-Cole, 2012; Shakespeare, Barnes, Priestly, Cunninghambirley, Davis & Watson, 1999). The emphasis on applied, service-orientated research has sometimes meant that less attention has been paid to the methodological aspects of research with this group of children and young people and the context in which the 'talk' of the research encounter is produced. Watson (2012), for example, notes that research rarely examines the interplay between disabled children's experiences and their social setting. I have written about this elsewhere in relation to the dynamics of the interviewer/interviewee relationship (Abbott, 2012), as have many others, but less has been written in the social science literature on childhood disability about the detail of other aspects of the interactions, and notably questions about where interviews happen and who else is present. In particular, and the focus of this chapter, there is little discussion in the literature about the context of the family home as a primary site for research with disabled children and young people. How does the researcher and the research participants manage the dynamics of the family home? How do the various actors – researcher, parent(s), carers and child/young person – relate to each other, and what kind of roles does the researcher need to perform in order to secure a 'successful research encounter' – and what counts as success?

As both Carpenter (2010) and Davies (2008) note, research often ignores the fact that most children, including disabled children, live with their families and are part of families but have been treated as somehow separate or autonomous in the way in which their lives are portrayed in research:

> There has been a theoretical shift in considering children as 'conceptually' separate from their families to reconsidering children's roles as active negotiators of family life. As such, children are now viewed as both independent actors and members of a family unit. (Davies, 2008: para 4.5)

In reality of course, access to meet and interview disabled children and young people at home is mediated through parents/carers who may also be research participants, either formally taking part, or informally by monitoring, interrupting, adding or smoothing the encounter with their son or daughter. So a researcher has to build relationships with everyone they encounter in the family home, even though very different kinds of things may be required – often almost all at once. So, on the one hand, the researcher needs to introduce, contextualize and lead the encounter that she or he has set up and brought about and which is largely foreign to the child/young person and their family. On the other hand, the researcher is keen to equalize (or disguise) their power in the hope that the interview will elicit 'good stuff' (about which, more later). In addition the researcher needs to demonstrate both adult competency to adults in the house and a non-authoritarian and inclusive approach to children and young people, which demonstrates that they are not the 'usual professional' but there to try to do something a bit different. What is different is the desire to produce 'meaningful talk' and create a space in which people feel safe and comfortable enough to share their experiences. A space described in these terms is very similar to the task of creating a safe therapeutic space. Rogers (1961), for example, writes about the creation of a safe, non-judgemental and supportive environment in which three core conditions are required for a successful therapeutic space and relationship: congruence – realness and genuineness; unconditional positive regard – respect for the client; and empathy – an attempt to understand the client's thoughts and feelings. I would suggest that a 'good' researcher tries to produce something very similar, and I want to discuss whether trying to emulate such a space is a good or a problematic thing – or indeed both.

In negotiating the space of the family home, Davies (2008) suggests researchers have to be sensitive to the family norms, rules and requirements that exist there. This sounds desirable but, as we shall see, research interviews can cut across and disturb all kinds of family conventions and norms. Although the ethical imperative of research is to leave people unharmed, I would suggest it rarely leaves them unchanged, so what kinds of responsibilities do we have when we go to family homes to do research? Underpinning this chapter is the assertion that the research encounter is inherently relational (Kitzinger, 2004; Smart, 2009; Abbott, 2012), so that the role of the researcher matters, that is, they are not invisible and their humanity, ideology, prejudices and personality are generally not left at the doorstep:

> Many proponents of qualitative research have recognised that the interview is a distinct type of social relationship. This relationship may involve, disguise, use and create many differing aspects of social interaction, such as power, friendship, reciprocity and shared understandings. (Birch & Millar, 2000: 190)

This chapter will draw on research carried out with young men with Muscular Dystrophy, their parents and other family members in which I was the main researcher and responsible for collecting data. Research interviews were in the family home, and the negotiation of that space and with different research participants, discussing issues of pretty significant emotional substance, provides a useful lens with which to explore the key themes this chapter seeks to address.

Transition to adulthood for young men with Duchenne Muscular Dystrophy

This chapter draws on a recently conducted study carried out with colleagues at the University of Bristol and Newcastle, and in conjunction with user groups in the field of Duchenne Muscular Dystrophy (Abbott & Carpenter, 2010). The focus of the study was on 'transition to adulthood', with emphasis on the young person's own experiences as well as those of parents and other family members. 'Transition' is a term with ordinary use, that is, denoting the change from boy to man/child to adult, but is also a term with legal meaning in the UK and denotes the point at which the various agencies that support disabled children should make plans and offer guidance to disabled young people (and their families) about what they will do in terms of education, work, training, support, housing etc. as they reach adulthood.

Duchenne Muscular Dystrophy (DMD) is a life-threatening condition that affects boys and men. In recent years average life expectancy for men with DMD has significantly increased to around 27 years of age (Eagle, Baudouin, Chandler, Giddings, Bullock, & Bushby, 2002; Eagle, Bourke, Bullock, Gibson, Mehtaa, Giddings, Strauba & Bushby, 2007). Our research found that there had been a significant lack of planning and preparation for this 'unanticipated' and marginalized young adult population (Rahbeck, Werge, Madsen, Marquardt, Steffensen & Jeppesen, 2005; Gibson, Young, Upshur & McKeever, 2007). So much so that all of the young men in our study who had finished full-time education were at home without work, and many with very restricted social lives and a strong 'dependence' on close family members for physical care and social interaction. Other key findings related to tensions and difficulties relating to the emotional and psychological adjustments and challenges of growing up with and living with a life-threatening condition, and how this had affected family relationships and families' willingness to communicate openly with each other about these adjustments and challenges (or not).

The study took place in three regions of England between 2007 and 2009. In the qualitative component, we spoke to 102 members of 40 families with a son aged over 15 living with DMD, an age at which planning for transition to adulthood would be current or recent. Having obtained ethical approval from a National Research Ethics Service, we wrote to every family with a son with DMD aged over 15 years via research partners in three specialist muscle health services in England. Parents who replied saying they would take part in interviews were then contacted to arrange a convenient time, and also asked if their son would be willing to take part in the study and if there were other members of the family who might also be interested.

On arrival at the family home, there was discussion about who exactly would take part, whether the young person with DMD wanted to be interviewed on his own or at all, as contact had been made via parents/carers, or with other family members, and how much time the family had available for the interviews. We wanted to include a range of family members, to try to ensure fathers were well represented, and to put the young person with DMD at the centre of the interview process. This was achieved to a greater or lesser extent, but, in some cases, family events surfaced once the researcher arrived. Sometimes a family might say they only had a short amount of time available and the researcher would have to quickly prioritize who to interview and which questions were most important to cover. At other times, households were busy and sometimes noisy as the interviews were going on. Although we tried to be flexible with families about times, offering evening appointments so that working parents could be included, evenings were sometimes difficult, given that families needed to relax after school or work, eat and get homework done. In addition some young men became less well as the day went on and preferred morning interviews. This meant that day-time interviews were more usual, which had the effect of excluding some parents, particularly fathers, who were at work. In an ideal world, we might have visited families more than once, to build rapport and to have more time to speak to more family members. However, in practice, families were generally willingly to give up one chunk of time to take part in the research, but reluctant to offer more.

Twelve young men elected to see the researcher on their own, and twenty-five with their siblings or parents. In a number of cases, young men started the interview with their parents and then, by mutual agreement, conducted the rest of the interview on their own with the researcher. The majority of interviews were, in effect, family interviews with parents and sometime siblings joining in. This was helpful if the young person was shy or unsure of contributing their own views. However, there were parts of the interview where different and sometimes competing perspectives were clearly possible; these needed careful handling. The researcher generally started questions by stating that it was fine for people to have different points of view and offered time alone with the researcher if anyone wanted to express their views in private. As some interviews progressed, it was clear that brand-new information was coming to light within a family, for example, what a young person did or did not know about DMD and its prognosis.

Interviewing in the family home: Being a 'good guest' and managing difference

As suggested, little has been written about how interviews in the family home operate and how the dynamic is managed (although Bushin, 2007 is an exception and particularly helpful). In my experience the opportunity to meet a disabled child or young person at home is always negotiated through the parent/carer. Thereafter, as in our study, family members may then also be respondents in their own right, or take part in family interviews if they elect to do so. Davies (2008) suggests that the researcher has to have respect for the 'conventions' in the place in which they have been invited. In the family home this means deferring to the parent whose house it is, and to 'leave unaffected the relationships that existed in the field prior to the research' (Davies, 2008, para 3.6). In these kinds of situations my sense is that a number of different things have to happen to help facilitate a 'good' interview. Firstly, on arrival the parent has to be reassured of my professionalism, my credibility, my adult knowledge and my interpersonal skills. They need a sense that their child will be 'okay' with me, including whether I can be attuned to any particular communication style their child has, and that I am likely to interact with their child in a thoughtful and respectful way. Secondly, either also on arrival, or some time later, the child or young person probably wants to be reassured (or at least I want to reassure them) that the encounter will not be boring, that I am not an authoritarian adult, that it will be safe to tell me things. For everyone I also have to be a 'good guest' (Davies, 2008) and fit in with whatever is happening domestically at the time that I arrive. Of course, the idea of being a 'good guest' is mostly my own fantasy and projection. It is not something I actually 'test out' with family members. So my own sense is that if I can work out the cues I am being offered about, for example, whether to say yes to a cup of tea, whether to take my shoes off at the door, whether to offer a comment on the person's house, whether to join in some talk about, say the weather or something on TV, then I am 'smoothing' my arrival and my presence and putting people at ease.

These different ways of being – adult-focused and then child- (or young person-) focused are rarely the same, and while they can be managed and switched between when children and parents and being interviewed separately, it is much harder to manage in the real-life encounters where some or much of the talk may happen together and where much of the 'action' precedes the interview, for example, while a cup of tea is being made or when things are being set up – the crucial time in which people are making decisions about each other. Holt (2010) draws an analogy with being a researcher in school settings where she is clearly an adult but wants to avoid being seen as a teacher and has to negotiate her position both with the child participants and the adult gatekeepers (the teachers themselves and the institution of the school). She notes the:

> ... complex negotiations in order to perform my identity in non-authoritarian ways with children, without transgressing institutional expectations on adult behaviour. (Holt, 2010: 14)

Power issues and relations are of course central to this, and there is a significant body of work that reflects on the inherent inequality of the research relationship as well as the inherent power differentials between adults and children (see, for example, Tisdall, Davis & Gallagher, 2009). While some writers suggest that adult researchers should seek to minimize their power when researching with children and young people, Holt (2010) writes instead about adopting a 'least-adult' role with children in an attempt to not repeat and act out unequal relationships in the research encounter. Cree, Kay & Tisdall (2002), on the other hand, endorse Mayall (2000), who suggests that it is naïve to think we do not have power over children, and should instead 'invite children to help us understand childhood' (Cree et al., 2002: 52).

Power is complex, and I have written elsewhere (Abbott, 2012) about being asked by young men to take part in video games before an interview gets under way, an activity in which I lose any semblance of credibility or expertise, and which actually makes me feel silly and uncomfortable. In this vein, Holt (2010: 19) notes:

> When an adult wishes to participate in children's social worlds, s/he is placed in a relatively powerless position. Children are the gatekeepers to their own games … and can allow or deny adults' participation.

While I may want to demonstrate something about my approach to power to a child or young person and show that I am a particular type of adult, that is, essentially a safe person who can be trusted, who is there to listen and who is essentially on 'their side', this is often mediated by how a parent either describes or interacts with their child in front of me and involving me. In my experience, in the setting up and 'checking out' part, some families are clearly anxious about how their children will 'do' or perform in the interview. This may well be related to past, negative experiences of encounters set up by other professionals that were run in a way that did not allow the child or young person really to participate, or where the outcomes are crucial and under-, or over-performing can have significant consequences (especially in terms of accessing support or services). Additionally, parents may have been forced to develop default 'deficit scripts' given the inherently negative ways in which families often have to describe their disabled child in order to access support. So a parent may project some of these fears, and for whatever reason present information about their child in particular ways: sometimes positive or sometimes rather negative. Morris (2003) writes about this in relation to how some staff in residential special schools talked about some children in negative ways in relation to a planned research encounter ('You won't get anything out of him'). We rightly construct this as an unhelpful and disabling attitude towards the

child: 'In these instances, it was the adult's attitude that had to be tack-
led first ...', as Morris writes (2003: 340). But, for all kinds of reasons, as
mentioned above, this can also happen with parents, and this is much
harder to write about as we normally don't want to be critical of parents
and we want to remain 'on-side' with everyone in the family unit.

Woolfson (2004) (as cited in Carpenter, 2010) argues that underlying
societal attitudes towards disability are very likely to influence parents
who have a disabled child and these may well (or may not) affect their
parenting approaches. So as Bushin (2007: 243) argues:

> It must be acknowledged that homes are not always places in which
> all children have a voice and feel as though they are listened to.

So in our study, some parents suggested that their son wouldn't say
much or be a 'good' interviewee, and sometimes also described their
son's life in a fairly bleak way – 'shaming stories', as I came to think of
them (see below). This was sometimes to the obvious embarrassment
of the young person. In these instances I had to maintain 'good terms'
with the parent but signal to the young person that I was not necessarily agreeing with their parents' interpretation.

In these three examples the difficulties around 'shaming stories'
(as it seemed to me that they were experienced by the young person)
are illustrated. In the first excerpt a young person felt offended by his
mother's description of him as 'disabled', a word I had introduced and
used during the interview myself:

> Mother: Because [son] is the first I suppose very disabled person in
> the school.
> Young person: Yeah but I still don't think I'm very disabled. That's a
> very negative view.
> Mother: Okay he's not disabled but he needs a little bit extra support.

In the second excerpt an interaction took place that was mirrored in
many interviews in which family members described the lack of social
opportunities the young men with DMD had. In many of these cases I felt
that the young person was embarrassed by (and sometimes resisted) the
suggestion that they were lacking in friends or a social life:

> Mother: There's nothing round here for him to do.
> Sister: You haven't really got any mates round here have you?
> Mother: But there's nothing here ... all he can do is go bowling.

Sister: You can't even go cinema and stuff.
Mother: He can't get into the cinema, he can't go swimming.
Interviewer: Is the cinema not accessible?
Young person: No.
Mother: And he can't go swimming 'cos that's not accessible either.

Finally, in this third excerpt, my sense was that a mother and father were using the interview to convey something to their son that they had wanted to say before but not felt able to. While their approach was a relatively gentle and measured one, I felt very aware that I did not want to convey that I was on the side of the adults and hence be a third adult in the room commenting on the young person's 'wasted days':

Mother: What annoys me and his dad is they've got so much potential and so much to give – why waste it? But having said that, we aren't in his position. To me and his dad from our generation, it's just a complete waste. The whole waste of all this intelligence and knowledge that they've got and … but it's like they say, if it's what [son] wants to do, well that's fine, but it just sometimes niggles you a bit … but they don't want to do it. And it's like as if they're giving up and you just want to shake them and …
Young person: Well I wouldn't mind doing stuff with my intelligence, but sometimes.
Mother: It gets too much. We do understand … we understand that. It's just when me and your dad are having conversations with you and you're so knowledgeable about this and that and the other, you can understand from the parents' point of view. So you can understand we're a frustration that you've got so much to give. But we understand if that's the way you want to be. We don't mind, I don't mind about you being in the house and doing what you want to do, if this is where you feel comfortable. It's just, we feel that you have got so much potential, and it's just being wasted.

One of my concerns in these exchanges was not to reinforce the idea the young people had lives that were wholly negative or deficient and in which they would be left feeling that the adults were all focused on what was problematic. At the same time, the issues and barriers being described were real and significant. Cree et al. (2002) highlight the different dimensions of the parental interjector or 'gate-keeper' role. So, for example, parents may (rightly) feel that the losses to their children associated in taking part in a potentially unsettling or upsetting research interview may not be outweighed by any gains (if there are any). Citing Masson (2000), they suggest that parents:

> ... may have a positive function, protecting children and young people from potentially damaging research ... but also use their position to censor children and young people.

I have discussed in this section my concerns about being a 'good guest' and the challenges associated with negotiating different positions with different people. My quest to be a 'good guest' is closely linked with my over-arching desire to get at 'good stuff', that is, for the research encounter to yield meaningful data. The next section of this chapter will reflect on what might constitute 'good stuff' and the quasi-therapeutic context in which this might occur.

Research or therapy? Getting to the 'good stuff'

In writing up our research and describing the study, we said that, in interviews, I, as the interviewer, had to be particularly sensitive to discussion topics that were potentially upsetting and try to manage discussion of these so that the experience stayed, as far as possible, firmly within the context of a research interview, rather than turning into a therapeutic session. In one instance the family asked directly if I could facilitate a family discussion about a sensitive topic, and I steered away. But in fact we had already covered such 'intimate ground' that I wonder in hindsight whether I had any clarity of my own about what the boundaries of the research encounter were. Interviews often feel therapeutic, and sometimes people say they have been, either explicitly, or by suggesting they have spoken of things for the first time. Birch and Millar (2000) draw similarities between a psychotherapeutic encounter and a research interview in the way that they can both potentially enable people to understand something of themselves differently by virtue of the sharing of their story. This certainly occurred in several interviews when different perspectives were shared and sometimes for the first time openly. In this excerpt the mother has suggested that her son going to university would be the biggest change he had ever faced:

> Young person: I'm not sure if it's like the biggest change.
> Mother: Well, it is going to be the biggest ...
> Young person: Well, I think probably the biggest change I think is going from like being able to walk to being wheelchair bound.
> Mother: That all happened ... I mean that was a big change, but that happened relatively smoothly ...

Young person: You think?

Father: You don't?

Young person: Well that's past now, there's not really that much point talking.

Mother: I mean you accepted all that pretty well.

Young person: No but … it doesn't matter.

Mother: No, well say what you think sorry. If that's okay … [to interviewer] if you're okay to analyze.

Young person: I mean it is a big change.

Mother: Yeah, I mean obviously we were dreading when [son] wasn't going to be able to walk any more. But that just all …

Young person: I know, well I think it's probably logistically the biggest change. But probably the biggest emotional change would probably be from going to walking to being wheelchair bound. So it really depends on what way you look at it.

Mother: But it was a gradual thing. I mean what was very difficult because we went through the call- … well [son] went through the calliper stage, and that was horrific. That was really, really hard. Wasn't it? I mean that was hard on you as well. And I think that was harder than actually going into the chair.

Young person: Okay.

Mother: Well I mean that's … okay, as you say it's different perceptions.

Young person: But that's all part of the same bit.

Father: Uhuh. Yeah it is.

Mother: Yeah, yeah uhuh. Yes.

Talk about the consequences and prognosis for Duchenne meant that of course what we were often either talking about or skirting around was people's thoughts and feelings about death. Sometimes it seemed to be that some of what was being said had not been said before, and it is hard to see how the research encounter could not stray into something that was close to a therapeutic encounter.

Here are just three extracts in which it seemed to me that some quite profound level of reflection and talk was going on. Firstly, in a small number of families there was talk of the hope for future treatments or cures, albeit tentatively. Such talk was imbued with quite a lot of intensity and emotion, as in this exchange between a mother and a sister where the young person is present, but not commenting:

Mother: And we're hoping that [son's] DNA is on the right page so that we can see if that works. So we've got everything crossed.

Sister: That'd be fantastic wouldn't it?
Mother: Um. So that'd be really good. Other than that, no we don't really ... [now addressing her son] we just take every day as it comes don't we, mate?

In the second extract, one mother shared her thoughts about her own future, which were linked inexorably with her son's:

Mother: It's not nice to plan ahead, but you have to. We've bought a house in Spain ... if anything happened that's where I'm going.
Interviewer: To stay?
Mother: Oh yeah! Big time. Wouldn't stop here. Couldn't live here anyway, cos [son's] been here, you know. And God willing, that'll be a long, long time, but that's the plan. And you can't really plan. You know like people say, 'Are you going to live there?' And you think, 'Yeah yeah'. Then you think, 'But what's got to come before?' You know.

In this third extract, a 15 year-old talks about difficulties in talking about living with Duchenne alongside his passionate desire to drive a car:

Interviewer: Do you talk to your mates about it ever?
Young Person: No, we don't really talk about it. They know I've got a problem but they don't talk about it a lot, talk about other stuff.
Interviewer: Is that how you like it, or would you sometimes like to talk about it?
Young Person: I'd rather talk about that than people not talking about it, I suppose. I just can't wait till I can learn to drive. People are saying at school, that if you're disabled you can learn to drive earlier than anybody else. I don't know if that's right, 'cos I haven't spoken to anyone about it, you're the first person I've ever said anything to, but that's what I've been told and that's what I heard on the radio.

Looking back at these extracts and remembering these research encounters, I am reminded at how I tried hard to create the conditions in which talk of a certain quality might be possible. What I mean is, talk that went beyond the superficial. In these moments I feel I have 'succeeded', that the interview is 'going well'. But in retrospect I am left wondering how far I have strayed into the 'therapeutic' and also how participants are left feeling. Birch and Millar (2000) describe their uncertainty about whether they 'unleashed' research participants' experiences as opposed to 'collecting' them. Cree et al. (2002) argue that because we often regard a 'successful' interview as one that has elicited a deeper level of personal reflection and/or disclosure, then the onus of responsibility to keep negotiating the boundaries of the encounter rests squarely with the researcher:

> ... to negotiate and re-negotiate with participants and to make ethical judgments about what is (and is not) a necessary line of investigation in a given research study. (Cree et al., 2002: 51)

But in practice does this happen and how easy is it? We usually do not know at the outset of an interview where the talk will take us and what is 'relevant'. My own research training some years ago warned me against 'mining' in interviews, that is, the danger of not sticking to the specific issue and question at hand because it was thought to be unethical to let people get deeper and deeper into subjects that may not really be what the research was about. Now the trend in qualitative research is for more open-ended and less structured encounters. How fair is it of me to cling to the so-called boundaries of a 'research interview' while clearly in pursuit of sensitive, private, potentially upsetting and conflicting talk? I clearly think a 'good interview' is one that leaves me and/or the interviewee feeling that something that matters has been discussed, that an intimacy has been shared, something disclosed or worked through, that someone has said things of significance, sometimes that they have said something that immediately translates into a powerful on-the-page quotation in my head. How does this affect the responsibilities of the interviewer and the ethics of the encounter, which may well go beyond anything presented on an ethics application form written sometime before interviews ever get started? The question of ethics is a good one, and it is highly doubtful that a successful application to an ethics committee has a great deal of bearing on whether a researcher goes on to be an ethical researcher (Beresford, 2012). Holt (2010) argues for an ethical approach that adopts and produces 'empowering research relations'.

If we are, albeit by stealth means, making everyone feel okay (even good) about the encounter and giving strong cues that the encounter is 'special' and a 'chance to talk', then we are trying to create something intimate. Given the technocratic approach we are often forced to take in terms of obtaining consent – even with the most accessible techniques – I think it's unlikely that children and young people (or many adults) really understand what is either being done to them or what they are agreeing to. Mishna, Antle and Regehr (2004) argue that if we 'over-do' creating an environment in which a child or young person feels comfortable or relaxed, then they might lose the capacity to make decisions about what they do and do not want to share. While we may routinely tell children and young people that they can choose to not answer any question they don't want, this rarely happens:

> Children and young adolescents may have difficulty anticipating the range of personal experiences that will be addressed in a qualitative interview, and their potential reactions to the kind of in-depth discussion inherent in qualitative interviewing. (Mishna et al., 2004: 455)

I notice the tendency, which I think is both right and questionable, to leave people feeling okay at the end of the research encounter. One way of doing this is with a positive closing question or to actually check that people are feeling okay. On one hand, this seems right and seems to concur with Davies (2008), who says we should try and leave the family unit unchanged by the research experience. On the other hand, it also seems like a kind of deception – persuading everyone that despite what has been said things can go back to the way they were, and also that I am free to go without having to feel either responsible or overly concerned. I can see, for example, that in closing one interview in which quite a lot of sensitive topics were covered, I am keen to be told that the mother and son are 'okay' or unscathed, and in actual fact I don't think I am leaving much scope for them to say, if it were true, that it had been a difficult or negative experience:

> Interviewer: Right. So what was it like to talking to me about all of that then [name], was it alright?
> Young Person: Yes. Yes.
> Interviewer: Not too boring?
> Mother: Not too boring?
> Young Person: No.
> Mother: Was David alright?
> Interviewer: But a little bit boring maybe?
> Young Person: Yes. You're cool David.
> Mother: You're cool, there you go! [Laughing]
> Interviewer: Thank you [name] let's turn this [recorder] off and ...

Concluding reflections

In this chapter I am trying to reflect on the importance of the home as a social and research setting, the power dynamics and differentials between different 'actors' and some of the methodological and ethical issues associated with trying to create an environment in which the encounter is a 'good' or meaningful one – with the associated questions that goal poses. The word 'actors' is helpful when we think of the performances that everyone are likely to be playing within an encounter as inherently foreign and strange as a research interview. Birch and Millar (2010: 200) remind us of this when they caution that, 'We need to try to suspend the belief that a more personal story reveals a more authentic story.' My concerns are that we understand the talk that emerges more usefully when we understand the context in which it was created. But my other concern is about the transparency and ethics of the research encounter in which the researcher often feels that they have to perform different roles, in different ways, with different goals – and with the aim of coming away with 'good stuff'. Four concluding points about this occur to me:

1. In trying to find out more about the lives of disabled children and young people, are we trying to 'mine the souls' of disabled children rather than 'letting them be'? (Murray & Penman, 1996). Is our quest one in which we find it hard to respect the privacies of disabled children and young people (or in fact any research participant), and only regard encounters as 'successful' if we feel the person or people opposite have really bared all? Or, in trying to create ways in which people can choose to reflect and share their intimate stories, are we trying to be more creative and respectful?

2. In questioning our research motives it has to be pertinent to ask why we need more research when we already know a great deal about substantive barriers to equality faced by disabled children, young people and their families and when so little is done at a political level with what we already know. 'Research weary families' (Cree et al., 2002) are likely to become more and more unsure of the benefits of research, particularly in times of cuts to support and services. In the study reported here I was pressed on this point (the usefulness of the research) by families more than any other study I can recall. Researchers have to continue to be very honest with research participants about the likely limits of change and/or personal benefit associated with taking part in research.

3. This is a fairly reflective piece of writing, and I am arguing, as I have done elsewhere (Abbott, 2012), that hearing more from the adult researcher may help us understand research findings more fully. Reflexivity is a good and useful endeavour in my view, but does it

run the danger of becoming 'all about me'? As Davies (2008, para 3.1) notes:

> There is a potential to be overly reflexive which may result in the researcher conveying more about themselves than the knowledge created through the research.

Holt (2010: 15) also reminds us that it is not right to 'suggest that the researcher can be all-knowing about her or his intentions and motivations'. Her description of the encounters as 'dynamic research performances' (p. 24) is helpful to me, as is her acknowledgment that such self-reflexivity, which shows the fallibility of the researcher and the research process, can be problematic in the world of academic research.

4. In trying to understand research encounters, one thing we rarely do is ask research participants what they have made of it all, and especially after they have had a chance to reflect on the process and what they have or have not shared. We generally do not ask children and young people in particular if the experience matched their expectations and how they understood the encounter.

Bushin (2007) concludes that the fluidity of action in family homes requires researchers to revisit, revise and renegotiating their ethical stance, their methods and their reflexivity with regard to their own positioning and stand- points. She also encourages researchers to be more honest and frank with each other about real-life research practice with children and young people so that we can learn from each other. I hope this chapter makes a small contribution to that endeavour.

Note

I want to acknowledge and thank all the young men, brothers, sisters and parents who took part in the research. The study was designed by Professor John Carpenter at the School for Policy Studies (University of Bristol) and carried out with the co-operation of Professor Kate Bushy at the University of Newcastle as well as our partner organizations, the Duchenne Family Support Group and the Muscular Dystrophy Campaign. The research was funded by the Department of Health in England as part of a Research Initiative on Long Term Neurological Conditions (Project 0530009). The views expressed in the chapter are those of the author and not necessarily those of the Department of Health.

References

Abbott, D. (2012) 'Other voices, other rooms: Talking to young men with Duchenne Muscular Dystrophy about the transition to adulthood', *Children & Society*, 26, 3, 241–250.

Abbott, D. & Carpenter, J. (2010) *Becoming an adult: Transition for young men with Duchenne Muscular Dystrophy (DMD)* (London: Muscular Dystrophy Campaign). http://www.bristol.ac.uk/norahfry/research/completed-projects/becominganadult.pdf [accessed 17 July 2012].

Beresford, B. (2012) Ethical issues and research with disabled children and young people, Presentation to 1st UK Disabled Children Research Network, University of Bristol, 16 May.

Birch, M. & Miller, T. (2000) 'Inviting intimacy: The interview as therapeutic opportunity', *International Journal of Social Research Methodology*, 3, 3, 189–202.

Bushin, N. (2007) 'Interviewing with children in their homes: Putting ethical principles into practice and developing flexible techniques', *Children's Geographies*, 5, 3, 235–251.

Carpenter, J. (2010) Disabled children growing up in families: Perspectives from developmental psychology and family systems theory. Presentation to ESRC Seminar Series: Researching the Lives of Disabled Children and Young People, with a Focus on Their Perspectives. Seminar 1: Theoretical Perspectives, University of Strathclyde, 29 January. http://www.strath.ac.uk/humanities/schoolofappliedsocialsciences/socialwork/esrcseminarseries/, [accessed 17 July 2012].

Connors, C. & Stalker, K. (2003) *The views and experiences of disabled children and their siblings: A positive outlook* (London: Jessica Kingsley).

Cree, V., Kay, H. & Tisdall, K. (2002) 'Research with children: Sharing dilemmas', *Child and Family Social Work*, 7, 1, 47–56.

Davies, H. (2008). 'Reflexivity in research practice: Informed consent with children at school and at home', *Sociological Research Online*, 13, 4, 5.

Eagle, M., Baudouin, S., Chandler, C., Giddings, D., Bullock, R. & Bushby, K. (2002) 'Survival in Duchenne Muscular Dystrophy: Improvements in life expectancy since 1967 and the impact of home nocturnal ventilation', *Neuromuscular Disorders*, 12, 10, 926–929.

Eagle, M., Bourke, J., Bullock, R., Gibson, M., Mehtaa, J., Giddings, D., Strauba, V. & Bushby, K. (2007) 'Managing Duchenne Muscular Dystrophy: The additive effect of spinal surgery and home nocturnal ventilation in improving survival', *Neuromuscular Disorders*, 17, 6, 470–475.

Gibson, B., Young, N., Upshur, R. & McKeever, P. (2007) 'Men on the margin: A Bourdieusian examination of living into adulthood with muscular dystrophy', *Social Science and Medicine*, 65, 3, 505–517.

Goodley, D. & Runswick-Cole, K. (2012) *Does every child matter, post-Blair? The interconnections of disabled childhoods* (Manchester: Manchester Metropolitan University). http://post-blair.posterous.com/ [accessed 18 July 2012].

Holt, L. (2010) 'The 'voices' of children: De-centring empowering research relations', *Children's Geographies*, 2, 1, 13–27.

Kitzinger, C. (2004) Feminist approaches, in C. Seale, G. Gobo, J. Gubrium & D. Silverman (eds), *Qualitative Research Practice* (London: Sage), pp. 125–140.

Masson, J. (2000) Researching children's perspectives: Legal issues, in A. Lewis & G. Lindsay (eds), *Researching children's perspectives* (Buckingham: Open University Press), pp. 34–45.

Mayall, B. (2000) Conversations with children: Working with generational issues, in P.H. Christensen & A. James (eds), *Research with children: Perspectives and practices* (London: Falmer Press), pp. 120–135.

Mishna, F., Antle, B. & Regehr, C. (2004) 'Tapping the perspectives of children: Emerging ethical issues in qualitative research', *Qualitative Social Work*, 3, 4, 449–468.

Morris, J. (2003) 'Including all children: Finding out about the experiences of children with communication and/or cognitive impairments', *Children & Society*, 17, 5, 337–348.

Murray, P. & Penman, J. (eds) (1996) *Let our children be: A collection of stories* (Sheffield: Parents With Attitude).

Rahbeck, J., Werge, B., Madsen, A., Marquardt, J., Steffensen, B. & Jeppesen, J. (2005) 'Adult life with Duchenne Muscular Dystrophy: Observations among an emerging and unforeseen patient population', *Developmental Neurorehabilitation*, 8, 1, 17–28.

Rogers, C.R. (1961) *On becoming a person: A therapist's view of psychotherapy* (Boston, MA: Houghton Mifflin).

Shakespeare, T., Barnes, C., Priestly, M., Cunninghambirley, S., Davis, J. & Watson, N. (1999) *Life as a disabled child: A qualitative study of young people's experiences and perspectives* (Leeds: Disability Research Unit, University of Leeds).

Smart, C. (2009) 'Shifting horizons: Reflections on qualitative methods', *Feminist Theory*, 10, 3, 1–14.

Tisdall, K., Davis, J. & Gallagher, M. (2009) *Research with children and young people: Research design, methods and analysis* (London: Sage).

Watson, N. (2012) 'Theorising the lives of disabled children: How can disability theory help?', *Children & Society*, 26, 3, 192–202.

Woolfson, L. (2004) 'Family well-being and disabled children: A psychosocial model of disability-related child behaviour problems', *British Journal of Health Psychology*, 9, 1, 1–13.

7

Remembering School in Different Historical Worlds: Changing Patterns of Education in the Lives of Disabled Children and Young People

Sonali Shah

Introduction

The right to education for all, including for disabled people, has been enshrined in international law for many years. A number of global policy instruments have asserted that everyone is entitled to enjoy equal rights and fundamental freedoms in different aspects of social life. In 1948, Article 2 of the *Universal Declaration of Human Rights* expressed that 'Everyone is entitled to all the rights and freedoms set forth in this Declaration,' one of these being the right and freedom to access education, outlined in Article 26. The right to education has also been asserted in later policy instruments such as the first protocol of the 1950 *European Declaration of Human Rights*, which stated: 'No one shall be denied the right to education.' This was followed by the *United Nations Convention on the Rights of a Child* in 1989 and the 1994 Salamanca *World Statement on Special Needs Education* (UNESCO, 1994), which called for the international community to adopt strategies and resources to enable disabled children and young people to be educated in mainstream schools.

However, in 2006 the United Nations reached new heights in terms of how it viewed disabled people, recognizing them as social actors with rights and choices as opposed to objects of charity, medical treatment and social protection. It adopted the *Convention on the Rights of Persons with Disabilities* (UNCRPD). With fifty binding articles, this is the first international human rights treaty designed to protect the human rights and fundamental freedoms of disabled people in all aspects of social life, including those with respect to accessibility, right to life, dignity, participation and inclusion in society.

Most relevant to this chapter are Articles 7 and 24, which promote inclusive investments into the future of disabled children. Specifically Article 7 emphasizes their entitlement to enjoy full human rights and fundamental freedoms on an equal basis to non-disabled children. It requires State Parties to ensure that the views of disabled children are given due weight and assistance is provided (appropriate in terms of age and impairment) to enable the children's rights to be realized. Article 24 reaffirms the right to education and requires States to ensure that disabled people are 'not excluded from the general education system on the basis of disability, and that children with disabilities are not excluded from free and compulsory primary education, or from secondary education, on the basis of disability' (United Nations, 2006: 18).

However, the declarations of policy rhetoric have not always been easily achieved in reality, especially when Governments reserve the right to implement policies or at least parts of them (as has been the case in the UK with regard to Article 24 of UNCRPD). Therefore the possibility of full educational inclusion for disabled children and young people remains contingent on the investment in enabling practices and breaking down of disabling barriers within and beyond the school gates (Armstrong, 2003; Shah & Priestley, 2009). This is apparent from the biographical material presented in the latter part of this chapter.

This chapter draws on remembrances from adults with physical impairments who grew up between the post-war period and twenty-first century in England (collected as part of a larger study funded by the Nuffield Foundation: Shah & Priestley, 2011) as a lens to explore how changing educational policies and practices shaped their choices and chances as they moved into adulthood. It connects vacillating philosophies and policy changes with personal narratives, and shows how this public–private interface influenced three key issues in the education lives of disabled children and young people: choosing pupils, choosing school; educational expectations and achievement; and the school environment. It also affords an opportunity to understand the ways private resources, particularly personal agency and familial capital, can resist and challenge professional authority and expected policy outcomes, thus triggering key turning points in life trajectories. However, before presenting these findings, the chapter outlines the significant policy shifts that have taken place in relation to the education of disabled children and young people from the Second World War to the present day.

Developments in the education of disabled children from post-war times

Education, like many social institutions, reflects the norms and value systems of the macro-level society in which it is embedded. In general, education is the vehicle by which social, academic and economic learning can be transmitted from one generation to the next. Further, education has been argued as being the mechanism by which young people are taught the skills necessary to participate in their community and actively engage with civic society (Shah, 2008). However the interplay of competing political, social and economic discourses and policies, on which the education system is based, dictates who is taught as well as how and when such teaching is administered. Given this, it is no surprise that the education for disabled children and young people between the post-war period and the present day has had a history steeped in vacillating practices, reflecting the social interests of the time (Oswin, 1998).

So, for instance, during the first half of the twentieth century education was driven by the reins of the eugenics movement, and later the philosophy of normalization. While encouraging the maintenance of social order and social improvement of the general population, it also promoted the control and exclusion of the so-called 'defective' minorities who were deemed a threat to such an achievement (Duncan, 1942; Stiker, 1999). These ideologies had great impact on policies of assessment and selection, in particular the 1944 Education Act, often called the Butler Act (Ministry of Education, 1944). The policy did bring radical reforms to the British education system by introducing a tripartite system, offering free compulsory education for all and encouraging disabled and non-disabled children to be educated together. However, it paradoxically perpetuated the segregation of disabled children into special schools that reinforced a medicalized approach and separated children into administrative categories of 'handicap'. Following the 1944 Act, the Handicapped Pupils and School Health Regulations in 1945 increased the categories of children 'who cannot be educated satisfactorily in ordinary school' to eleven (reduced to ten in 1953). These categories included 'partially sighted', 'partially deaf', 'delicate', 'epileptic', 'diabetic', 'physically handicapped' and 'educationally subnormal [ESN]' (Barnes, 1991). This shaped the nature of post-war educational institutions, prompting a rise in the number of those in special schooling from 38,499 in 1945 to 106,367 in 1972 (Topliss, 1975).

Since the Butler Act in post-war Britain, various attempts have been made to legislate for the educational inclusion of disabled children. Publication of the Warnock Report (Warnock, 1978), and the subsequent 1981 Education Act (DfE, 1981) are widely acknowledged as significant turning points towards integration. The 1981 Act replaced the above categories of 'handicap' with categories of 'special educational need' (SEN), gave a legal entitlement to assessment and promoted greater parental involvement in the process. Its inclusion drive was promoted by subsequent policies, including the 1996 Education Act and the Special Educational Needs and Disability Act (SENDA) of 2001 (DfES, 2001). In September 2005, Part 4 of the Disability Discrimination Act came into effect, advocating the idea that children and young people with special educational needs (SEN) should, where possible, be educated in mainstream schools alongside their non-disabled peers and siblings. This was also asserted by the Disability Equality Duty (2006), which further increased pressure on schools and colleges (CSIE, 2005), and the Equality Act 2010 (replacing the 1995 Disability Discrimination Act). The legal duties made it unlawful for education providers to treat disabled children 'less favourably' than their non-disabled peers, and required them to make 'reasonable adjustments' to enhance disabled children's participation in education.

Although such policy initiatives have injected schools with the aspiration to provide young disabled people with the means to participate in education on more of an equal playing field to their non-disabled contemporaries, the regime of the 'education market' (Ball, Bowe & Gerwitz, 1994) and the perception that disabled children have a low value or are a drain on teaching resources fuelled schools' opposition to inclusion. Statistical data from the Pupils Level Annual School Census (PLASC) evidenced that in the years 2006/7 there were 89,400 pupils enrolled in special schools in England. Despite the plethora of policies advocating educational inclusion for disabled children, figures taken from the School Census and SEN Survey between 2007 and 2011 show an annual increase in the number of pupils attending special schools. In 2011 there were 94,275 pupils in the 1,048 special schools (maintained and non-maintained) across England (DfES, 2011a). This represents 1.2 per cent of the school population (counted as being 8.1 million in 2011). The percentage of disabled children across all schools (both with and without statements of educational needs) was recorded as 2.8 per cent and 17.8 per cent respectively.

The Coalition Government in 2010 decided to reverse the drive to close special schools put forward by the previous Labour administration.

When in opposition they criticized Labour's support for inclusion, referring to the proposal as 'absurd' as it allowed many pupils to be 'inappropriately placed in mainstream schools' (BBC News, 29 November 2006). This incited the current Prime Minister's own manifesto commitment to a 'moratorium on the ideologically-driven closure of special schools', with a pledge to 'end the bias towards the inclusion of children with special needs in mainstream schools' (Conservative Party, 2010: 53). So, despite the radical policy changes since the post-war period, data from 2011 School Census suggests that over 45 per cent of all pupils continue to attend special schools. Moreover, with 1,048 special schools in England in 2011 it is evident that the number is greater in the twenty-first century than in the early 1970s (Office for National Statistics, 2000).

The changing nature of impairments is said to account for the continuation of special education. Since 1975, children aged 0–16 have formed the fastest-growing group of children in the UK, rising from 476,000 in 1975 to 772,000 in 2002 (Haines & Ruebain, 2011). This suggests a 62 per cent increase (Prime Minister's Strategy Unit, 2005). However, over the years the profile of disabled children has changed as a consequence of advancing medicine, which has enabled the survival of children with complex cognitive and physical impairments (Glendinning, Kirk, Guiffrida & Lawton, 2001; Shah & Priestley, 2011). Many of the maintained and non-maintained special schools are housing children with the label of Behaviour, Emotional and Social Difficulty (EBSD), followed by Autistic Spectrum Disorder (ASD). Data taken from the School Census in 2011 (DfE, 2011b) indicates that out of the eleven categories of need highlighted above and used to identify children with SEN, there are 353 schools for pupils with 'physical disability'.

Furthermore, while most special schools are day schools, boarding schools have been described in various reports as having an important role since the post-war period (Cole, 1986). For instance, in the Warnock Report of 1978, boarding schools were suggested as being important, especially in situations where a disabled child required coordinated provision of medical treatment, education, therapy and care

> ... which it would be beyond the combined resources of a day school and his family to provide but which does not call for his admission to hospital. (Cole, 1986: 5)

Residential schools were also considered useful in bringing respite to families of disabled children. There are still around 10,000 disabled children attending residential special schools (Shah & Priestley, 2009).

This equates to 4 per cent of all students with SEN. Data from the Family Resource Survey reveals that disabled children are significantly over-represented in looked-after children (see also Priestley, Rabiee & Harris, 2002). According to the report *Disabled Children in Residential Placements* (DfES, 2003), of the 1,320 residential placements for disabled children just under half were in schools.

The location and physical structure of these institutions has changed since the 1940s, when several were converted country mansions situated in the countryside, many miles from pupils' family homes (Cole, 1986). The distance of these schools from children's families was considered to impede parent–child relationships. This idea has been suggested by a number of authors, including Shakespeare and Watson (1998), and Shah (2005), who argue that residential schools may cause detachment from the child's family and home community. Fuchs and Fuchs (1998) concur, suggesting that the removal from the common culture of childhood contributes to later isolation in adulthood. Although this situation has officially changed under the persuasion of official guidance, including the 1989 Children Act (which encourages the maintenance of regular contact between children and parents/guardians), evidence shows that a significant number of disabled children who reside in boarding schools neither go home nor are visited by family on a regular basis (Gordon, Parker & Loughran with Heslop, 2000).

However, although the above evidence indicates macro-level change in terms of policies and practices in the education of disabled children, it is only through the connection of public policies and the private lives of disabled people that the actual impact of these policies can be determined. Focusing on the relationship between private lives and public policies provides a lens to examine social change, as well as both the intended and unintended consequences of policies, beyond the public purpose. For example certain educational policies for disabled people had a profound impact on family life, social relationships and self-identity. It further enables an understanding of the interplay between structure and agency in determining real-life outcome. Intertwining biographical narratives with a macro-level historical analysis of the education system for disabled children, this chapter explores the impact of public policies on private lives of individuals with physical or sensory impairments, born in the 1940s, 1960s and 1980s. In particular the chapter pursues three themes: (1) choosing pupils, choosing schools; (2) academic expectations and achievements, and (3) the school environment.

The narratives illustrate the structures of control under which the private lives unfolded over time, and how they interacted with different institutions, polices and environments. They also reveal key points at which individual agency and familial resources collided with professional authority or with institutional barriers to inclusion, enabling individuals to resist expected life course trajectories and follow new ones. Connecting these narratives with historical policy analysis permits an examination of how educational regimes and institutional provision dominating different historical times framed the life course expectations and social relationships of disabled children and also their social, academic and economic opportunities in subsequent adulthood. First, however, a note on the methodological approach adopted to conduct the research on which this chapter is based.

Methods

The methodological approach adopted for the research reported in this chapter is innovative and forward-thinking, in that it facilitates connections between individual experience and the social context, between biography and history, and between structure and agency. It provides disabled people with opportunities to become autobiographers and social historians by combining their biographical narratives with historical policy analysis to generate evidence of disability history and social change from the Second World War to the present day.

Grounded in a social model of disability (Oliver, 1990), the method reconnects the 'individual' experience of disability with its 'social' context in post-war Britain by enabling the history of disability and education to be known through disabled people's narratives. In this way, the empirical focus for narrative research moves beyond the 'life experiences of disabled people' and towards the 'experiences of disability in people's lives', responding to Finkelstein's reminder that 'disabled people are not the subject matter of social interpretation of disability' (Finkelstein, 2001: 1). Thus, the primary purpose is to reveal and challenge the network of social relations, institutions and barriers that inhibit the full participation and equality of disabled people in society.

Thomas (1999: 8) supports the use of micro narrative as a lens to view macro change with her contention that 'experiential narratives offer a route to understanding the socio-structural'. Reismann (1993) concurs that narratives uncover a wealth of knowledge about the socio-cultural world in which an individual lives and grows. Thus, through personal narratives, society and culture can 'speak for itself' (Smith & Sparks, 2008: 18). Moreover, in terms of disability research, narratives are particularly useful as they offer insights into how impairment and disability is negotiated and constructed (i.e. either as a personal or social phenomenon), by different biological subjects (Goodley & Tregaskis, 2006).

The method of analysis used for the research reported here is guided by Priestley's 'individual-biographical' (2001) and 'structural-normative' (2003) approach to disability and the life course, and by Shah's (2005, 2008) approach to disabled people's 'careers'. In this way, the research seeks to evidence the ways in which different environments and barriers, institutions and policies, personal characteristics and relationships shape particular life course trajectories, pathways and turning points in individual lives. This approach generates biographical 'traces' of social history and social patterning in the lives of young disabled people over time as well as instances of individual agency, resistance and resilience that initiate particular turning points in life course pathways. It presents young disabled people as critical social actors, helping them to make a contribution as social historians by contextualizing every aspect of their story and relating it to the social world of today.

Looking at the history of education through the perspectives of young disabled people, rather than via a positivistic lens derived with a specific focus in mind, not only 'gives voice' to those frequently left out of official educational discourse, but also offers opportunities to engage with the past in new ways (Armstrong, 2003). Using these insider perspectives in critical ways reveals hidden, often contested histories of segregation and inclusion that sometimes collide with dominant ideology about the educational histories of disabled children. Therefore bringing history alive allows new understandings of the past to frame future policy agendas for inclusion, indicating what works and avoiding negative outcomes for future generations.

The biographical narratives used for illustration below have been selected from longer life history interviews conducted (by the author, a disabled researcher) as part of a larger empirical research project, funded by the Nuffield Foundation and based at the University of Leeds. Sixty life history interviews were conducted with three cohorts of men and women who volunteered to participate in the project. They grew up with physical or sensory impairments within different socio-historical contexts in England between the 1940s and the twenty-first century. The oldest generation were born in the 1940s – during or shortly after the Second World War – and grew up with attempts to more systematically address disability in British social policy (in the emergence of the post-war welfare state with major legislation prompted by an analysis of social need – education, employment, health and social assistance, for example). The second generation, born in the 1960s, experienced childhood and early adulthood at a time when assumptions about the social exclusion of disabled people were being radically reviewed (for example, in critiques of residential institutions and segregated schools, in moves towards integration and community living, and in the rise of the early disabled people's movement). The youngest cohort, born in the 1980s, were the first generation of disabled people to reach early adulthood in the era of international non-discrimination and human rights legislation affecting all aspects of their lives.

The selection of the three cohorts was significant both generationally and historically. The primary aim of the research was to examine how life had changed for disabled people since the Second World War, with a particular focus on young disabled people who are experiencing adulthood in an era of international disability rights legislation.

The life history interviews were conducted in 2007 and 2008 using a topic guide covering five themes – *family life, education, medical treatment, employment* and *identity*. Semi-structured interviews were conducted by a disabled researcher who, like the participants, had experiences of challenging oppression, disablement, segregated education and inclusion. This shared experience, or 'epistemological privilege' as Stanley and Wise (1993) put it, facilitated rapport between the researcher and the researched, encouraging the latter to be more honest and lucid with their responses (Shah, 2006).

Participants were encouraged to tell stories of their lives, in a chronological order (typically from their birth stories to those of life in the present). These stories included perceptions of their past, present and future selves, revealing the interface between the social structures and personal agency in the construction of these possible selves. This chapter draws on some of the discussions from the larger study. They are intended to be illustrative, rather than representative, of the experiences of education and schooling across the three generations. They also demonstrate the interplay between structure, agency and resources in the shaping of outcomes. All the quotes used below are from real people who gave written consent for their stories to be used in the public domain, although their real names have been replaced with self-selected pseudonyms.

Findings

Theme 1: Choosing schools, choosing pupils

The oldest generation were born during and after the Second World War, during a time of significant policy change and a time when the first attempts were made to address disability systematically within British social policy. This had a substantial impact on the choices and experiences of future generations of disabled children and adults.

Education was identified as central to the social reconstruction of post-war Britain, stemming from Beveridge's wartime analysis of social need in which 'Ignorance' was a particular concern. The 1944 Education Act was conceived as one of the three pillars of the new welfare system (along with the 1948 National Health Service and 1946 National Assistance Act), bringing optimistic changes to how education was organized and provided to children and young people. The innovative reforms offered free secondary education for all, raised the school leaving age to 15 and encouraged inclusion or, at least, integration. However, it soon became apparent that the reform of the 'new' Education Act was principally targeted at the middle classes (Tomlinson, 2001). Further, despite its stated commitment for local authorities to provide an equal education for all children, and a greater understanding and public concern towards the educational inclusion of disabled children, it also permitted professional authorities to exercise greater control over the selection and admission of pupils (via the Eleven Plus examination). This gateway determined whether pupils went to secondary modern schools or to grammar schools. The academic selection process also facilitated an expansion of special education. Although schools for 'the deaf' and 'the blind' have been established since the late 1700s, and for all disabled children since the 1920s, more special schools were required to accommodate children identified by one or more of the eleven categories of need stipulated by the 1944 Act (see also Borsay, 2007). So, as Barnes (1991: 29) argued, 'selection by ability sanctioned selection by disability'. Moreover medical authorities were given powers to remove disabled children from the mainstream sector, even where this did not comply with parents' wishes. There was no unitary system of selecting pupils to attend special schools. Rather it was based on Intelligence Quotient (IQ) results and completion of the Handicapped Pupils Form, which included opinion from educational and medical authority. The involvement of medical authority in educational placement of disabled children was revealed in some of the self-told stories of the oldest generation.

Bob started residential special school at the age of five in the 1950s. He believed medical professionals had a prominent role in shaping educational trajectories of disabled children at that time:

> ... the education of disabled children going up to the 1960s was actually controlled by the health service and not by education, so they

had quite a large say in where disabled children went ... they felt it was best to send me away to a special school, for my mum and for me.

Similarly, May, born in 1946, went to a special school at an early age following a medical consultation. She recalls:

> I think it was the consultant who we saw, yeah. And it was them that said I should go to this school, yeah, it was down to the consultant really, that I should go there. Because you had physiotherapy, which you could have had anywhere really. Could have gone to the hospital for it. But that was one of the reasons. I don't really know what other reasons were ...

A number of disabled children initially went to their local mainstream school with non-disabled peers from their neighbouring community, as promised by the 1944 Education Act. However their placement was often curtailed after they were labelled 'educationally sub-normal' and thus deemed, by teachers and Local Education Authorities, to be incapable of receiving an 'ordinary' education (Hurt, 1988). This can be exemplified by Ray's experience of spending two weeks in a local mainstream primary school before his parents were advised to send him to special school because his visual impairment was deemed a health hazard:

> ... my mum and dad took me to a mainstream school when I was 4½. I was there for two weeks and the teachers decided that it was unsafe to have a blind kid or, that was how they referred to it, partially sighted kid in their school, so they sent to me a residential school. It will have been what 1949/50 and I was there till I was nearly 8 basically, so I was there for 4 years ... it was a school for blind kids and deaf kids ...

Hilary, born a year prior to Ray in 1945, recalls how she was at mainstream school for a term, before her parents were persuaded to remove her and consent to her going to a residential school specifically for children with cerebral palsy (the most common childhood impairment of the time after the decline in tuberculosis). In the early 1950s parent groups and philanthropists established the Spastic Society charity, which set up schools for children with cerebral palsy:

> When I was five, the LEA suggested that I should go to the local primary school for three mornings a week. My parents were happy

with the choice. But my mother soon recognized that it wasn't working. For example, at playtime the other children bullied me and
segregated me from their games. When they did include me, the
children would delight in playing 'push and shove' with me as I sat
in my buffer chair, which was on wheels. ... After a few weeks, the
Headmistress admitted that having me in the school wasn't working
and I need personal one-to-one teaching. So I left after a term and
I had a home tutor. She was hopeless. ... Now the local school and
home tutor had failed me, the LEA had to provide financial support
for me to be educated out of the county ... a school in Edwardian
mansion seventy miles away from where we lived. I was at the school
for ten years ...

Worton shared a similar memory of attending the local mainstream
primary school before her parents were advised that her 'needs' would
be better catered for in a residential special school. However, given the
eleven categories of impairment on which educational provision for
disabled children was based at the time, there were difficulties finding
placements for children with multiple impairments:

Basically when I went blind I spent a couple of months being towed
round all the boarding schools and being turned down by them
because the blind ones didn't want me because I didn't walk very
well and the physically impaired schools didn't want me because
I was blind, and some schools didn't want me because once I went
blind it became obvious that I was actually quite deaf ...

Dan was also enrolled in a local mainstream school at the start of his
educational career. This enabled him to go to the same school as his
brothers and neighbourhood friends. However, as a consequence of
extensive orthopaedic surgery when he was seven and eight years old,
he missed out on large part of schooling. Thus doctors suggested to him
that he should attend the 'local' special school:

I can remember, I should imagine possibly 7 or 8, being in and out of
hospital, and it was suggested by the medical profession that I should
go to a special school, and I always remember this school ... it was a
real big old type of building and we used to be taken on a blue single-
decker bus with the City Council Education Department written on
the side.

Contrary to Hilary, Ray and Worton, Dan's placement at the special school was a temporary one. He was disappointed with the lack of academic challenge and keen to join his friends in the local mainstream school. The strong family relationships that featured throughout his story played an influential role in his subsequent pathway, enabling him to avoid following a trajectory of segregation and go on to live an ordinary life among his family and community:

> I used to complain, at home you know, saying 'I want to go to school with all the others' and I don't know what happened, whether my parents had put pressure on or whatever, but I remember leaving the school and then going to an ordinary secondary school, where you know, it was more Maths and English and what have ya', rather than making raffia baskets.

There were other examples of resistance and resilience among the oldest generation. Several members of the cohort indicated how parents had resisted professional authority so their children could follow an inclusive life pathway. Such was the case with Maggie who, like Dan, briefly encountered the idea of special schooling (advised by the school and doctors) before her mother directed her towards a more 'ordinary' childhood and adulthood.

> I think why I had the life I had was because me mum wouldn't let me go to a special school. ... The council, or whatever they call them, and the school wanted me to go to a special school. And my mum put her foot down and said 'no way, she will go to that school'. ... And I remember her sort of saying [to me] 'you're bright enough to cope and so I know you can do it'. And I think I must have said I don't want to go to a special school. Because my friends were here, it was a village, we knew everybody, and people would say 'oh, we'll look after her'. I suppose when you think about it my life could have been totally different, totally different.

Such resistance came with informal and creative support interventions, which, in the absence of public structures of support, were required to protect young people from disability discrimination and help them to overcome barriers to achievement. Such support was often provided by family, friends or individual teachers. This was apparent from the remembrances of some participants from the oldest cohort, (including Grace), who completed their compulsory education during a time when disability was considered more as a 'personal trouble' rather than a 'social issue' (Mills, 1959):

> I learned later that I was to go to a special school but dad refused, bearing in mind this is [mid-1950s]. Dad absolutely refused point blank. I wasn't to go to special school. I was to go to mainstream school. ... I went to the same school as my brother. ... There was no way I could have managed to walk to school, and mum also arranged for me to go to school on a bike. Nobody else was allowed to go to school on a bike but I was allowed to go on my three-wheeler so that's quite, quite good ... bearing in mind it was the 50s, the school was quite receptive to disability. The classrooms were upstairs and I was allowed extra time to get upstairs, (*Grace.*)

As well as parents, teachers were identified as significant to participants' future trajectories. This was evidenced in stories from the youngest generation too. For instance, Helen (born in the 1980s) attributes her inclusive educational pathway to a teacher at the special school she used to attend who recognized her academic potential. The agency of this teacher triggered a critical turning point, from segregation to inclusion:

> I was very, very lucky because the only reason I left my special school was that the teacher who had – that had been assigned to my class and had the most to do with me throughout my time at my special school saw that I had the potential and the ability to survive in a mainstream environment. So she took her free periods off when she wasn't teaching, she took me to the local primary school and made sure that I did maths and science along with kids at the local primary school. But the – she fought against the rest of the school and to some extent the apathy of my parents to get me out of the school.

Even though proposals for the 1976 Education Act had sought to implement Labour's comprehensive education pledges, there were continuing loopholes in the placement of disabled children. If a child's placement in mainstream school was deemed to disturb the education of other pupils, or result in expense perceived as 'unreasonable' they were advised to go to special school. These same constraints were included in the 1981 Education Act and, to some extent, the 1996 Education Act. Further, although in theory educational psychologists had been given responsibility for making placement decisions, the majority of decisions were still made by Chief Medical Officers (Segal, 1961). So despite shifts in policy goals, the inclusion of disabled children, like Helen, into mainstream schools was more the outcome of personal agency and social capital rather than public policies.

However, the biographical narratives also highlight how resistance and choice was sometimes constrained by the limited inclusion policies. Eileen, for instance, was born in 1968. She had a mobility impairment from childhood, although it was not diagnosed as Hyper-mobility Syndrome until she was 15. In practical terms the impairment meant that she 'didn't walk normally ... fell over more than is normal and was falling down staircases, couldn't run without falling over'. Eileen attended mainstream school for all of her compulsory education, although, as her tendency to fall over was perceived as 'dangerous' for the school she was 'excluded' from school on a regular basis. As mentioned above, disability was considered a private affair as opposed to public issue, so if Eileen was not physically fit enough to participate in the curricular activities there was no learning support for her to draw on. Rather she was 'told to go home' and to 'come back when [she] was better'. Her reflection below draws comparisons between her own experience of schooling compared to her perception of what she believed should happen under the Disability Discrimination Act (the dominant legislation at the time she was interviewed):

> I had both of my legs operated on. I had both of them done when I was 15. I was at the end of the first year of doing my O levels and it was the beginning of the second year of doing my O levels. And I was off school for between four and six months each time. And there was no support whatsoever. So actually it was only that a friend brought all of the notes (she took notes in class, she photocopied them and gave them to me) that I actually did my O levels ... when I think about it now, it's bloody ridiculous. ... I would make an assumption now that under the DDA I would have been able to go along and say you have to make provision for me; whether it be home tutoring or just sending notes home, or telling me what you're studying. There was nothing, nothing at all.

The 1981 Education Act did introduce greater parental involvement in school placement decisions. This, coupled with increasing political activism (from disability advocacy groups and from parent advocacy groups), encouraged greater resistance to advice provided by health professionals in relation to the education of disabled children. Parental 'choice' was further promoted by the Conservative Government, in the 1993 and 1996 Education Acts, which saw the emergence of a new Code of Practice and a Special Educational Needs Tribunal system. The system presented parents with new rights and opportunities to appeal the educational placement of their disabled child, enabling a move away from a policy framework that gave professionals maximum decision-making power (see Riddell, Adler, Mordaunt & Farmakopoulou, 2000; Harris, 1997). The practical workings of such a policy shift are illustrated by some of the biographical narratives from the youngest cohort, who were born during the Thatcher Conservative Government and completed compulsory schooling between the 1981 Education Act and the Special Educational Needs Disability Act (DfES, 2001).

For example, Rachel was born in 1985. She went to a special school when she was 5, under the recommendations of medical authority and the LEA, who did not consider it to be appropriate for a child with a significant speech impairment to go to mainstream school. As is evident from the biographies of the oldest cohort (i.e. Dan and Maggie), Rachel's mother recognized her academic potential and fought to get Rachel transferred to a mainstream school. Although Rachel spent the final year of her primary education in a mainstream school, her transition to secondary school, in the mid-1990s, was not straightforward, as articulated by her mother:

> because the LEA said there was no accessible secondary school so she will have to go back to special school. ... So off we went to the High Court and Special Needs Tribunal, and they agreed that she should go to the local comprehensive.

However, in the event, the local comprehensive school were not prepared to accept Rachel as their pupil.

This story of resilient and compassionate parents of disabled children fighting against dominant institutional policies and opportunity structures is not a unique one. Such a narrative was also conveyed by Harvey, who, describing his upbringing as 'working class', recalls that his mother's agency has been critical to his own academic drive and ability to move beyond expectations of class and disability:

> my mother has been the one that's motivated me to succeed, to be where I am today. ... She was like: 'son, you can't be a bricklayer, you can't be a fisherman. You know, there's only one thing you can do and that's to use your brain. You know, so you've got one way out of here.

You know, you've got one way to succeed and that's by using your education, you know,' so that's what I did.

Harvey remembers the contradictory policy changes that were implemented by the Thatcher Government in the 1980s, promoting inclusion while steering disabled children towards educational segregation. He suggests how his mother caused a critical turning point in his life pathway by resisting professional authority to secure a place at mainstream school:

> ... when I first started at school the Tory Government had introduced mainstreaming disabled people in education. However, my mother still had to fight the entrenched values of the education system to enable me to go into mainstream education. There was a lot of pressure on me to go into a special needs school ... round about the time when I was starting school there was this kind of accepted thing that disabled children went to special school. ... I'm really pleased that my mother fought against that to put me into mainstream school and to ensure that I had the support to succeed, because there was a lot of doubt amongst the professionals as to whether I would be able to succeed. For example, when I was about 3 or 4 [I didn't know it at the time] but I went to see an educational psychologist who obviously did tests on me to see if I could cope in a mainstream environment.

Although there were more stories of inclusion placements from the youngest cohort, this could be attributed to the social capital and support mechanisms available in the 1980s, 1990s and twenty-first century, which have motivated the growth of parents and families as 'change agents' for disabled children, and encouraged parent–professional partnerships (Wolfendale, 2004). Further, support networks for parents and disabled children, as well as positive disabled role models in public spaces, gave them the confidence to contest decisions of professional authority. Unlike parents of disabled people in the oldest and middle cohort, parents of the youngest cohort were making decisions in a climate more informed and supportive of disability rights and equality (with the disabled people's movement, the inclusion movement and advocacy groups). Although educational inclusion is dependent on the availability and willingness of local schools to accept disabled children, in some instances it is more determined by parental advocacy. This was indicated in some of the narratives from each generation. They suggested that, in the absence of statutory frameworks of disability, practical creative solutions were negotiated between some families and schools Not all families, however, had the capacity to resist professional decisions and in such cases children were more likely to be directed by public policy frameworks of segregation.

Theme 2: Achievement and expectations

The biographical narratives from across the three generational cohorts revealed the impact achievement and expectations in childhood had on their choices and chances in adulthood. They suggest how institutional relationships and regimes frame expectations, influence patterns of achievement and direct future trajectories (Shah, 2008; Furlong & Biggart, 1999). There were ample references, in the narratives, to the poor standard of education and unchallenging curriculum offered at special schools. For example, May expresses how the limited academic opportunities offered to her in special school influenced the low expectations she had of herself:

the standard of education was very poor. They never had any expectations of you at all. Never was entered for the 11+, didn't do any O levels, it was very basic education. ... I mean, you did reading, maths, things – you know, things like that. But it was very sort of basic things. I used to try and stay off school as much as possible. I used to pretend I was ill. Or I'd go to school and get myself worked up as though I'd got a temperature so they'd send me home, just hated it. So I didn't have any expectations of myself, I just wanted to – couldn't really wait for the day until I left school. ... I left at 16.

Dan presented a similar recollection of his schooling in the 1950s when he was '7 or 8', drawing comparisons between special and mainstream school:

it was more about doing things like making raffia baskets and playing with, you know, clay and they had gardens at the back and used to let us potter about, digging things up or planting things, but it didn't seem to be you know, really academic type of thing ...

Like Dan, Daisy had a taste of special education at the age 7 when it was suggested that she should go to an 'open air' school. These schools, which grew in number during the 1930s, aimed to provide children with a temporary haven, with a regime of sunshine and fresh air, to recuperate from diseases like tuberculosis or poliomyelitis, before returning to mainstream school (Oswin, 1998; Cole, 1986). However, these institutions only offered basic education so disabled children, like Daisy, were academically behind their peers when they returned to mainstream school:

> ... it didn't seem like a school, we had to go to bed in the middle of the day and things like that! (laughs) It was horrible really, I didn't learn a thing in those two years. Through Friends Reunited, I recently met up with a friend that I made there. And she came down here with her dad and he said to me as well, the couple of years that she spent at that school left a big gap in her learning. So I think it really is better if children can go to mainstream schools.

Ray expressed a similar memory of his schooling in residential special school. He tells a story of his enthusiasm and aspiration to read aloud being quashed by teachers' low expectations:

> I remember distinctly once, there was a chap in charge of the teaching and he brought somebody round the school and he brought them into our class, you know (you're always getting visitors and stuff, you know, people who peer at you) ... and asked me to come to the front and read and I was really pleased 'cause I could read, you know, like I was about 5 or so then, and he asked me to read, so I read very proudly, you know, and of course I heard him say something along the lines, 'As you can say he'll never do anything academically because he has to move his entire body to read' or something like that, you know, and I was really upset.

This was similar to Ian's experience, some twenty years later. Ian, born in the 1960s, recalls an encounter with a head teacher from his previous special school, which illustrates how teacher expectations can impede as well as facilitate the choices and chances of young disabled people:

> when I was at [FE college] and I can remember coming out of a lecture at break time, seeing my old head teacher, diving down a corridor to avoid him but failing miserably. And he caught me up and said 'what are you doing here?' And I said 'I'm a student' ... and his exact words were 'Oh, I never thought one of my pupils would be clever enough to do A-Levels.' And that summed up the entire ethos of that school. There was no motivation.

However, not all experiences of special school were negative. Catherine, like Hilary (mentioned above) went to a school run by the Spastics Society, where there was a great emphasis on fulfilling academic potential. Contrary to others in the oldest generation, Catherine gives a very positive account of staff expectations:

> It was the only grammar school in the country for people with cerebral palsy ... the original headmaster was the most exceptional man and he used to say 'you're all the cream of the cream'. And he fought for us to have exactly the same lifestyle as any other 11 to 18-year-old, and have the same chances. So the [school] is what made me what I am today.

Other participants from the oldest generation went to mainstream school but still identified gaps in their education as a result of regular periods of hospitalization. As noted elsewhere (see Shah & Priestley, 2011), post-war medical regimes caused significant interruptions to social and academic progression (see also Barker, 1974; Kornhauser, 1980). For example, Bella contracted polio as an infant and spent substantial blocks of her childhood and adolescence in hospital undergoing surgery. She believes that this put her at an academic disadvantage to her peers:

> I missed quite key things in my education, and very early on I must have been in hospital when they did the alphabet. And so I went back to school and it was almost like everybody had a secret code that I wasn't aware of, and I just couldn't understand how you worked this out, you know, what letters followed each other. ... So it was key things like that, that I just missed and I had to sort of constantly try and catch up ... my education as I said earlier was really disrupted because of all the orthopaedic surgery I had. And I once added it all up and I mean from contracting polio to the age of 17, I spent about 7½ years in hospital. So I was coming and going all the time.

This draws attention to the opportunities for schooling provided to children in hospitals. In the 1950s, James Robertson joined the British psychologist John Bowlby in his work to improve the rights and welfare of child patients in long-stay hospitals. Their work prompted the Ministry of Health to set up a formal inquiry into the welfare of children in long-stay and short-stay hospitals, and later led to the publication of the Platt Report (Central Health Services Council, 1959). Further, both were instrumental in the development of services that supported hospitalized children and offered them opportunities consistent with other school-age children (Murphy & Ashman, 1995). The provision of educational services within hospitals was perceived as critical to reduce the detrimental impact of educational deprivation on children's progression, and the emotional effects of falling behind in school, suggested by Barker (1974) as including low self-esteem and loss of self-confidence.

International interest in hospital schools grew during the 1920s, with the introduction of educational services and support within hospitals in several countries (Murphy & Ashman, 1995). Educational services and schools were considered to be a bridge between hospital wards and the outside world. Bella recalls what her hospital education was like in the 1950s:

> I was on a ward with, I think it was 0 to 14, and then you moved onto an adult ward at 14 and they taught almost the average age. So they would come in the mornings, and I know it's very different now for children who are in long-term hospital, but they would just come, they would arrive, and hand out a card with sums on or something like that, and because I think they were below the age I was at, you know my chronological age, it would take me a very short amount of time to do the work. And then there was nothing else, you see, even though I can remember asking if there was things that I could have or more work that I could have. So if the work hadn't been sent in from my school, which only came periodically, it would have been very minimal really. ... I mean in that sort of era occupational therapy seemed to be about making things, so I'd make 20 rabbits or something. I did a lot of basket work.

Eileen, from the middle cohort, has similar remembrances of her experience at a hospital school in the 1970s and 1980s. Her narrative reveals how the limited education of the hospital school constrained her ability to pursue the O-Level syllabus:

> They provide you with teachers when you're in hospital, er, if you're in for any period of time. But they couldn't do an O-Level syllabus. They could let you draw pictures and they could give you books to read, but I mean I – I could read a book! I could bring my own books to read but there was no syllabus.

In contrast, Amy recalled a positive experience of hospital school. Born in the 1960s, she spent much of her childhood and young adulthood in hospital as a result of childhood arthritis, but considers the school pivotal to a subsequent academic and career progression:

> ... the doctor who was in charge of this unit, she was very, very up on your education ... she absolutely wanted you to be as educated as you could be, and if I hadn't been in that hospital unit, and back at the daily boring special school, I never would've taken any exams, or I don't think any of my academic, um, or creative skills would've been recognized ... our days were literally split into three hours probably of physiotherapy, and three hours of schooling, every day. Every weekday. Um, on absolute standard term times, and that was one reason you were in there a long time, because she didn't like any disruption, the head honcho, she didn't like any disruption to your schooling, as much as to your physio ... it's just strange, because there we had about three teachers and not everyone was given the same chances. ... I went from my whole school life there, apart from the odd little bit of time where I did go back to the other day school.

Hospital schools were not included in any of the narratives from the youngest generation. However, those who went to residential special school did express dissatisfaction with the standard of teaching and low expectations of the staff. This was after the 1988 Education Reform Act, which proposed that children in special schools are entitled to have access to the National Curriculum like their peers in mainstream schools. Halpin and Lewis (1996) argue that, in actuality, it was not designed with special school pupils in mind, so was met with much resistance from special school teachers. Holly and Zoe, born in the 1980s, both attended residential special school from a young age. Like those in the oldest cohort, they made reference to the low expectations of teachers and limited academic opportunities of special schools.

However, Mickey's narrative suggests his experience in residential special school was a positive one. Born in 1985, Mickey started his educational career in 1990, in a local mainstream primary school. Although he was considered 'a bit of a high-flyer' by the teachers, he was also restricted from progressing as his sight had started to deteriorate and, while he could read Braille, his primary school teachers could not. Therefore Mickey went to a residential secondary school for young people with visual impairments, where he took his A-Levels and resided there as a weekly boarder:

> This was good in that it was supporting and had facilities for me to achieve academically. For instance, all teachers knew how to read

Braille. Also friends were always close by. I was trained how to use a white stick.

Harvey's narrative of educational inclusion identifies positive teacher expectations as significant to his subsequent educational success:

> They had very high hopes for me 'cos I did quite OK in the GCSEs, you know, I did above average for the school, you know, and they were like you – you know, Harvey, you go to the top for university. ... I think if I didn't have those teachers inspiring me, because that's what they did, I wouldn't have done what I've done today.

This indicates that the role of teachers can be significant in advancing the attainment levels of young disabled people. In 2010, the Department for Children, Families and Schools issued new guidance on *Breaking the Link between Special Educational Needs and Low Attainment*, emphasizing that 'interventions put in place should minimize any impact on attainment' (DCSF 2010: 9). Quantitative data produced by the Department for Education in 2012 (on Attainment and Pupil Level Characteristics) reported that 24.7 per cent of pupils with SEN without a statement achieved 5 or more A*–C grades at GCSE or equivalent (including English and mathematics). This is compared to 8.5 per cent of pupils with SEN with a statement, and 69.5 per cent of pupils with no identified SEN.

Theme 3: School environment

Remembrances from all three generational cohorts revealed how institutional regimes and the physical environment of the schools they attended as children had an impact on their subsequent adulthoods. Typically, isolation from mainstream community and family life was highlighted as a negative consequence of residential special schools. The narratives revealed scars of segregation arising from institutional environments and relationships. They also indicate that despite the policy shifts that have taken place special education since the 1940s, there are still a great many similar experiences of segregation across the generations. The stories reveal that such segregation was influenced by limited access to social capital required to resist professional authority. While some children had parents with the ability to turn around decisions taken by medical authority in relation to their educational placement, others did not. Rather some parents accepted the constant involvement of professionals in their child's life, believing their interventions were inevitably in the child's best interests. Such resignation to professional authority, however, often resulted in disabled children spending a significant part of their childhoods at residential school estranged from family and community.

As mentioned above, the post-war Education Act led to the growth of residential special schooling all over England. For the sake of affordability, country mansions previously owned by Victorian philanthropists were bought by local authorities and converted into schools for 'delicate children'. Stories from the middle generation offer insightful descriptions of these residential special schools in the 1960s and 1970s, where they spent a significant part of their childhoods:

> ... it was terribly cut off, it started off as a Victorian businessman's hunting lodge. And gradually worked its way to being a school for what were called 'delicate children' ... kids that were recovering from operations were often sent there because being in the county side not far from the Rudyard Lake, the air quality was better and was thought to be conducive to your recovery. (*Ian, 1960s.*)

> ... the school that I went to was originally in a place which is almost in the country, not quite, it had golf courses on one side in fact it had two golf courses with lots of green fields and things. (*Aton, 1960s.*)

The middle generation highlighted the trauma of being separated from their family for long periods of their childhood. While some participants overcame such scars in adulthood, others have them for the rest of their life. For example, Flora, the eldest child of ten, was sent to one of the residential special schools, funded by the Spastics Society, miles from comfort of family and life as she knew it. The perpetual physical and emotional detachment caused by segregation in her formative years did have significant repercussions in her later life, especially in terms of her mental health:

> I used to go for three months at a time and I never understood why I couldn't go home at weekends. ... That was traumatic being away so long when you are young. ... It was very bad because when I came home, they weren't used to having me around and it went pear-shaped. I didn't get on with my mum and I got very depressed. ... I was so depressed and I thought of killing myself.

Similarly, Sonia was removed from her family home at a young age although no one explained why she was being sent away from home to school. Like Flora, Sonia and others from her generation felt the strain of prolonged separation on her relationships with parents and siblings:

> I used to feel that you know, just so isolated and strange thoughts do go through your head like well, why am I here? You know, am I not wanted, kind of thing. ... I was only going home what, once every six, seven weeks. ... I used to go home to sit in my bedroom and not – not really communicate with them really, just a sulking teenager. Yeah. And I think it did upset my parents actually. But they didn't really know how to broach it and I was completely inarticulate.

With minimal contact with families, school became the social world of childhood for many of the disabled people who spoke to the author. They offered rich descriptions of the environments and regimes of the institutions they attended in the 1960s and 1970s:

> There was no carpets in the school, it was stone floors, wooden floors. There were hospital beds with rails on them 'cos when we little we had cots. And you were in a dormitory with probably about twenty other people in a room. ... We didn't have no tellys, no carpets, no ... you know, it was really horrible, hard blankets, there was hardly any heating 'cos the building was like, I don't know, it must have been pre-Victorian this building ...' (*Tan.*)
>
> Looking back it was horrendous behaviour, but at the time we just accepted it. The school was very institutionalized, and you got up at seven every day, including weekends, which I wasn't too happy about. And they had set meals, you had set bath times, set bed times, the day completely structured ... every break time we had to sit on the toilet, whether we wanted the loo or no. I couldn't understand this at all, and one day I said 'I don't want the toilet' and I got told off for that, and I did it again and I got a good spanking. (*Poppy*)

Such regimented practices were also noted in the narratives of some of the oldest generation. Ray attributes some of his personal habits today to the regimented social learning of his school days:

> ... I mean we'd get up at 6 o'clock, go downstairs into a big washroom, wash your hands and face, get dressed and stuff, and then you'd have to walk to another part of the school which was some way away to have your breakfast ... on Sundays they used to inspect your underwear and they used to do it in the dormitory so you know

they'd look at your knickers and – or your underpants in a dormitory and of course if you'd not cleaned yourself, they would make a – a thing out of it so that everybody would know, you know, which is very good 'cos it gave me this obsession with hygiene which I've always had since. ... I always get up early as well.

Themes of isolation and estrangement of mainstream culture were also evident in the narratives of the youngest generation who attended special school. Holly attended the same special school from infanthood to adulthood. School became her primary social world:

I went to a special needs nursery and then started a special needs school at the age of 5. So a lot of the people I went to nursery school with that I actually went to my main school with. I've actually been with the same bunch of people from the age of 2 to the age of 18. ... A lot of students spent two weeks at home, then a week boarding at the school, which is what I did. It was nice staying at school because I got to spend time with friends. Because with mainstream schools you're within a catchment area and so you live near your friends. The school I went to, because it was special needs school, it really wasn't like that. People came from all over the place ... when I got home I was at home and there was nothing for me outside of home so it was quite nice to actually spend that week at school boarding.

Several stories from Holly's generation comment on how the sheltered environment of special school failed to prepare them for adult life in the inclusive community:

I left school when I was 18 and we were very cocooned. ... We weren't told about the outside world and things as a disabled person, the kind of attitudes we were going to come across. ... At that point I still didn't know things like the DDA and stuff like that.

This was concurred with by Mickey who went to a residential school for young people with visual impairments. Although it supported him to progress academically, it prevented him from learning the skills required to make a smooth transition into the adult world:

... it was quite a sheltered environment, so going to university was quite a shock. ... I think, in a way, the sheltered environment of the secondary school made me a little weaker as everything was done for us. It may have been easier for me at university if the school was not so sheltered.

The biographical narratives, from across the generations, suggest that although there appeared to be some improvements in academic expectations over time, there appeared also to be a lack of social expectation towards community inclusion in adulthood. Similar conclusions were reached by the British Council of Disabled People in the 1980s (BCODP 1986) – that the special education system was constraining young people from learning the skills and social knowledge they needed to live as independent adults.

Conclusion

This chapter has explored the interplay between public policies and private lives, with a particular focus on the shifting educational and schooling opportunities available to young people with physical impairments growing up between the post-war period and the twenty-first century. Through personal narratives it has illuminated how young disabled people born in the three generations were subject to the vacillating practices of educational exclusion, integration and inclusion on different levels. Adopting biographical methods in this way also gives a presence to the voices of disabled people and allows them to document their own history, rather than it being written/invented by those in power. As demonstrated in this chapter, personal narratives are not simple anecdotal evidence, but sources of knowledge that needs to focus not on the individual, but on the institutions, policies, environments and relationships that shape them.

The biographical reflections provide traces of social change in relation to how pupils were selected to attend particular schools and the personal impact of these schooling choices within and beyond the school gates. They also reveal the extent to which personal agency and familial capital (particularly the resilience and resistance of the mother) interacted with public policy to trigger turning points in the expected future pathways for young disabled people. So, for instance, the oldest generation went to school at a time when the 1944 Butler Act encouraged the expansion of special schools and gave medical professionals authority to dictate the educational placement of disabled children. While, within this policy context, it was expected that young disabled people would follow a trajectory of educational segregation, the stories reveal turning points in these expected pathways, often triggered by familial agency, resulting in the pursuit of more inclusive lives. Interestingly, this was more apparent for the oldest and youngest generations, rather than the middle generation. Despite the significant social reforms introduced by the Labour government in the 1970s, the narratives suggest that the growth of residential special schools, their isolated environments and weak family structures directed the middle generation towards segregated lives. It is worth noting that recent policies have gone some way to limiting the estrangement of disabled children from family life. Standard 4 of the National Minimum Standards for Residential Special Schools (DfE, 2011c: 7) asserts that:

> Children can contact their parents/carers and families in private and schools facilitate this where necessary. ... Schools are sensitive to individual children's circumstances such as restricted contact with families. Communication aids should be available for children who need them.

While this suggests that disabled children today have opportunity structures to enable them to live more inclusive lives compared to their predecessors, it is important to examine the real impact these policy frameworks are having on individual lives. When comparing generational stories it is worth noting that there are surprising similarities in terms of estrangement and isolation for those from the oldest and youngest generation. However, these comparisons also reveal the new forms of cultural capital available in recent times, which have allowed parents to contest professional advice and make informed choices about their children's future. Such evidence prompts the need to understand the extent to which changes in public policies impact change in the private lives of disabled children and young people. The recent establishment of the Department for Education's promotion of 'joined up' practice between education, health and social care authorities has gone same way to acknowledge these connections. As outlined in the SEND Green Paper (DfE, 2011a) *Support and Aspiration*, there are plans to regularly monitor the impact of services for disabled children, young people and their families by different measures. For instance, accountability measures will be put in place to track the improvements of schools to support young people who have low achievement scores. Further, a new body, HealthWatch, has been prepared to give young people and parents a voice in the development of health services.

However despite the UK Government's overhaul of the SEN system, with the introduction of a single assessment process and specific plans to give parents greater choice and support as outlined in *Support and*

Aspiration (DfE, 2011a), the immediate future does not look too rosy for disabled children and young disabled people who, with the increasing anti-disability provisions, are significantly less likely to have the support they require to achieve their educational aspirations on a par with their non-disabled contemporaries. This is further impeded by the UK Government's reservation on Article 24 of the UNCRPD, which has been evidenced as the way forward for improving the educational and life outcomes of disabled children (EHRC, 2012). In this regard, therefore, the connection of micro-level lives with macro-level policy structures is important in the development of future provision for disabled children and young people as it offers a means to identify what facilitates and constrains their future choices, aspirations and life outcomes..

References

Armstrong, D. (2003) *Experiences of special education: Re-evaluating policy and practice through life stories* (London: Routledge Falmer).

Ball, S.J., Bowe, R. & Gerwitz, S. (1994) Market forces and parental choice, in S. Tomlinson (ed.), *Educational reform and its consequences* (London, Institute for Public Policy Research and Rivers Oram Press).

Barker, P. (1974) *Psychological effects on children of admission to hospital*, Update, 7, 1019–1024.

Barnes, C. (1991) *Disabled people in Britain and discrimination: A case for anti-discrimination legislation* (London: Hurst/BCODP).

BBC News Channel (29 November 2006) *Special schools closures absurd.* http://news.bbc.co.uk/1/hi/education/6196098.stm [accessed 10 January 2010].

BCODP (British Council of Organisations of Disabled People) (1986) Disabled young people living independently (London: BCODP).

Borsay, A. (2007) Deaf children and charitable education in Britain, 1790–1944, in A. Borsay & P. Shapely (eds), *Medicine, charity and mutual aid: The consumption of health and welfare in Britain, c. 1550–1950* (Aldershot: Ashgate), pp. 71–90.

Central Health Services Council (1959) *The welfare of children in hospital: Report of a committee of the CHSC (Chairman: Sir Harry Platt)* (London: Ministry of Health/HMSO).

CSIE (2005) *Working for inclusion in 2005.* Bristol: Centre for Studies in Inclusive Education. http://uwe.ac.uk/csie05.htm [accessed 14 June 2007].

Cole, T. (1986) *Residential special education: Living and learning in a special school* (Milton Keynes: Open University Press).

Conservative Party (2010) *Invitation to join the government of Britain* (London: Alan Mabbutt on behalf of the Conservative Party).

DCSF (Department for Children, Schools and Families) (2010) *Breaking the link between special educational needs and low attainment: Everybody's business* (London: DCSF).

DfE (Department for Education) (2011a) *Support and Aspiration: A new approach to special educational needs and disability.* https://www.education.gov.uk/publications/eOrderingDownload/Green-Paper-SEN.pdf [accessed 8 November 2012].

DfE (Department for Education) (2011b) *Schools, pupils and their characteristics.* http://www.education.gov.uk/rsgateway/DB/SFR/s001012/index.shtml [accessed 8 November 2012].

DfE (Department for Education) (2011c) *Residential special schools – national minimum standards.* https://www.education.gov.uk/publications/eOrderingDownload/nms%20rss%20september%202011.pdf [accessed 18 November 2012].

DfES (Department for Education and Skills) (2001) *Special educational needs code of practice* (Ref: DfES/0581/2001) (London: DfES Publications).

DfES (Department for Education and Skills) (2003) *Disabled children in residential placements.* https://www.everychildmatters.gov.uk/_files/D652D71766 58D23D115B9AD445D6B673.pdf [accessed 17 May 2009].

Duncan, J. (1942) *The education of the ordinary child* (London: Nelson).

Equality and Human Rights Commission (EHRC) (2012) *The Commission's work on the UNCRPD.* http://www.equalityhumanrights.com/uploaded_files/humanrights/uncrdP_mar2012.pdf [accessed 14 February 2012].

Finkelstein, V. (2001) *The social model of disability repossessed*, retrieved January 2007. http://www.leeds.ac.uk/disability-studies/archiveuk/finkelstein/soc%20 mod%20repossessed.pdf [accessed 14 February 2012].

Fuchs, D.& Fuchs, L.S. (1998) 'Competing visions for educating students with disabilities: Inclusion versus full inclusion', *Childhood Education*, 74, 5, 309–316.

Furlong, A. & Biggart, A. (1999) 'Framing choices: A longitudinal study of occupational aspirations among 13 to 16 year-olds', *Journal of Education and Work*, 12, 1, 21–36.

Glendinning, C., Kirk, S., Guiffrida, A. & Lawton, D. (2001) 'Technology dependent children in the community: Definitions, numbers and costs', *Child: Health, Care and Development*, 27, 4, 321–334.

Goodley D. & Tregaskis C. (2006) 'Storying disability and impairment: Retrospective accounts of disabled family life', *Qualitative Health Research*, 16, 5, 630–646.

Gordon, D., Parker, R. & Loughran, F., Heslop, P. (2000) *Disabled children in Britain: A re-analysis of the OPCS disability surveys* (London: Stationery Office).

Halpin, D. & Lewis, A. (1996) 'The impact of the National Curriculum on twelve special schools in England', *European Journal of Special Needs Education*, 11, 1, 95–105.

Harris, N. (1997) *Special educational needs and access to justice* (Bristol: Jordans).

Haines, S. & Ruebain, D. (2011) *Education, disability and social policy* (Bristol: The Policy Press).

Hurt, J. (1988) *Outside the mainstream: A history of special education* (London: Routledge).

Kornhauser, P. (1980) 'Preschool and school programs in humanizing children's hospital stay', *Paediatrician*, 9, 231–241.

Mills, C. (1959) *The sociological imagination* (Oxford: Oxford University Press).

Ministry of Education (1944) *The Butler Act* (London: HMSO).

Murphy, J. & Ashman, A. (1995) 'The education of children in hospital schools', *Australasian Journal of Special Education*, 19, 1, 29–36.

Office for National Statistics (2000) *School pupils: By type of school, 1970/71–1998/99*: Social Trends 30 (London: Office for National Statistics).

Oliver, M. (1990) *The politics of disablement* (Basingstoke: Macmillan).

Oswin, M. (1998) A historical perspective, in C. Robinson & K. Stalker (eds), *Growing up with disability* (London: Jessica Kingsley Publishers), pp. 29–41.

Priestley, M. (ed.) (2001) *Disability and the life course: Global perspectives* (Cambridge: Cambridge University Press).

Priestley, M., Rabiee, P. & Harris, J. (2002) 'Young disabled people and the "New Arrangements" for leaving care in England and Wales', *Children and Youth Services Review*, 25, 11, 863–890.

Priestley, M. (2003) *Disability: A life course approach* (Cambridge: Polity Press).

Prime Minister's Strategy Unit (2005) *Improving the life chances of disabled people: Final report* (London: PMSU).

Riddell, S., Adler, M., Mordaunt, E. & Farmakopoulou, N. (2000) 'Special educational needs and competing policy frameworks in England and Scotland', *Journal of Education Policy*, 15, 6, 621–635.

Riesmann, C. (1993) *Narrative analysis* (London: Sage).

Segal, S. (1961) 'Dull and backward children: Post-war theory and practice', *Educational Research*, 3, 3, 171–194.

Shah, S. (2005) *Career success of disabled high flyers* (London: Jessica Kingsley).

Shah, S. (2006) 'Sharing the same world: The researcher and the researched', *Qualitative Research*, 6, 2, 207–220.

Shah, S. (2008) *Young disabled people: Choices, aspirations and constraints* (Surrey: Ashgate).

Shah, S. & Priestley, M. (2009) 'Home and away: The impact of educational policies on disabled children's experiences of family and friendship', *Research Papers in Education*, 25, 2, 155–174.

Shah, S. & Priestley, M. (2011) *Disability and social change: Private lives and public policies* (Bristol: The Policy Press).

Shakespeare, T. & Watson, N. (1998) Theoretical perspectives on research with disabled children, in G. Fairbairn & S. Fairbairn (eds) *Integrating special children: Some ethical issues* (Aldershot: Avebury).

Smith, B. & Sparkes, A.C. (2008) 'Narrative and its potential contribution to disability studies', *Disability & Society*, 23, 3, 17–28.

Stanley, L. & Wise, S. (1993) *Breaking out again: Feminist ontology and epistemology* (London: Routledge).

Stiker, H.-J. (1999) *A history of disability*, translated by William Sayers (Michigan: University of Michigan Press).

Thomas, C. (1999) *Female forms: Experiencing and understanding disability* (Buckingham: Open University Press).

Tomlinson, S. (2001) *Education in a post-welfare society* (Buckingham: Open University Press).

Topliss, E. (1975) *Provision for the disabled* (Oxford: Blackwell/Martin Robertson).

UNESCO (1994) *The Salamanaca Statement and Framework for Action on special needs education* (Paris: UNESCO).

United Nations (2006) *Convention on the Rights of Persons with Disabilities – Optional Protocol*. http://www.un.org/disabilities/documents/convention/convoptprot [accessed 14 February 2012].

United Nations Committee on the Rights of the Child (2008) *Consideration of reports submitted by states parties under Article 44 of the Convention, Concluding observations: United Kingdom of Great Britain and Northern Ireland*, CRC/C/GBR/CO/4) (New York: United Nations).

UPIAS (Union of Physically Impaired Against Segregation)/Disability Alliance (1976) *Fundamental principles of disability* (London: UPIAS/Disability Alliance).

Warnock, M. (1978) *Meeting special educational needs: A brief guide by Mrs Mary Warnock to the Report of the Committee of Enquiry into Education of Handicapped Children and Young People* (London: HMSO).

Wolfendale, S. (2004) *Getting the balance right: Towards partnership in assessing children's development and educational achievement*. Discussion paper commissioned by DfES, London: DfES. www.teachernet.gov.uk/workingwithparents [accessed 2 November 2011].

8
Disability, Childhood and Poverty: Critical Perspectives on Guatemala

Shaun Grech

Introduction

Up till recently, it was claimed that 10 per cent of every population was disabled. The new *World Report on Disability* (WHO/World Bank, 2011) has pushed up this global figure to 15 per cent – around 1 billion people. Around 82 per cent of these disabled people are said to live in the countries of the global South (some 800 million people), and are among the poorest of the poor. Many live in rural areas, with little or no access to healthcare, rehabilitation or employment, and where living and working conditions pose a constant threat to health and well-being. A bulk of these disabled people are children, experiencing poverty in disproportionate and multidimensional ways.

The relationship between disability and poverty (often depicted as a mutually reinforcing one) is now well documented, and guesstimates suggest that 20 per cent of the world's poorest are disabled people, that is, 1 in 5 of the poorest people (WHO/World Bank, 2011). Others suggest that none of the politically charged Millennium Development Goals (MDGs) will be achieved by 2015 unless the needs of disabled people are flatly addressed in all the target areas (Groce, 2009).

But Disability Studies remains critically disengaged from the global South, despite the fact that the bulk of its constituents are located in this specific geopolitical and historical space. This is evident in the virtual absence of the global South from mainstream Disability Studies literature (see, for example, Oliver 1990, 1996). The lack of engagement with the global South in much of its content comes, though, as no surprise, given that the field remains dominated by White, Western, middle-class academics, and the focus of their work, almost invariably, is the same post-industrial urban settings they operate from and write

about – work imbued with ideological, theoretical, cultural and historical assumptions and specificities (Grech, 2009, 2011).

But this distance from the global South has not stopped the almost
wholesale and indiscriminate exportation of ideas and models, such
as the social model of disability, from global North to global South,
together with inferences from the Western context about the presumed
situation of disabled people in the so-called 'developing' countries – all
disabled people, all disabled children 'out there' – realities and lives the
discipline never intended to listen to or even address in the first place.

This scenario unfortunately meets one where mainstream international development continues to exclude disabled people, an exclusion
marked at policy, research and practice levels. Disabled children are often
left out of broad-based poverty-reduction measures, such as the provision of education and healthcare, as well as efforts targeted at specific
populations such as children and young people living in conditions of
extreme poverty.

In this chapter I draw from ethnographic work in Guatemala to address
in a critical manner a number of issues that remain as Disability Studies is
faced with the global South, its disabled children and childhoods within
these very particular spaces of poverty. As the word 'global' is becoming
fashionable as a means of selling this West European and North American
(WENA) discipline, it is perhaps more important than ever to engage with
some of the lacunae that emerge at these epistemic intersections.

Where is the 'global' in disability studies?

As the 'majority world' or the 'global South' is all too often neatly pack-
aged by Western theorists, one is immediately struck by the way in
which the very complex and heterogeneous socio-economic, political,
historical, cultural, ideological, religious/spiritual and landscapes that
make up these complex hybrid spaces (temporal, material and discursive) within which these lives are lived are hardly considered or subject
to complete lack of interest. For many theorists, the global South remains
an object of fleeting curiosity and occasional 'study', written about from
the safe and very detached comfort of their Western offices. From this
position all the world is made to look the same, simplified, reduced and
homogenized, in the rat race to sell one's epistemologies and practices
to everyone, everywhere, indiscriminately but discriminatingly. Instead,
the politics of location, or rather the geopolitics of knowledge (Mignolo,
2002) of these Western writings, and which ultimately make this knowledge, its creation and imposition possible and 'legitimate' – complicit

in the neocolonial – are conveniently shelved. The 'global' sells, but the historical baggage that endows the neoliberal globalization of knowledge and practices, replete with inequality and epistemic violence, is hardly interrogated in Disability Studies. And it is here that even metanarratives such as the rights-based discourse diffuse in much theory and 'activism' become questionable, when indeed 'human-rights discourse coexists uneasily with the exercise of imperial power' (Rao & Pierce, 2006: 2).

The epistemologies exported are not so much tools for listening, understanding, learning and transformative change from below, as much as metanarratives to fetishize and exoticize to the end of disciplining these spaces and subjects and their narratives. And again the imperialistic trail of Western 'knowledge' and practices, the academic neocolonalism, continues unabated. In this process, debates are perpetually re/neocolonized, discourses simplified and generalized, contexts (places and spaces), cultures and histories (temporalities) homogenized, and many critical issues are left ignored or intentionally resisted. As I highlight elsewhere, Disability Studies perhaps becomes even complicit in the neocolonizing of the Southern space and subject (Grech, 2012). More specifically, dynamics such as these could mean a Disability Studies that not only excludes, but that paradoxically may be disabling by discursively silencing them and their lives, even if indirectly by relegating them to the margins of the epistemological and ontological. Indeed, as Said (1993: 35) puts it,

> [t]he difficulty with theories of essentialism and exclusiveness, or with barriers and sides, is that they give rise to polarizations that absolve and forgive ignorance and demagogy more than they enable knowledge.

Poverty matters: Disability and childhood in the hybrid 'spaces of poverty'

The lack or absence of interest in these spaces (material and discursive, spatial and temporal), and consequently of the lives within them, is no by no means a small negligence considering that disabled people and their families live in them, because they shape their experiences, possibilities and lives. This is the reality they are bound to speak about and from:

> How can you know anything about us, when you don't know where we live, how we eat, how we love, how we care, how we touch? ... many come here, much of our reality is not known, we remain faceless, people pretend to know us, but all they know is what they want

to believe about us ... which is more of their own reality and where they come from ... this is all *they* want to know. (Alfonso)

It is even more interesting how poverty, a critical defining aspect of this Southern space (at least to many), the lineage of empire, the neo-colonial, is little more than a narrative stripped of historicity, which continues to be abused not only in Disability Studies, but also in the accounts of organizations working with children under the auspices of 'development'. This is indeed a profound contradiction when it is this same assumed (and disproportionate) poverty that to many defines the 'global South' – an ontologically separate (but consistently homog-enized) space from that constructed as the West. It is also the reference to this poverty that draws attention to disability and childhood in the global South as an academic and practice project. Within this proc-ess, much that varies from or is not known within the individualist, welfarist, secular, urban, industrial mindset is therefore ignored. One could, perhaps, be speaking about *spaces of poverty* and life therein, spaces that are as material as they are discursive, and that ultimately are critical in understanding how disability and childhood are con-structed and lived (see the section below), and how these are never detached from the geopolitical and the historical – notably colonialism (see Grech, 2011, 2012). One may include here a number of examples that not only differentiate these spaces of poverty from those in the West, but that call for a grounded knowledge. This is no way meant as an exhaustive list or one that characterizes all the spaces of poverty in the global South, but simply as some aspects that suggest a 'different' space and a different poverty from that customarily found in the glo-bal North, and how these are negotiated, lived and often survived on a daily basis:

- Around 55 per cent of the population in the global South live in rural areas, hosting some 75 per cent of those in extreme poverty.
- Around 80 per cent depend on agriculture.
- Many poor people, particularly those in rural areas, are often both producers and consumers. As producers they are involved in complex and diverse livelihood activities (rather than the one job), activities that are not always remunerated. These are almost invariably per-formed in the informal sector.
- Many of the poor (especially those in remote rural areas) are not entitled to benefits, and have little or no access to any form of social protection (e.g. health, disability benefits etc.).

- Between 50 and 70 per cent of the budget of a poor household is used simply to purchase food. In rich countries, this figure is 10–15 per cent.
- Around 1 billion people are hungry and 2.6 million lack access to adequate sanitation.
- 1.5 million people (90 per cent of which are children under the age of 5) die every year from diarrhoeal diseases (including cholera).
- Around 75 million children are out of school (IFAD, 2010; FAO, 2008; World Bank, 2008; WHO, 2009, 2010; UNESCO, 2010).

By positioning disability within these spaces of poverty, myriad issues emerge as we attempt to talk about disability and childhood in the global South. I will be discussing these in the rest of this chapter. But before addressing some of these, it is perhaps important to frame back these spaces of poverty within the complex narrative that is the global South. This is because the hybrid that emerges pushes us to problematize boundaries and totalizing forms of cultural understandings and notions of identity, place and space at the most basic levels. Where do agrarian societies fit in the materialist pre-capitalist/capitalist dichotomy? How does a materialist model explain a situation in which a substantial proportion of livelihoods remain dependent on home-based subsistence production? Importantly, how are disability and childhood lived within spaces that are not necessarily impervious to the penetration of Western ideologies, influences, work and consumption patterns and so on? García-Canclini's (2005) work on hybrid cultures emphasizes the cultural mixtures or hybridizations between the traditional and the modern, providing powerful analytical power to the condition of societies and people at various intersections and crossroads. As he explains, 'neither the "paradigm" of imitation, nor that of originality … nor the one that lazily wants to explain us by the "marvellously real" or a Latin American surrealism, are able to account for our hybrid cultures' (2005: 6). People ultimately operate at various (and interacting) margins of capitalism, globalization, markets etc. Using some of the examples above, for example, the fact that many of the rural poor have one foot in the market and the other in subsistence, means that they enter and exit the market but still survive. This, though, does not mean that they remain unimpacted by its pressures (e.g. price hikes of staple foods). The hybrid is also manifest in the presence of non-unitary households, not necessarily blood-related and not always sharing access and control over resources. This perhaps suggests a renegotiation of what we understand by family, a re-examination of households of different formations and compositions, relationships, control of assets and even conflicting interests. Acknowledging the possibility of intra-household variations remains especially important, since it helps counteract an essentially Western view of the household as composed of a nuclear family and where all resources and power are distributed equally to the benefit of all members. At a more functional level, it may highlight how the provision of services or other benefits directed at the household may not necessarily reach disabled people, and this implies that we first need to understand how issues of power, identity and access are negotiated within households, and the functions of roles, norms and ideology in creating and sustaining these. And even more questions arise here: what does disability mean in these different families? How is childhood lived, and how does it face up to the whole gamut of intra-household dynamics and perhaps even disadvantages (see also Bolt & Bird, 2003)? How are (if any) disabling narratives and practices shaped within and through these intra-household relationships? And how do children and disabled family members negotiate and survive through this hybrid household? Can this hybrid household also be a source of resistance and resilience?

The emphasis on the hybrid does not imply the fetishizing of the local and the traditional, but is useful in steering away (at least momentarily) from the notion that these spaces and people are necessarily impenetrable to global influences and unwilling/unable to participate (or are simply assimilated or antagonistic) to global factors and processes. Furthermore, it implies that local people may not necessarily want to revert to whatever is perceived as pre-modern, pre-industrial, pre-capitalist, or anything perceived as the pure or pre-hybrid (if this ever existed at all). Instead, they may be constantly borrowing and negotiating in the process of transculturation, sometimes even as resistance. Arias (2008) notes how the constructions of an authentic Maya identity in Guatemala, one that is autonomous or bound to that prior to the conquest by the Spanish, is not only inauthentic, but ignores the fact that Mayas and their identities reflect the influence of modern technology and globalization, which not only impact them, but are being utilized by communities (e.g. modern communication strategies) for their own benefit. A number of questions arise, which have a variety of implications for disabled children. Where do these local people and spaces fit within the materialist construction of universal history, and how realistic is the project of removing capitalism when this (or renegotiations of it) is on occasion already incorporated within the hybrid? Can ignoring hybridity be dangerous when it is within the hybrid that communities often renew themselves, when it is within the local that the global is processed and experienced, and within and through which meaning (e.g. of disability, poverty and childhood) develops? How do these hybrid post/neocolonial spaces connect with the disabled body, itself hybrid and constituted by 'transgressed boundaries, potent fusions, and dangerous possibilities' (Haraway, 1985: 69) – that consistently refute and resist dominant ontologies, epistemologies and discourse?

The construction and definition of disability and childhood: On personhood

Positioning disability and childhood within these hybrid spaces of poverty, within the hybrid global South, means that other complexities emerge. In fact both the definition of disability and childhood become hugely con- troversial, and indeed there is no single definition of either of these across cultures. Not only is there no homogeneous category called 'disabled' or 'child', but the meanings of these are dependent on the hybrid contexts in which they are placed. The implication is that what disability means in specific spaces involves first engaging with what is valued in these same locations (physical and ontological), and how this varies across complex, multiple and fluid geographical (rural and urban, for example), spatial, social, cultural and economic dimensions, themselves bound to broader notions of ideology, spirituality and cosmology. This is what constitutes and is understood as full personhood in very specific contexts and tem- poralities and by very specific populations at the most micro levels. It is therefore against this background that the meaning of disability is shaped, lived and experienced – against the hegemony of 'normality' (see Davis, 2010). This means that rather than analyzing the experiences of the disa- bled child in isolation, individualizing them, it is perhaps more important for any analysis to start off by understanding what surrounds the child, what it means to be a 'full' child and a 'full' person, because this is what disability is positioned along/against and how it is defined and interpreted by both disabled people and those around. At the most basic level, it renders the endeavours to go in the field armed with any definite model and conceptualization of disability (whether the social, medical or other) and childhood, highly problematic if not irrelevant.

In rural Guatemala, for example, these notions of personhood often varied by gender. For men, full personhood included getting married, having a house, children, and most importantly labouring hard to support the family as the main and often sole breadwinner – the critical source of survival:

> One has to be able to demonstrate that he is capable of doing many things, especially to struggle for his family. ... I am an agricultural

labourer ... yes only this ... we work very hard because agriculture is the work of real men, and because of this, you have to have faith in God and love for work, to keep on struggling for everything. (Rolando)

For women, full personhood often involved the ability to get married (preferably to a suitable candidate who could support her financially), bear and raise children, attend to household and other tasks, and where possible supplement (not replace) the husband's labour and earnings, and maintain familial and social relationships:

I did what a normal person does, I washed, I ironed, I cooked, I took care of the children, and I helped my husband with some work here and there to make some extra money to keep the family going, to help with buying the tortilla. I did what a normal person does. (Maria)

Probing further permits the opening up of the analysis towards the wide range of beliefs, responses and attitudes towards disabled people in these hugely complex and varied contexts (socially, economically, politically and culturally). This is further complicated by the fact that disabled people themselves are not a homogeneous group, and their experiences are invariably shaped by other social microcosms, including gender, religion, group affiliation, roles, age, rights and so on at micro levels, implying that we also need to engage with other social issues such as patriarchy, machismo and racism among others.

But it is also important to frame what childhood means within specific notions of personhood, again in specific spaces. In Guatemala, within these spaces of poverty, participants emphasized the family as the most important institution for the poor, and within this, children, participants highlighted, are socially and culturally valued and expected. Children satisfy emotional needs, enable the continuation of the family, and most critically are the only insurance mechanism possessed by the poor. Children are a source of labour power that comes to replace that of the ageing parent, to feed and attend to some or all of the basic needs, and to intervene in times of adversity, including illness, and hence to ensure survival.

How the disabled child relates to these constructions of personhood, and how experiences are defined and impacted, are mediated by aspects such as the type of impairment. It is highly unlikely, for example, for a child with dyslexia to be oppressed in a community where livelihoods involve agricultural labour and/or construction. One must also be

alert to the fact that this child labour may not necessarily be exploita-
tive. Indeed, in rural Guatemala, children contribute a range of labour
power during key stages in the agricultural cycle to compensate the
labour power of other family members and/or to replace it when other
members are engaged in other tasks or are unable to (e.g. on account of
ill-health). This labour input is so normalized that even schools make
concessions to allow children to work, for example, leaving school early,
or many not turning up, for example, when sowing, fertilizing or during
harvest time. Much of this work is not a matter of luxury in contexts
of extreme poverty, or 'bad' or 'negligent' parenting but a question of
growing enough of the subsistence crop to pull them through the 'hungry period' (dry season).

These hybrid spaces of poverty, it is important to note, do not imply
the domestication, elimination or 'sell-out' of the traditional in favour
of the modern, since these beliefs and practices are often employed as
counter-hegemonic forces or simply as enablers of survival. For example,
studies (see e.g. Whyte & Ingstad, 1995) show how, despite its physically
arduous nature, agricultural work performed by the rural poor redeems
itself by providing a wider breadth of tasks, less specialized and less
formal than those in urban areas and cities. Many of these tasks are in
fact also performed by disabled people, including children (e.g. sowing,
fertilizing etc.). This is especially the case when families (and communities) work together as the basic unit of production and live in close prox-
imity; working conditions are flexible (e.g. family members compensate
each other's labour); and activities are largely subsistence- (rather than
market-) oriented:

> There is much that is difficult here, much that is really hard, but we
> survive because we have each other, because we know our environ-
> ment, and we can *all* help. My son, even with his physical disability,
> is helping us so much, he feels good that he is doing so, and we value
> his input – every task that everyone can do is beneficial to us as a
> collective. (Rigoberto)

This is where one must question, (re)negotiate and challenge the construction of these spaces and people as 'uncivilized' and in need of
outside intervention. Within these spaces, so are a plethora of myths
constructed about the presumed treatment of *all* disabled people in
all countries of the global South, a global South that is as lacking as it
is cruel, where disabled people are consistently hidden, killed, aban-
doned or neglected – much of this a result of 'strange' and 'bizarre'

religious and other beliefs and practices. Though ill-treatment does exist and can never be justified and should even less be ignored, such discourse remains predicated on and continues to proliferate only on the basis of the homogenization of these spaces and people as inferior, exoticized and desiring of external intervention, where much of this assumed ill-treatment is indeed *expected*. Such discourse is similar to that of Western feminists in the 1970s, who repeatedly depicted the women of the so-called 'third world' as powerless, backward, uneducated victims – discourse that continues to enrage feminists in the global South (see e.g. Mohanty, 1991). These are the spaces, subjects and their cultures too often collectively demonized by the 'superior West', and like much of the colonial enterprise, predicated on homogenizing, subjugating and constructing a subject *in need* of correction, while contemporaneously legitimizing the exercise of power and domination (epistemic and material) over it – disabling it. Escobar (1995), for example, notes how development discourse and practice 'relies on the perpetual recognition and disavowal of difference' (1995: 54), violence naturalizing the subjugation of the global South through a host of tools and organizations embodying empire (see Hardt & Negri, 2000).

Homogenizing the experience of disability and childhood is an impossibility, because contexts vary even within single countries, including what is conceptualized as full personhood, as well as individual, family and social circumstances – themselves constantly interacting, and importantly, dynamic. One may include here a number of factors: the type of impairment; prices and price hikes (e.g. of food and medication); family (if any) composition and number of dependants (compared to those engaged in remunerated activities); rurality and geographic isolation; types of livelihood; age; class (or caste), to name but a few. The implication, and to conclude this section, is that what disability and childhood might mean, and the experiences flowing from these, are not only complex and intensely heterogeneous. They are, most critically, fluid and constantly (re)negotiated, implying that they can hardly be encapsulated in models or grand metanarratives, however open or comprehensive they claim to be.

Families and communities of poverty and the agency of the poor: Beyond individualism

Engaging with the global South through a secular and individualist Western Disability Studies raises other key concerns in the hybrid spaces of poverty, notably the collective, or rather the families and communities of poverty. Substantial poverty literature highlights how networks of families, relatives, friends and neighbours often remain the most important and valuable institution in the lives of poor people, facilitating access to food and money (for example, through informal micro loans), labour and information, among others (see Narayan, Patel, Schafft, Rademacher & Koch-Schullem, 2000). This is especially the case for those in deep and chronic poverty, where formal safety nets are inadequate, absent or fragmented, and where social and cultural life remains family-based. This horizontal type of social capital between poor people is characteristic of resource-poor communities, who are more often than not 'best linked, socially, with other poor households rather than to the "gatekeepers" to important goods and services' (Bird, Hulme, Moore & Shepherd, 2002: 28). In contexts such as rural Guatemala, disability is almost exclusively a family responsibility, and is lived as a family in settings where the idea of a community exists firmly within people's psyche and lifeworlds, real and imagined (see Bauman, 1992):

> We eat, we work, we survive together ... we cannot pull throughout without our families and communities, they are our brick and mortar. In this land of nothing, where the government does not exist or care, where you have nothing, you have God to warm your soul, and your neighbours to feed your body, that is how you manage to survive. (Oscar)

Positioning disability and childhood within a relational context provides a much-needed contribution to evaluating the applicability of the discourse on rights and antidiscrimination legislation, emanating from and often based on a Western individualistic perspective. While it is important to note that in theory rights holders also have obligations towards others, critics contend that these policies and slogans (e.g. 'rights not charity') are often far too detached from the social, historical and cultural realities of the majority world, where community ties persist, and where individual rights may not be present or are overshadowed by relationships of mutual obligation and reciprocity (see e.g. Miles, 2000; Ghai, 2002). In such circumstances, the notion of an independent individual as a rights holder may be idiosyncratic to the strong social bonds and ways the individual is embedded therein. Therefore it may be more pertinent and responsible to speak of *community rights*. In this case, addressing collective needs may provide better opportunities for all, even though this requires greater political commitment, resources and addressing the structural causes of poverty. Collective interests may also not necessarily overcome individual ones, especially when efforts targeting the family (e.g. better health) translate into better care for the disabled family member.

Across cultures, the complexity and heterogeneity of individual, social and family circumstances, and other factors and processes, make the assumption of a unified global move towards Western individualism (and the valorization of autonomy and self-determination) often untenable. Furthermore, at the intersection of the local and the global, the hybrid contexts adopting in various degrees, modalities and levels, elements of the old (the traditional) and the new (the modern), means that one can speak of multiple traditionalisms and modernities (see Garcia-Canclini, 2005), as well as families. This may be evident in the patterns of families in newly emerging economies (especially urban areas) retaining strong cultures of relatedness and community, blending elements of both individualism and collectivism. Finally, the stronghold of resistant cultural beliefs and ideologies over people's perceptions, attitudes and behaviours is also a critical factor in the debate, since these will not be changed through legislation alone. Instead, they continue to coexist and condition the applicability and possible outcomes of the rights language alongside the nuances, opportunities and limitations offered by the social, economic and political environment at the most micro levels.

Looking at disability within cultural contexts such as rural Guatemala, where the communal envelopes the individual, means that we need to look at the impacts of disability on the whole family rather than solely the disabled child, where disability in the absence of any formal safety nets is exclusively a family responsibility and lived as a family affair. Caring for a disabled family member in conditions of extreme poverty in rural Guatemala often implies less time and opportunity to engage in remunerated productive labour (especially for mothers, sisters and other female caregivers), and therefore household capacity to earn an income is often reduced when directs costs (especially those of medication and transportation) are increasing. In turn, the resources available for the satisfaction of basic and other needs of other household members, including health, food and education are severely reduced, impoverishing and for some opening the possibility of impairment. These impacts are so strong that perhaps we should be speaking about a *disabled family*. Writers in critical disabled studies have spoken extensively about the impacts on families of disabled people in Western spaces (see Goodley & Runswick-Cole, 2010). The implication is therefore that any analysis looking at disability, childhood and poverty in the global South needs to engage from a family perspective or more precisely a household analysis. These voices and lives cannot be stifled or ignored since they not only impact how disability and childhood are constructed, experienced and lived, but also because they live the constant risk of impairment. Dependence on and the ensuing impacts on the household implies that intervention or rather poverty-reduction efforts should be focused more broadly on supporting families (as opposed to focusing exclusively on the individual, e.g. through one-off job skills training programmes) while never losing sight of broader structural problems impacting whole communities. Ultimately, healthy, food-secure and economically stronger families should be able to be a reliable informal safety net for their disabled members, without compromising their own health, consumption levels and well-being:

> The important thing is that my family did not abandon me, they have been with me at every moment, every day, even if only some food, and when they can, they buy me a pill for the pain, from the little they can, very poor all of us, my brother cries because he can't do more for me. Take away my family and I am dead in this misery you can see. (Ismael)

Framing disability within these social and familial networks of support sheds light on the resilience of poor people as agents of change and actors in their own right. But it also permits some or other challenging of the generalizations discursively constructed about the presumed treatment (generally oppressive) of all disabled people in the majority world at the hand of their households and communities (highlighted earlier). Perhaps the major problem with such discourse is that it continues to ignore and render invisible the care of families who historically have ensured and continue to ensure the survival of their disabled members, families that like those in the West are indeed capable of loving their children in the same way, and indeed do try their best. Unlike many families in the West, though, they do this single-handedly with no access to the most basic of services and support, constrained not by their will, but by the most extreme and violent poverty and material deprivation. It is within these situations of despair that disabled children continue to survive, and if this is not a reflection of love, one is hard pressed to question what love and care really do mean.

Again, this is not to suggest that ill-treatment does not exist or to even exoticize and idealize these families and the care they provide. But there is now substantial cross-cultural evidence to show that there are indeed both positive and negative responses to disability even within single countries (see e.g. Ingstad & Whyte, 2007). It is surely problematic to homogenize these complex spaces, cultures and people we often write about from a distance and often know little. It is problematic to forsake much-needed critical engagement with the varying attitudes and behaviours on the ground and how these are mediated by a host of socio-economic, cultural, political, personal, ideological/spiritual, situational and many other dynamic variables. Suggesting that ill-treatment is all that faces disabled people in the countries of the global South renders invisible the agency, resilience, love and care of families, dehumanizing and often demonizing them. Importantly, discourse such as this renders the disablism caused by poverty itself invisible and perhaps even irrelevant. To reiterate, this is not about ignoring oppression (of all forms) when it does exist, but it is about giving back to these families the same agency, heterogeneity and humanity awarded to (or taken for granted) among Western families. It is also about making sure that their efforts at surviving and enabling the survival of their disabled children are understood, learnt from and built upon, and never ignored or trampled on, whether discursively or materially.

Conclusions

In this chapter I have attempted to discuss some critical gaps as Disability Studies is confronted with disability and childhood in the global South. My argument is that this debate is too complex and we know too little, and what we think we know is often premised on and developed in specific spaces, places and temporalities, within the confines of specific disciplines imbued with their own historical baggage, much of which is imperial and colonizing. Too many debates continue to be colonized, even when tenets from Disability Studies are thrown at a global South they never intended to address, so what chance is there for a field of thought, perhaps a genuinely 'global' Disability or Childhood Studies, that still struggles to emerge?

We urgently need an approach in Disability Studies that is genuinely global and critical, which encourages listening and questioning rather than simply transferring discourse and methods, where uncertainty, contingency and (self)reflexivity are key. It is about learning about the contexts, cultures, ideologies and most critically the knowledge, experiences and lives of those we talk about – the way they interpret and know themselves and their world – because they are the ultimately the real 'experts' in their own lives.

Much of this is not possible without a Disability Studies ready to be interdisciplinary, where debate and collaboration across disciplines, fields and practices is consistently prioritized, and where monolithic approached are constantly challenged. The voices from the global South must never be stifled – especially those that challenge the fixities of our own positions and practices. Indeed, cannot we do without a type of Disability Studies prepared to be hybrid, inter/transdisciplinary, adopting the philosophical nomadism highlighted by Braidotti, the vision of the subject that is non-unitary, and a philosophy 'played out on this juxtaposition of Sameness and specular Otherness' (2006: 21).

Framing disability and childhood within the global South in an open way, though, is not possible without decolonizing the debate, without being critical and challenging our own dominant epistemologies. We need to decolonize our own minds – to acknowledge that there are different worlds and different ways of knowing these worlds, and how these kick up different ways of learning, talking about and acting upon the world. This is what we owe to those we so often construct as voiceless and powerless.

References

Arias, A. (2008) The Maya Movement: Postcolonialism and cultural agency, in M. Moraña, E. Dussel & C.A. Jauregui (eds), *Coloniality at large: Latin America and the postcolonial debate* (Durham, NC: Duke University Press), pp. 519–538.

Bauman, Z. (1992) *Intimations of postmodernity* (London and New York: Routledge).

Bird, K., Hulme, D., Moore, K. & Shepherd, A. (2002) *Chronic poverty and remote rural areas*, CPRC Working Paper No. 13 (Manchester: CPRC).

Bolt, V.J. & Bird, K. (2003) *The Intrahousehold Disadvantages Framework: A framework for the analysis of intra-household difference and inequality*. CPRC Working Paper No. 32 (London: ODI).

Braidotti, R. (2006) *Transpositions: On nomadic ethics* (Cambridge: Polity Press).

Davis, L.J. (2010) Constructing normalcy, in L.J. Davis (ed.), *The Disability Studies reader* (New York and London: Routledge), pp. 3–19.

Escobar, A. (1995) *Encountering development: The making and unmaking of the Third World* (Princeton, NJ: Princeton University Press).

FAO (2008) Soaring food prices: Facts, perspectives, impacts and actions required. Prepared for the High-Level Conference on World Food Security: The Challenges of Climate Change and Bioenergy, Rome. 3–5 June, 2008.

Garcia Canclini, N. (2005) *Hybrid cultures: Strategies for entering and leaving modernity* (Minneapolis, MN: University of Minnesota Press).

Ghai, A. (2002) Disability in the Indian context: Post-colonial perspectives, in M. Corker & T. Shakespeare (eds), *Disability/Postmodernity: Embodying disability theory* (London: Continuum), pp. 88–100.

Goodley, D. & Runswick-Cole, K. (2010) Parents, disabled children and their allies, in L. O'Dell & S. Leverett (eds), *Working with children and young people: Co-constructing practice* (London: Palgrave), pp. 69–79.

Grech, S. (2009) 'Disability, poverty and development: Critical reflections on the majority world debate', *Disability & Society*, 24, 6, 771–784.

Grech, S. (2011) 'Recolonising debates or perpetuated coloniality? Decentring the spaces of disability, development and community in the global South', *International Journal of Inclusive Education*, 15, 1, 87–100.

Grech, S. (2012) Disability and the majority world: A neocolonial approach, in D. Goodley, B. Hughes & L. Davis (eds), *Disability and social theory: New developments and directions* (London: Palgrave Macmillan), pp. 52–69.

Groce, N. (2009) 'Disability, poverty, human rights and the need for accurate data to promote action', *ALTER: European Journal of Disability Research*, 3, 3, 185–187.

Haraway, D. (1985) 'A manifesto for cyborgs: Science, technology and socialist feminism in the 1980s', *Socialist Review*, 80, 65–107.

Hardt, M. & Negri, A. (2000) *Empire* (Cambridge, MA: Harvard University Press).

IFAD (2010) *Rural Poverty Report 2011: New realities, new challenges* (Rome: IFAD).

Ingstad, B. & Whyte, S.R. (eds) (2007) *Disability in local and global worlds* (Berkeley, CA: University of California Press).

Mignolo, W. (2002) 'The geopolitics of knowledge and the colonial difference', *South Atlantic Quarterly*, 101, 57–96.

Miles, M. (2000) 'High level baloney for Third World disabled people', *Disability World*, 5, Oc.–Dec. http://www.disabilityworld.org/10-12_00/news/baloney.htm [accessed 19 July 2006].

Mohanty, C.T. (1991) Cartographies of struggle: Third World women and the politics of feminism, in C.T. Mohanty, A. Russo & L. Torres (eds), *Cartographies of struggle: Third World women and the politics of feminism* (Indianapolis, IN: Indiana University Press), pp. 1–47.

Narayan, D., Patel, R., Schafft, K., Rademacher, A., & Koch-Schullem, S. (2000) *Voices of the poor: Can anyone hear us?* (Washington, DC: Oxford University Press).

Oliver, M. (1990) *The politics of disablement* (Basingstoke: Macmillan).

Oliver, M. (1996) *Understanding disability: From theory to practice* (Basingstoke: Macmillan).

Rao, A. & Pierce, S. (2006) Discipline and the other body: Humanitarianism, violence, and the colonial exception, in S. Pierce & A. Rao (eds), *Discipline and the other body: Correction, corporeality, colonialism* (Durham, NC and London: Duke University Press), pp. 2–35.

Said, E. (1993) *Culture and imperialism* (New York: Knop).

UNESCO (2010) *EFA Global Report 2010: Reaching the marginalized* (Paris: UNESCO).

WHO (2009) *Diarrhoeal disease*, Fact sheet No. 330. http://www.who.int/mediacentre/factsheets/fs330/en/index.html [accessed 6 February 2010].

WHO (2010) *Trends in maternal mortality: 1990 to 2008* (Geneva: WHO).

WHO and World Bank (2011) *World Report on Disability* (Geneva: WHO).

World Bank (2008) *Global Monitoring Report 2008 – MDGs and the environment: Agenda for inclusive and sustainable development* (Washington, DC: World Bank).

Whyte, S.R. & Ingstad, B. (1995) Disability and culture: An overview, in B. Ingstad & S.R. Whyte (eds), *Disability and culture* (Berkeley, CA: University of California Press), pp. 3–32.

9
'Wearing It All with a Smile': Emotional Labour in the Lives of Mothers and Disabled Children

Katherine Runswick-Cole

Introduction

This chapter explores emotional labour in the lives of mothers and disabled children. It draws on data from a recently completed research project, 'Does Every Child Matter, post-Blair? The interconnections of disabled childhoods', a two-year project funded by the Economic and Social Research Council (http//post-blair.posterous.com).

Including a chapter that has a focus on the experiences of *mothers* and disabled children in a childhood studies text is controversial. Approaches rooted in a 'new sociology of childhood' (James & Prout, 2001) mean that children are no longer considered to be simply the 'property' of their parents/carers. In research and in work with children, the importance of listening to the voice of the child, rather than talking to children's proxies, including parents/carers and practitioners, has rightly been emphasized. Indeed, the 'rights' of the child as 'active social agents' in their own 'social worlds' (James & Prout, 2001) have been enshrined UK national and international legislation in the form of the Children Act, 1989 and the UN Convention on the Rights of the Child, 1989 (UNICEF, 1989). A discussion of the lives of non-disabled mothers of disabled children in the context of a disabled children's childhood studies text might then be seen as problematic.

Yet non-disabled mothers of disabled children have occupied a liminal position as non-disabled people who have been described, at worst, as 'oppressors' of their disabled children and, at best, as no more than 'allies' to their disabled children in the same way that professionals have been described as 'allies' to disabled communities (Ryan & Runswick-Cole, 2008a; Finkelstein, 1999). This is despite the fact that mothers of disabled children experience disablism directly and by proxy through their relationship with their disabled child (Ryan & Runswick-Cole, 2008a). Indeed, this experience of disablism has been recognized as a form of discrimination, known as 'discrimination by association', in the UK Equalities Act following the case *Attridge Law and S. Law* v *Coleman* (2007). The European Court of Justice found that Sharon Coleman had been discriminated against in the workplace on the grounds of her association with her disabled son.

My aim in this chapter is to argue that despite the clear tensions inherent in focusing on the experiences of (often) non-disabled mothers' experiences in the context of disabled children's childhood studies, this is, nonetheless, an important and legitimate area of enquiry. Not least, because, as we shall see below, the emotional work of mothers and disabled children often intersects.

Mothers and emotions

Talking about emotions is a slippery business. Emotions are multidimensional, and cannot simply be reduced to biology, or to discourse; they are formed through ongoing relationships (Reay, 2000). It is widely argued that mothers' and children's emotions become 'enmeshed' so that mothers' and children's emotional states become mutually dependent (ibid.: 574). This meshing of mothers' and children's emotions is, perhaps, unsurprising in Western cultures where, despite shifts in women's work patterns and opportunities, the majority of childcare is still carried out by mothers (Moss, 1991). Although childcare is often assumed to be the responsibility of *parents*, it continues to be the case within families that mothers usually carry the major responsibility for childcare; they are held responsible for their child's well-being and life options and for their child's physical and emotional care. Under the New Labour government (1997–2010) there were shifts in 'policy speak' (Ball, 2009), which attempted to renarrate fathers' contributions to parenting. For example, *The Children's Plan* (DCFS, 2007: 20) acknowledged that:

> Fathers, in particular, say that they often feel invisible to health and children's services professionals and find that many services are not offered at times that fit with their working patterns.

Yet it continues to be the case that it is mothers, more than fathers, who are expected to prioritize day-to-day care for their children in their lives (Moss, 1991).

While there is a wealth of literature that suggests that mothers carry the main responsibility for childcare, there is also evidence to show that mothers of disabled children are even more likely than other mothers to engage in complex, skilled and prolonged aspects of care (Traustadóttir, 1995; Read, 2000; Cole, 2004). Frequently, mothers of disabled children engage in mothering with an intensity of level of involvement that is beyond what other mothers usually experience (Traustadóttir, 1995; Ryan & Runswick-Cole, 2008b). While childcare is made up of a complex mix of practical, care and educational work (Reay, 2000), it is the emotional work associated with mothering that is the focus of this chapter. I approach this topic cautiously, however, conscious of the fact that focusing on mothers' emotional labour may only serve to sustain the 'myths of motherhood' – that mothers have innate caring abilities that fathers neither have, nor can learn (McLaughlin, 2008) – yet at the same time I want to argue that mothers' emotional labour is an area that needs to be recognized both in their lives and the lives of their children (Hochschild, 1983).

Emotional labour

When mothers of disabled children 'wear it all with a smile' they are engaging in emotional labour. Emotional labour is usually understood to mean that a person is hiding or changing his/her feelings in an attempt to show a more 'acceptable' emotional front to those around them. Hochschild (1983: 7) discusses emotional labour as a form of work, describing it as 'the management of feelings to create a publicly observable facial and bodily display'. Emotional labour describes the relational rather than the task-based aspects of work (Steinberg & Figart, 1999); in other words, the focus is on feelings rather than a simple description of the (care) work involved. Hochschild's (1983) original discussion of emotional labour was in the context of flight attendants' service work. Hochschild describes the requirement that flight attendants be 'nicer than natural' in order to perform their service work. However, emotional labour has since been discussed beyond the service industry, particularly in relation to care (see e.g. Staden, 1998), and it is the relational aspects of mothers' care-giving and the impact on their children that form the focal point of this chapter.

Hochschild (1983: 7) explains how service work, such as the work carried out by flight attendants, requires employees to 'induce or suppress feeling in order to sustain the outward countenance that produces the proper state of mind in others'. In other words, service workers are required to show one emotion, while suppressing another, for the sake of those they serve. At times, employees are also required to absorb not only their own emotions but the emotions of those around them, for the good of others (Steinberg & Figart, 1999). The requirement to 'induce' or 'suppress' feelings and to absorb emotions can take place in different workplaces (aircraft cabins, shops, school and hospitals). Emotional labour also takes place across different structures as employees have to manage emotions across hierarchical divisions, managing the emotions of superiors, peers and subordinates in the workplace (Steinberg & Figart, 1999).

The focus here is on mothers' and children's emotional labour as they 'induce' or 'suppress' feelings and absorb others' emotions in a variety of contexts including: the park, the supermarket, schools, hospitals, clinics, assessment meeting, within the home and across different hierarchical divisions as they interact with professionals, friends and family.

Ashforth and Humphrey (1993: 90) define emotional labour in service roles as 'the act of displaying the appropriate emotion', or conventions of emotional display (Jarzabkowski, 2001) as a means of managing norms in a given context (e.g. on a plane, in a shop, in a school), and which also involve routine scripted performances. Some of the scripts are so detailed that they become tied to specific responses. For example, McLure and Walker's (2007) analysis of parent–teacher consultation evenings revealed scripted conversations in which, McLure and Walker argue, teachers constrained parents' responses through the use of carefully structured scripts, which were designed to limit parents' responses. This scripted nature of emotional labour has led Steinberg and Figart (1999) to describe emotional labour as a cultural performance.

Hochschild (1983) makes a useful distinction between the 'surface acting' and 'deep acting', which takes place during the performance. 'Surface acting' describes a situation where the employee merely feigns the emotion required, which differs from what they feel, whereas 'deep acting' requires the actor to focus on their 'inner feelings', actually resulting in changes in how they feel.

Of course, the quality of performances may vary; performances can go 'wrong' or fail to be carried off convincingly. The audience necessarily interacts with the performance, either to support it by abiding by the display rules and (re)producing the expected scripted responses, or by unsettling how the performance will be played out, by going off script or finding some other way of disrupting the performance. Of course, sometimes it is the actors who disrupt the performance: they 'corpse', they become distracted, they laugh or they freeze and can no longer sustain the illusion of the performance (Steinberg & Figart, 1999).

The focus within this chapter is on the function of 'display rules' and scripts in the mothers' and children's day-to-day encounters with quasi-intimates such as teachers, shopkeepers, doctors, psychologists and social workers, as well as with intimates, such as family members, friends and children, and, indeed, complete strangers who they encounter in the street, supermarkets, parks and other public spaces. The questions this raises about mothers' and disabled children's emotional labour children include:

- To what extent are mothers and their children required to 'induce' or 'suppress' feelings in order to produce the proper state of mind in others?
- Which scripts do the mothers and their children follow, and what are the responses tied to these scripts?
- What happens when the mothers and/or children 'corpse' or go off script?
- What happens when the audience (friends, family, children, professionals, strangers) disrupts the mothers' and children's performance?
- What consequences does disruption have for the mothers' and children's emotional labour?
- What impact does the mothers' emotional labour have on children and vice versa?
- How might recognizing and valuing the mothers' and children's emotional labour impact on their mothers and children's lives?

The study

The focus on emotional labour in the lives of mothers of disabled children is in the light of a recently completed research project, 'Does every child matter, post-Blair: Interconnections of disabled childhoods', a two-year project funded by the Economic and Social Research Council (http//post-blair.posterous.com). We explored with disabled children and young people, their parents/carers and professionals, families' experiences of education, health, social care and leisure. This chapter is primarily supported by interviews with mothers and children conducted between 2008 and 2011 in the north of England.

The data for this chapter is drawn from the mothers' accounts of parenting disabled children. Each of the mothers' accounts has been written up into narratives. These include life stories, biographies, vignettes, composite narratives and ethnographic tales (see Goodley, Lawthom, Moore & Clough, 2004). The interviews were open-ended and covered a range of issues related to the families' experiences of health, social care, education and leisure.

In the course of the analysis of these narratives, the research team visited and revisited the mothers' stories, searching for themes or 'nodes' (Snow, Morrill & Anderson, 2004). The team subjected the narratives to points of analysis or themes that were drawn together as the data was collected (Snow et al., 2003). The range of analysis and discussion allowed ongoing consideration of how forms of interviews were developing; it allowed us, we hope, to capture some of the complexity of the cultural performances we were exploring. It also allowed us to reflect on our research questions, and through it we began to make the connections between the nodes and the broader literature. Emotional work was frequently referred to by mothers in the narratives, which led us to explore 'emotional labour' within the lives of mothers of disabled children. It is not, perhaps, surprising that the emotional labour of parents emerged as a key theme within the narratives given that one of the research team is the mother of a disabled child and another is a father. We were, perhaps, already sensitized to the emotional labour work of parents.

Pen portraits of mothers

The majority of mothers in the study were recruited by requests for participants advertised in the magazines and newsletters of a range of voluntary organizations, including impairment specific support groups, parent support groups, fathers' support groups, minority ethnic support groups and others. We requested that *parents* of disabled children aged 4–16 take part, but responses to the publicity were largely from mothers.

What follows is a series of pen portraits of the mothers whose narratives are referred to here. All the names used are pseudonyms in order to protect the participants' anonymity.

- Sally is in her 40s. She has one child, her 13-year-old daughter, Hilary. Hilary has been given the label of moderate learning disabilities. Susan does not have paid work outside the home. She is married and her husband runs his own business.
- Susan is in her 40s. She has three sons aged 17, 14 and 11. Laurie, who is 14, has a label of Profound and Multiple Learning Disabilities. Susan works occasionally as a cleaner and her husband runs his own business.
- Harriet is in her 30s. She has a 6-year-old daughter diagnosed with cerebral palsy. Harriet works part-time as a solicitor. She is married to a policeman.

- Natalie is 40 and her daughter Nadia is 4. She has the label of Downs Syndrome and epilepsy. Natalie is married, and has two sons aged 7 and 9. Her husband's work means that he is away from home half the week. Natalie cares for Nadia full-time, and has no paid work outside the home.
- Kate is in her 40s. Her son Rob is 11, and he has a physical impairment that will require surgery as he reaches adulthood. Kate works for a carers' organization in the North-West. She is married and has three other children: two sons who are young adults and a daughter aged 9.
- Rachael is in her 50s and is married. She has nine children, including three adopted children (who she calls her 'chosen' children), aged 9, 14 and 21, who are all disabled. Five of her children have grown up and left home. All her disabled children live at home with Rachael. Rachael is married and her husband works part-time.
- Rebecca is in her 30s and is married with two boys. Laurie is 7 and has the label of Profound and Multiple Learning Disabilities. Oscar is 9 and is going through the process of being diagnosed with Attention Deficit Hyperactivity Disorder.
- Jane is in her 40s and teaches at a university. She is separated from her husband and has a son and a daughter. Helen is 13 while Greg is 11 and is a wheelchair user.

Cultural performances with strangers

The mothers in the study were acutely self-conscious of their performances in a variety of contexts, but public spaces seemed to be the most difficult environments for the mothers as it was here that they encountered strangers. Anticipating and managing the emotions of strangers was a huge source of emotional labour for mothers of disabled children. For example, Harriet told us that her daughter wears a bib because she dribbles but apart from that she looks 'normal'. Harriet said that she used a wheelchair for her daughter when she is in a hurry, but she then confided that her daughter 'didn't really need the wheelchair' and that 'I almost chose it so people realize that something is wrong'. Harriet used the wheelchair as a very visible prop, which symbolizes 'disability', to support her performance as a mother of a disabled child. In this way, Harriet escapes prolonged negotiation of her child's identity, and her own, in public spaces while at the same time hoping to pre-empt possible negative comments or responses from strangers.

Whereas a wheelchair functions very effectively as a symbol of disability, Susan describes what happens when a prop, like a large buggy, fails to signify disability:

> ... you've got people looking, well I don't mind the looking it is the staring and you've got people staring and then there's children saying 'what's that big boy doing in a buggy, mummy?' 'I don't know, darling' ... then walking off. It is 'well, let's not confront it, it is too awful'. And I feel like saying: 'well that's my life, you know'. But going to town with Laurie makes me this person I'm actually not.

She vividly describes having to suppress her feelings of anger and frustration, and the impact this has on her turning her into 'someone she's not'. This is a powerful example of a mother suppressing her own feelings for the sake of others and the impact that this 'deep acting' has on her and her relationship with her child.

Another mother, Natalie, talked about the reactions her daughter, Nadia, received in their home town. She said that:

> I would say that, I think, I feel fine living here with Nadia. It is a small town it is a nice place to live. I mean she's highly visible, people look at her and occasionally ... they just sort of look at her and they give me this sort of 'ahhh', which is really 'ahhh, glad she's not mine!'

Natalie describes the reactions of strangers and comments on *their* emotional labour as they try, unsuccessfully it seems, to mask one feeling for another. For Natalie, the outcome of this uncomfortable interaction was that she took the role of being 'nicer than natural' by not challenging the strangers' negative comments about her daughter.

Natalie also talked about her worries about the impact this will have on Nadia in the future:

> ... when you have a child that is disabled in this way most people wanna talk to you. To initiate some kind of interaction, I think when your child is older, things are different, they're embarrassed by it.

Natalie seems to be anticipating possible emotional work she may have to do in the future, and this potential emotional work is a source of worry for her. She also worries that Nadia will be excluded in her community.

Cultural performances with friends and family

Encounters with strangers were not, of course, the only relationships where emotional work took place. Relationships with friends and family also led to significant emotional labour for the mothers. Rebecca described suppressing her feelings when a friend commented on the support she received:

> I have a friend who is always pointing out my failings for sending Oscar to mainstream school or saying 'it is alright for you, you get free pedro boots we don't get those' and 'it's alright for you'. Well, nothing is alright for me, my husband works damn hard to pay into the system, so really I don't think we're really getting anything we're not entitled to.

Support groups, although generally considered to be positive for parents of disabled children (McLaughlin, 2008), also brought mothers into environments where they were doing significant emotional work. Sometimes mothers simply absorbed emotions as they listened to other mothers talk about their children. However, Kate describes the emotional work she did with another parent:

> I made friends with a couple there who had a 14-year-old daughter who was supposedly in remission ending up ... rushed her to theatre, she never made it, she died. ... I thought 'oh my God! I can't do this any more', but I had to do it.

Again, she suppressed her own feelings to support another person.

The mothers' narratives also revealed the emotional labour that occurred within families, not least with their partners. The mothers often talked about the 'cause' of their child's impairment. Two mothers in the study, Kate and Rebecca, were told by doctors that their children's impairments were a direct result of their genetic inheritance from their mothers. This caused tension between parents. Kate told us that her husband said: '"oh well, it has come from your side then!" I remember him saying the words to me and I just went "yeah".' Rebecca also felt that her husband and his parents might blame her for their son's impairment, and yet she also suppressed her feelings of anger and hurt.

Scripted performances

There were examples of heavily scripted performances within the parents' narratives. However, unlike the service workers in Hoschild's

(1983) original study who initiated the scripts, mothers described their reaction to scripts initiated by others.

> Researcher: There is that thing [that other people say] about 'it is a good job it happened to you, I wouldn't ...'
> Natalie: Aaaargh! Yes I know. You are obviously the right person, you've been chosen! You have to wear it all with a smile because people don't want you to be unhappy, they don't want to look after you, they say, you're alright because ... anyway back to me, do you know what I mean?

Natalie plays along and, in doing so, is expected to deny her emotions.

Disrupted performances

There were examples of in the mothers disrupting the performances and failing to conform to the expected 'scripts'. For example, Rachael said:

> Some people look at them [her three disabled children] going down the street and walked into bushes before, especially when I've got the three of them. They look at me and go [open-mouthed]. Their face, their mouths fall open ... and sometimes, my older children get very upset when I do this, I say 'do you want a photo of my beautiful children? Is that why you are looking? Is there something I can help you with? Is there a question you'd like to ask me that you haven't had answered?' Or 'would you like a photo next time, pet?'

Kate also described disrupting the performance in hospital with her new-born son:

> I lost my temper because everyone wanted to look at him, it was like being a guinea pig so people from all over the hospital came to look at him. In the end me mum lost her temper and shouted 'would you all get out of this room, it's not a freak show!' So they all toddled off then. That really got on my nerves because they didn't ask me, they just turned up 'we're just looking at your baby, we're just looking at your baby, we've heard through the hospital', so I thought oh they are all discussing it, and one said well you learn from it and I thought well at the end of the day it's nice to ask! You know people have to learn but at the end of the day they just turned up in droves, gangs of them just looking, and that really annoyed me, so I had that to cope with.

But Susan described what she saw as the risks of disrupting the performance especially in the context of managing professional encounters. Susan said:

> I only once swore at a meeting when I told everyone to ... and walked out.

She felt that professionals were very critical of her now and that they 'don't like me'. Susan paid a high price to pay for 'going off script' and failing to suppress her emotions for the sake of the professionals.

Cultural performances with children and by children

Mothers talked about suppressing their emotions for the sake of their children. Kate described going to the operating theatre with her son Rob:

> The morning of the operation he said to me 'I don't want to go', so I said to him 'don't you?' 'Well, I want the operation, mummy, but it is just the thought of it', which I knew, so I said to him I thought I've got to play a game here, I've got to be quick, so I said 'I tell you what, would you like me to have the operation with you?' 'Ah, could you do that, mummy?' 'Do you want a bet? Course I can! So when the porter comes I'll get on the bed with you and I'll ask them can they do me a special hole there so I can have a tube like you?' 'That would be great, mummy, if you could do that'. So when the porter come, I told him. So I got on [the trolley] and all the mums are laughing and they are going 'where you going Kate?' ... and I'm 'oh I'm having an operation with my son'. And me and Rob went dead proud of ourselves. ... I said 'we are going to have an operation, aren't we?' And Rob said 'yes, my mummy is having the same operation as me', and that is the way I coaxed him.

Kate worked hard to reassure Rob to support him through the operation. However, the mothers' needs to manage the emotions of others may also have less positive outcomes for disabled children as in the case of Harriet, whose daughter used a wheelchair although she didn't really need to. When mothers go 'off script' this also impacts on children as, for example, when Rachael openly challenged people staring at her children, her children were embarrassed and would rather that she had said nothing.

Some mothers and disabled children talked openly about their emotional labour with each other, and jointly negotiated strategies for managing their emotions and those of others. Greg, a young wheelchair user, and his mother Jane told us about being stared at when they went out. On one occasion in a fast food restaurant, Greg felt so uncomfortable at being stared at by another child that he couldn't eat his burger. In the end, he stared back until the child looked away. In their conversation about managing being stared at, they discussed possibilities – among them gesturing or swearing at the person doing the staring. But Greg and his mother concluded that a 'stare cam' – hidden cameras that caught people staring at disabled people – was a good solution. People would be fined for staring, and if they repeated the offence they would have to 'go to prison'.

Conclusion

The narratives reveal the mothers and children engaged in demanding emotional labour. Like the flight attendants in Hochschild's (1983) original study, there were examples of mothers being 'nicer than natural', suppressing and inducing emotions and absorbing the emotions of those around them, even when others expressed hostile attitudes towards their children. Mothers and children carried out their emotional labour in a range of contexts, including shops, hospitals and playgrounds, and with a variety of others, including strangers, professionals and family members.

The mothers in this study were clearly attuned to the emotional labour of others, including strangers who tried (and often failed) to mask their feelings about disabled children. Mothers of disabled children also seem to anticipate future emotional labour as they worry about what the future will hold for their children.

The impact of mothers' emotional labour on the lives of their disabled children is complex. At times, disabled children experience their mothers' emotional work as supportive, at times as embarrassing, but significantly emotional work was also sometimes a shared experience between mothers and children that allowed them to develop strategies and responses to managing the emotions of others.

Finally, Hochschild (1983) suggests that emotional labour should be honoured. The task-based aspects of the care given by mothers of disabled children have often been the focus of research. And yet, the emotional labour carried out by mothers and disabled children often goes unnoticed. Noticing emotional labour opens up two potential opportunities. As we saw above, it offers an opportunity for mothers to share their experiences and perhaps to support their children. In addition, a recognition of mothers' emotional labour also raises important questions about the behaviour of the 'others' – those people whose comments cause mothers and children to work hard to manage their own emotions and the emotions of others. Mothers' accounts of their emotional labour reveal what Campbell has described as the omnipresent 'ableist gaze' (Campbell, 2009). A form of 'compulsory able bodied-ness' (McRuer, 2006) permeates cultures in the global North. Ever-narrowing definitions of normativity and a failure to value difference and diversity within children and childhoods create the day-to-day, mundane encounters described by the mothers in the stories above, which require them to work hard to manage their own emotions and the emotions of others.

Recent interpretations of the experiences of mothers of disabled children have rightly moved away from accounts that emphasize the 'burdensome' aspect of caring for disabled children focusing on models of 'grief' and 'loss' (Lazarus & Folkman, 1984) towards more affirmative and celebratory understandings of parenting disabled children (McLaughlin, Goodley, Clavering, & Fisher, 2008; Ryan & Runswick-Cole, 2008b). It is not my intention here to imply that a recognition of emotional labour in the lives of mothers and disabled children should provoke a move back towards the deficit model of mothering disabled children. Rather, a recognition of the emotional labour of mothers of disabled children teaches us as much about the emotional worlds of the 'others' as it does about the emotional worlds of mothers (Goodley, 2011). After all, it is 'others' who cast mothers and disabled children in the role of service workers, who, like flight attendants, are required to attend to their emotional responses. For mothers and children, 'clients' include family and friends, professionals and strangers, the hours are long and often unsociable, and their work goes unnoticed and unrewarded.

Acknowledgements

I would like to thank the Economic and Social Research Council for funding the study on which this chapter draws, and the Research Institute of Health and Social Change at Manchester Metropolitan University for their support for the research. I would like to thank Dan Goodley, whose ideas have hugely influenced my thinking about mothers' emotional work, and, finally, I would like to thank the participants in the study for their time and their expertise and for sharing their stories about their lives.

References

Ashforth, E. & Humphrey, R. (1993) 'Emotional labor in service roles: The influence of identity', *The Academy of Management Review*, 18, 1, 88–115.
Attridge, S. & Law v *Coleman* [2007] ICR 654 EAT.
Ball, S.J. (2009) *The education debate* (Bristol: The Policy Press).

Campbell, F.K. (2009) *Contours of ableism: The production of disability and abledness* (Basingstoke: Palgrave Macmillan).

Cole, B. (2004) *Mother-teachers: Insights into inclusion* (London: David Fulton).

DCSF (Department for Children, Schools and Families) (2007) *The Children's Plan: Building brighter futures* (London: The Stationery Office).

Finkelstein, V. (1999) A profession allied to the community: The disabled people's trade union, in E. Stone (ed.), *Disability & development: Learning from action and research on disability in the majority world* (Leeds: The Disability Press), pp. 21–24.

Goodley, D. (2011) *Disability Studies: An inter-disciplinary introduction* (London: Sage).

Goodley, D., Lawthom, R., Clough, P. & Moore, M. (2004) *Researching life stories: Method, theory and analyses in a biographical age* (London/New York: Routledge).

Hochschild, A. (1983) *The Managed Heart: Commercialization of human feeling* (Berkeley, CA: University of California Press).

Home Office (1998) *Supporting families* (London: Stationery Office).

James, A. & Prout, J. (2001) *Constructing and reconstructing childhood* (London: Routledge).

Jarzabkowski, L. (2001) 'Emotional labour in educational research', *Queensland Journal of Educational Research*, 17, 2, 123–137.

Lazarus, R.S. & Folkman, S. (1984) *Stress, appraisal, and coping* (New York: Springer).

McLaughlin, J., Goodley, D., Clavering, E. & Fisher, P. (2008) *Families raising disabled children: Enabling care* (London: Palgrave).

McLure, M. with Walker, B. (2007) Interrogating the discourse of home–school relations: The case of 'parents' evenings, in M. Hammersley (ed.), *Educational research and evidence-based practice* (Milton Keynes: Open University).

McRuer, R. (2006) *Crip theory: Cultural signs of queerness and disability* (New York: New York University Press).

Moss, P. (1991) 'School-age child-care in the European Community', *Women's Studies International Forum*, 14, 539–549.

Read, J. (2000) *Disability, the Family and Society: Listening to mothers*, Buckingham: Open University Press.

Reay, D. (2000) 'A useful extension of Bourdieu's conceptual framework?: Emotional capital as a way of understanding mothers' involvement in their children's education', *The Sociological Review*, 48, 4, 568–585.

Ryan, S. & Runswick-Cole, K. (2008a) 'Repositioning mothers: Mothers, disabled children and Disability Studies', *Disability and Society*, 23, 3, 199–210.

Ryan, S. & Runswick-Cole, K. (2008b) 'From advocate to activist? Mapping the experiences of mothers of children on the autism spectrum', *Journal of Applied Research in Intellectual Disabilities*. http://www3.interscience.wiley.com/journal/121430934/abstract?CRETRY=1&SRETRY=0 [accessed 23 March 2012].

Snow, D.A., Morrill, C. & Anderson, L. (2003) 'Elaborating analytic ethnography: Linking fieldwork and theory', *Ethnography*, 4, 2, 181–200.

Staden, H. (1998) 'Alertness to the needs of others: a study of the emotional labour of caring', *Journal of Advanced Nursing*, 27, 1, 147–167.

Steinberg, R.J. & Figart, D.M. (1999) 'Emotional labor since *The Managed Heart*', *Annals*, ASPSS, 581, 8–26.

Traustadottir, R. (1995) 'Mothers who care: Gender, disability, and family life', *Journal of Family Issues*, 12, 2, 211–228.

UNICEF (1989) *UN Convention on the Rights of the Child* (Geneva: Office of the High Commissioner for Human Rights).

Part III
Contemporary Theories

In the chapters in Part III, the authors pick up on some common of the emergent themes from the first two parts of the book. Each study goes beyond critiques of the deficit productions of disabled children's development and aims to raise expectations around disabled children's childhoods. Several chapters question the spectre of the 'normal' child' and seek productive ways of moving beyond the 'normal'/'abnormal' binary. However, there are also some differences and distinct perspectives between the chapters. Some chapters embrace the dominant Western nature/social opposition that separates impairment and disability, highlighting social practices of oppression towards emancipatory action. Other chapters question the bracketing of 'the body' from 'the social', highlighting the social processes of impairment or drawing attention to the strategic power of oppositions as a practice.

The authors work with both historical and the current ideas about inclusion and participation, and question modern and postmodern worldviews as they engage with discussions of global relations. They bring theories from critical psychology, post-structuralism and postcolonial studies in recognizing disabled children's childhoods in the wider context and examining disability and childhood concepts as global and globalizing discourses.

In Chapter 10, Tillie Curran asks how disabled children's childhood studies can form alternative relations of authority to the dominant discourses of disabled childhoods that have emerged in the global North. She describes how disabled children's childhood studies, as we saw in Part II of the book, can deconstruct Western accounts of childhood by making visible disabled children's views in research spaces. She explains how these studies redefine vulnerability and discusses factors that encourage meaningful engagement with research in practice and professional education.

In Chapter 11, Harriet Cooper draws on the work of Lennard Davis (1995) in relation to normalcy to historicize the notion of the 'normal child'. In the first section, Harriet discusses the 'normal child' in terms of the British documentary series *Born to be Different*. She then turns her attention to five childcare manuals, published between 1839 and 1924, to explore a gradual shift of emphasis in the manuals from concerns about sickness to anxieties about normalcy. Harriet concludes her chapter by describing one mother's resistance towards normalizing practices, which sees her, instead, accepting her child for herself rather than trying to make her like others.

In Chapter 12, Tsitsi Chataika and Judy McKenzie explore how disabled children's childhoods can be theorized in 'African' ways of being and thinking. They draw on socio-cultural and postcolonial approaches to unsettle the dominance of theories from the global North. Tsitsi and Judy promote indigenous knowledge systems and ask for a dialogue, on equal terms, between North and South.

In Chapter 13, Dan Goodley and Rebecca Lawthom explore the reasons why 'the non-disabled' or 'normative' imaginary responds to disability in terms of the often contradictory processes of fear/fascination; attraction/repulsion; recognition/extermination. Adopting a social psychoanalytic account, they consider the ways in which disability becomes wrapped up in responses of the non-disabled through sharing disabled people's stories. They conclude by turning the pathological gaze, which has so often settled on disabled children, back on to the 'normals', and in doing so ask us to rethink how we understand humanity and its reliance upon normativity in children's lives.

In Chapter 14, Jenny Slater shifts our focus and encourages us to think about dis/abled youth. In her chapter, Jenny considers the theoretical and methodological approaches to research concerning youth and asks where disabled young people fit in. She describes the emergence of youth as a sub-cultural category, exposing the 'ableism' present in the view of youth as a period of transition to 'normal' adulthood. She challenges us to break away youth from adulthood expectation, and, in so doing, to relieve dis/abled young of the pressures of trying to become the mythical adulthood 'norm'.

10

Disabled Children's Childhood Studies: Alternative Relations and Forms of Authority?

Tillie Curran

Introduction

This chapter asks how disabled children's childhood studies constitute alternative forms of authority to the dominant discourses of disability and childhood. Studies concerned with impairment and child development discuss disabled children in problematic terms and, it is suggested, these are not studies of their childhood. The dominant discourses of childhood and disability that emerged in the global North continue to have worldwide authority and impact in presenting disabled children in deficit and negative terms (Oliver & Barnes, 2012). The authority of these discourses is based on the positivist methodologies used. In England, they continue to be endorsed by policy, patterns of service provision and professional practices, but the links between concepts, policy and practice, and how we can be as people, are complex, and Foucault's work is used to analyze these links.

Foucault, Dreyfus (2012) explains, was interested in interpreting practices that resist and shift dominant discursive relations. Practices that resist dominant discursive relations begin by critiquing the claim to there being one dominant version of truth and authority. Resistance entails making visible any discontinuities that have been discounted or made to fit a progressive single historical account (the orthodoxy of teleological history). The dominant idea of the person as an essential fixed subject (unfolding and confessional) is also rejected. In order to shift dominant relations, marginal practices are made central by clearing space for different possibilities: immediate, multiple plural local events and ways of being that resist the totalization of dominant discourses. These interpretive practices can be found in disabled children's childhood studies.

Disabled children's childhood studies generally open with a critical deconstruction of Western discourses and systems of welfare and disrupt a single progressive historical account of childhood. Practices excluding disabled children are made visible and disabled children's views are brought to the centre through new research spaces. The concepts of disabled children's childhood that are generated through these new relations make it possible to circumvent the authority of dominant discourses. Disabled children, like everyone, are embodied, not as a result of 'nature', but specific social practices of embodiment. The 'social/nature' opposition is discussed here as one of these practices that is both powerful and open to change.

The chapter shows how disabled children's childhood studies resist and shift dominant relations in the following sections:

- making practices of exclusion visible;
- centring disabled children's experiences;
- creating spaces for disabled children's views;
- conceptualizing disabled children's childhoods

The discussion looks at the impact of disabled children's childhood studies in health and social care. The use of research in health and social care is often viewed as a problem, but when practitioners engage in research activities, especially when children and young people are also involved, the impact described is exponential. I am writing as a social work academic in England, who has not been a disabled child or adult, and I finish with some reflections on the contributions of disabled scholars, trainers and researchers in professional education.

Relations of authority and resistance

Foucault's work helps to understand the connections between knowledge, power and subjectivity, their significance and possibilities for change (Hall, 2001). Power is viewed as immanent, dispersed and continually productive. Foucault (1974, 1982, 2005) recognizes acts of violence and torture as forms of domination, but analyzes exercises of power that are not so direct and visible. 'Governmentality' is the term he used to describe the management of the population that occurs through the combined effects of knowledge disciplines and systems of administration (Schwan & Shapiro, 2011). Governmentality operates through professionals' management of the family but most significantly through self-management by the family (Elden, 2006). Professionals also self-manage exercising 'autonomous' judgement while subject to the everyday practices that make up the apparatus of governmentality. As Rose and Miller (2010) argue, government acts upon professionals and also operates through the actions of professions. A critical view of 'autonomy' is key to this form of analysis:

> Personal autonomy is not the antithesis of political power, but a key term in its exercise, the more so because most individuals are not merely the subjects of power but play a part in its operations. (Rose & Miller, 2010: 272)

'Discourse' refers to the disciplines, practices and techniques we are all subject to and to which we subject ourselves (self-discipline) at the level of the body, the local and global (Danaher, Schirato & Webb, 2000). Knowledge power strategies are about the management of time and space, including going to school or work, buildings, institutions, city and rural land practices and all areas of life. Our subjectivities are produced through these continuous experiences, which not only limit us by constraint, but through practices that generate our preferences, options and choices.

In Britain, welfare emerged in the 1900s in what Philp (1979) describes as the 'social space' produced through the division of the private and public sphere. The social work domain, he explains, has a specific 'regime of truth'. The 'psy' discourses are used to give the 'deviant' a voice. The social worker uses the 'psy' discourses to give the 'deviant' a voice by speaking for their 'subjectivity'. The client is motivated to change rather than directly governed. In contrast, the medical regime of truth is characterized by its use of techniques to make 'objective' statements about the body that are authorized on the basis that they are independent from a person's subjectivity.

Analysis from this perspective is not concerned with the content of knowledge *per se* ('connaissance'), but identifying the *relations* of power and domination that are involved ('savoir') (Foucault, 1974). Power is viewed as ascending and productive; micro practices are 'taken up' and invested in (Foucault, 2005). The partial way in which the 'social model of disability' (Oliver, 1990) is taken up in policy and practice is discussed below as an example of this. Knowledge is not to be accepted as a form of liberation, and a sceptical approach to all knowledge is advanced, which is particularly important when discussing disability, childhood and welfare discourses. Tremain makes this point in her discussion of disability and governmentality:

> One of the most original features of Foucault's analysis is the idea that power functions best when it enables subjects to act in order to constrain them. (Tremain, 2001 in Tremain, 2005: 4)

The dispersed view of power and critique of liberal autonomy presents power and authority as far-reaching, and critics have read this totalization to imply a passive, determined view of the individual and the end of emancipatory aspirations. However, Foucauldian analysis is concerned with questions of 'how' and not 'why'; there are no claims of causality and, therefore, no suggestion of any scenario being necessary or inevitable (Kendall & Wickham, 1999). Foucault (1997 in Faubion, 1998)) explains that resistance is always part of the exercise of power, and he discusses this in terms of an ethics of the self in relation to others. As Dreyfus (2012) puts it, people can act; one has the power to question and capacity to change oneself and possibly one's context. The individual is not the inventor of thought, and analysis is not interested in any 'inner' explanation. However, changing oneself, in relation to others, is considered a practice of 'freedom'. 'Freedom' is the practice of 'thought about thought in relation to others'. It is a *social* practice:

> 'Thought' is not to do with thinking beings but the relations to selves, others and systems of 'truth'. 'Thought' is event, the threshold of positivity. (Faubion, 1998: xxxvii)

Foucault invites us to be specific and curious, and to seek 'signs of existence' of desirable alternatives to dominant discourses. Resistance as a reflexive practice with others is about forming alternative relations and ways of being. Concepts are practical accomplishments. When practitioners engage with research and research activities involving disabled children and young people, for instance, there is opportunity for such reflexivity and alternative ways of working.

Making practices of exclusion visible

Disabled children and their lack of visibility in society has been a long-standing concern recognized in policy literature in England. Disabled children were officially recognized as 'children' and 'children in need' with the introduction of the Children Act 1989 (Department of Health, 1991), but more than twenty years on, research continues to highlight their marginalization in all aspects of their lives. Disabled children are at a greater risk of experiencing abuse, adversity and institutional forms of education and care (Goodinge, 1998; Read, Clements & Ruebain, 2006; Woodcock & Tregaskis, 2006). Stalker, Green and Lister (2010) state that the higher risk of abuse experienced by disabled children is likely to be under-reported and has not received the attention it deserves at research, policy or practice levels in the UK and many other countries. In England, 'child protection teams' are often separate from 'disabled children's' teams in children's services, complicating and potentially compromising the protection of disabled children (Curran, 2010).

The links between dominant discourses of disability and childhood and exclusion have been made visible in disability and childhood studies. Disability activism and disability studies have been highly critical of individual models of disability. The individual model of disability locates the 'problem' within the individual through the scientific orthodoxy of 'methodological individualism', producing an individual tragedy view of disability (Oliver, 1990; Oliver & Sapey, 1999). Oliver and Barnes (2012) state that the personal tragedy view continues to be the dominant definition of disability in Western societies. Child development discourses use age-based stages and thereby fail to account for disabled children's 'normal' development (Oliver & Sapey, 1999). Child development, Burman (1994) argues, is constituted through bio-power strategies of normalization; 'universal' *and* 'special' needs are defined through arbitrary techniques such as the 'normal distribution curve'. Psychodynamic theory is less concerned with normative measures of development and regards the child's primary relationships as pivotal, though when applied to disabled children it is generally preoccupied with parental adaptation to 'bad news' and attachment reactions to their child (Philp & Duckworth, 1982; Howe, 2006).

A 'child first' view of the disabled child is advanced in professional literature to counter the above negative discourse (see Stalker, 2012), although caution is needed before adopting an uncritical notion of 'child' and 'childhood'. According to Clarke (2010: 9), childhood is characterized not by coherence or universality, as represented by Aries in 1960, but a contradiction between the Romantic idealized view of childhood and the 'brutal reality of most children's lives'. The gap between the ideal and reality is *productive*, he explains, fuelling a lengthy process towards the abolition of child labour and endorsing the necessity of philanthropic charitable work. Family-based 'child centeredness' emerged in its current form from the seventeenth century. Historically diverse views of children as 'sinful', 'vulnerable' or 'naturally innocent', he explains, are brought together as being in 'need for education' (education for the aristocracy while children of working families continued to labour or survive somehow). The 'standard child' is located as part of the Western apparatus of colonialization, with some authors arguing that the 'cultivation' of 'the child' and its authorities was *the* system of colonial governance (Garrett, 2009; Wells, 2009). Child rights discourse is also based on the 'standard child', yet groups of children are sidelined by targeted programmes of funding or 'saved' as victims or live in places and communities that have no recognized rights to nationhood (Ennew & Swart-Kruger, 2003).

When disabled children's normal development is not understood and recognized, their childhood is not conceptualized as a childhood, but is conflated with adverse social conditions experienced and practices of exclusion are made invisible. Disabled children are rarely the 'siblings' or sons and daughters in literature about 'families with disabled children' (Curran, 2010). Disabled young people are rarely mentioned in texts about trafficked children, youth offenders, child soldiers and so on. As Watson (2012) points out, disability is rarely found in generic childhood research that would recognize 'social markers' such as gender, ethnicity or social class. Disabled children's experiences of marginalization are normalized when their childhoods are constructed as if 'natural' and inevitable rather than 'social' and open to change.

Postcolonial analysis of disability is concerned with global North/ South relations, productions of inequality and forms of intervention. Mortality and morbidity rates, Meekosha (2008) argues, are closely linked to colonial land sequestration and imposition of regulated migration and immigration. Concepts of disability imposed from the 'metropole' do not recognize destruction and forced dependency of indigenous people's lives, and so she defines 'disability' as 'the taking of land'. She draws on Connell's (2007 in Meekosha, 2008) four textual moves of the global North to explain. These are universal claims; reading from the centre; gestures of exclusion; and grand erasure, which combine to produce 'other' indigenous people's discourses as 'peripheral'; normalize the legacy of colonial institutions; endorse the Western marketization of health and render events such as 'natural disaster', war and disease invisible in discussions of disability. The 'grand erasure' of colonialism is produced through an 'evolutionary' account of history that positions colonized lands as pre-industrial and in need of 'development'; constructions of gender, race, disability and childhood oppress and are used to 'liberate' as being in need of Western welfare. Resistance entails 'writing back', recognizing geopolitical location, historical contradiction and illuminating discontinuities and diversity of experiences.

Centring disabled children's experiences

Understanding disabled children's experience and hearing their views is an overarching aim in disabled children's childhood studies. Disabled children are respected as 'disabled children', active participants with their own experience. A variety of methodologies are used and ethics are generally considered throughout the research process. These studies show disabled children's presence and validate their *existing* involvement and contributions within their families, community and wider society. Studies are explicitly action orientated with respect to problematic practices of others.

The application of the social model of disability begins by listening to disabled children in order to identify and remove barriers to disabled children's opportunities to participate in all aspects of society. Disabled children are to be supported and protected by equitable levels of support, relevant definitions of abuse and accessible safeguarding practices (Marchant, 2001; Morris, 2001; Woodcock & Tregaskis, 2006). Segregation, exclusion, bullying and hate crime are highlighted as risk factors for disabled children's well-being and safety (Alderson, 2000). Disabled children of ethnic minority heritage experience marginalization from their community when placed in distant segregated services where their heritage is not recognized as an important aspect of belonging and identity (Flynn, 2002). Paradoxically, opportunities for disabled children to take positive risks are limited through segregated service provision, and at the same time adversity and trauma such as the death of their peers can go unrecognized.

Creating space for disabled children's views

Detail of the research design is often set out by disabled children's childhood researchers to show how space is created for disabled children and young people to participate and shape the agenda. Participatory action research, ethnography, narrative and advocacy research paradigms and the use of innovative, responsive methods, bring different relations as well as focus. Time is commonly committed for in-depth engagement with disabled children. Research methods include familiarization with research processes including reporting back stages to recognize the likelihood that disabled children are not used to being asked for their opinions by professionals (Morris, 2001).

Ethnographic studies seek out diversity, complexity and richness of disabled children's lives, and researcher reflexivity is a central feature (Shakespeare, Barnes, Priestley, Cunningham-Burley, Davis & Watson, 1999; Davis, 2000; Davis & Watson, 2001). Priestley's (1999) school-based study shows how disabled children drew on statements associated with medical and social models of disability in their negotiations with their teachers, and how they also used statements about gender and age that operated in the school, illustrating the relational and heterogeneity nature of disabled children's meanings.

Disabled children's words and pictures are often inserted in the studies to illustrate their capacity to participate in research and highlight the sophisticated quality of their insights (see Davis & Hogan, 2004). The meanings of disabled children who do not use verbal communication and who have diagnostic labels of learning difficulties are actively sought. Methods such as observation recognize the ways families and practitioners *already* communicate, and a wide range of theoretical work is brought to these studies to express intimacy of relationships and depth of experience (Simmons, 2011). Participant observation, Wickenden (2011) explains, is used to learn a wide range of forms of expression, to see their many selves and interests and to understand the perspectives of others in their lives. Disabled children and young people often view themselves as 'normal' and approach the same aspirations as other children pragmatically, 'wanting to be known as who they *are* rather than what they can do' (Wickenden, 2011: 172).

Conceptualizing disabled children's childhoods

The concepts of child development and impairment that are applied to disabled children are not studies of their childhoods. Oliver and Sapey (1999) suggest that parents are socialized into a grief response as a reflection of professionals' 'imagined experience'. A parent in a study of a web discussion site reflects on the fear she had of the moment her son would start to use a wheelchair. When she saw his pleasure from using it, she realized he might have had it earlier had she not been influenced by the negative attitudes of professionals (Avery, 1999). A very different socialization is offered in disabled children's childhood studies. Childhood is not bordered against adulthood as a natural or fixed category, and life span is a contested nosology. Disabled children share lived aspirations for their future and disabled adults share lived reflections upon their childhood experiences. Life course research into the impact of institutional care on disabled adults' career and family life highlights these continuities and the fluid nature of child/adult experiences (Priestley, 2003; Shah, 2007; Shah & Priestley, 2009).

Theories in disabled children's childhood studies contribute to and invigorate mainstream areas of social science. Normative assumptions of vulnerability are deconstructed and 'resilience' is contextualized, requiring social action and resources that disabled children and young people find supportive (Runswick-Cole & Goodley, 2012). Studies of disabled children's experiences challenge universal concepts illustrating the specific and partial application in practice. Disabled children's opportunities for play are limited by inaccessible facilities and the uses of play by professionals for therapeutic goals (Goodley & Runswick-Cole, 2010). Support for disabled children who are dying is found to be lacking in many ways that signal a lack of respect for the significance of disabled children's family life (Runswick-Cole, 2010). The wheelchair is not only to be valued, but is understood as 'cyborg', as a part of the body. Drawing on Haraway's work, the concept of cyborg is pushing and transgressing boundaries of body/object/technology/culture and traditional relations between these, and research methodologies inspired by this approach are again innovative (see Goodley, 2011; Goodley & Runswick-Cole, 2011).

The social model of disability is strengthened, extended and refined to reassure concerns that a social focus necessarily neglects the personal experience and to recognize diversity. Its emancipatory goals, though, are subject to further critique. Tremain (2001, 2005, 2006) is concerned by the way in which the social model separates 'nature' from the 'social'. 'Impairment', she explains, is produced as a category as if independent of the social, historical and cultural context and, in the same way that the categories of 'sex' and 'gender' establish nature as *prior* to culture, the model makes the category of impairment prior to the social. The nature/culture dichotomy is hierarchical, with the primary category *defining* the form of the secondary category. No attempt, she argues, is made to examine the notion of the body, the historical location of categories or its status as representation of 'reality' and of 'normality'. 'Impairment' acts as a regulatory system. 'Impairment' is determined through bio power – forms of knowledge/power used increasingly since the late eighteenth century to objectify the body and manage life and the life of populations. She states:

> In short, impairment has been disability all along ... the category of impairment emerged and in part persists in order to legitimize the disciplinary practices that it generated in the first place. (Tremain, 2006: 192)

Resistance entails refusal of dominant forms of individuality through a 'critical ontology of ourselves', a form of inquiry 'to liberate ourselves from both the state and the type of individualization that is linked to the state' through the formulation of 'what we want' (Tremain, 2006: 194).

Disabled children's childhood studies are about what disabled children want, and the reflexive research processes used illuminate the connections between disabled children's lives and services. Disabled children's vulnerability can be understood as the effect of social practices of embodiment; vulnerability is not equivalent or distinct from the body. Todd (2006) advocates the involvement of disabled children not as little citizens or consultants on welfare, but direct involvement in the analysis of the use of power, language and discourse. How might practitioners undertake 'critical ontology of the self'? What is the impact of disabled children's childhood studies in health and social care?

Impact, authority and cultures of learning

The identification and assessment of research impact in health and social care practice has been discussed as a problem for research funders and practitioners. There are, however, some indications of the impact of arguments for involvement of disabled children and young people. The need to listen to the experiences of disabled children is a current theme taken up in welfare policy and practice. Disabled children and young people have been more routinely involved in consultations, though Franklin and Sloper (2007) point out that disabled children have only relatively recently been consulted and are still excluded from many such exercises. Young disabled people consulted were in general agreement with the *Every Child Matters* (Department for Education and Skills, 2003) outcomes that inform children's services in England. However, they added prerequisite outcomes such as being pain-free and having people available who understand their forms of communication (Sloper, Rabiee & Beresford, 2007). Research into children's experiences of speech therapy stresses the need for therapists to facilitate the *listening* skills of all those involved in their lives and address exclusion as a central part of their role (Roulstone & McLeod, 2011).

A body of research aimed at emphasizing positive aspects of parents' coping identifies their strategies and the sorts of support that works for them (Beresford, Sloper, Baldwin and Newman, 1996). Children's rights and protection are brought together in the *Safeguarding Disabled Children Guidance* (Murray & Osborne, 2009). This guidance states that abuse occurs and goes undetected when welfare priorities are overly based on assumptions about impairment and parental support needs without effective attention to the disabled child's experience. It advances specific roles to ensure a focus for disabled children and calls for social change in order to address bullying and exclusion.

Studies of how research is used in health and social care view practitioner engagement as a multi-layered inter- and intra-organizational matter (Walter, Nutley, Percy-Smith, McNeish, & Frost, 2004; Gould & Baldwin, 2004; Fook, 2004; CWDC, NCSL & TDA, 2008). Nutley, Walter & Davies (2009) explain that impact can be instrumental around a specific goal, and it can also lead to conceptual development, though they rarely found the research culture necessary for this owing to barriers including accessibility and relevance of the research and lack of leadership and strategy. In their study of research use in children's services, Curran, Benjimen and Oliver (2013) found that the most developed research cultures were in the universal services provided for all children and the least developed in specialist services. The involvement of children and young people in research activities was a significant factor. Children and practitioners were conceptualized as active and capable, shaping the transformation agenda with a sense of integrity and child focus. A cycle of research production was apparent when external research acted as the impetus for local projects that were subsequently published for wider impact. Specialist practitioners attributed their lack of engagement with research to crisis conditions, and both children and practitioners were conceptualized as vulnerable. There were some research projects taking place in specialized services, and this suggests that support is more significant than service configuration per se. However both factors are especially relevant to disabled children, given the paradoxical effect of universal and specialized configuration discussed above.

The impact of research in professional education and the links between universities and practice organizations is important. Rossiter (2001), a social work educator, asks 'what do I want my students to do? I want them to move from deploying expert knowledge to assessing the governmentality of helping as a routine practice of ethics necessitated by the historical development of social work in Western capitalist countries' (2001: 3–4). Being a 'helper', Shakespeare (2000) suggests, constitutes colonial relations of 'othering', whereas being 'helpful' means that actions are experienced as helpful and, as every person can be helpful, the relation is reciprocal. The involvement of 'service users' and practitioners is built into health and social care education programmes, and though concerns have been raised about replications of personal tragedy relations and tokenism, learning *from* disabled people provides alternative relations and thereby opportunity for 'critical ontology of the self'. My connections with disabled scholars and trainers are a source of critical ontology of self to consider the impacts of intervention as potentially beneficial and harmful. It also provides a source of vigilance and confidence in the ways that we can influence the effects of power. Continuing local dialogue is needed to centre disabled children and young people and their families, to make visible practices of exclusion and to make links between the local and global to understand global significant experiences of inequalities, desires and helpfulness.

References

Alderson, P. (2000) *Young children's rights*, 2nd edn (London and Philadelphia, PA: Jessica Kingsley Publishers).

Avery, D.M. (1999) Talking tragedy: Identity issues in the parental story of disability, in M. Corker & S. French (eds), *Disability and discourses* (Buckingham: Open University Press).

Beresford, B. (1996) 'Coping with the care of a severely disabled child', *Health and Social Care in the Community*, 4, 1, 30–40.

Beresford, B., Sloper, P., Baldwin, S. & Newman, T. (1996) *What works in services for families with a disabled child?* (Ilford: Barnardos).

Burman, E. (1994) *Deconstructing developmental psychology* (London: Routledge).

Clarke, J. (2010) The origins of childhood: In the beginning ..., in D. Kassam, L. Murphy & E. Taylor (eds), *Key issues in childhood and youth studies* (Abingdon and New York: Routledge), pp. 3–14.

Curran, T. (2010) 'Social work and disabled children's childhoods: A Foucauldian framework for practice transformation', *British Journal of Social Work*, 40, 3, 806–825.

Curran, T., Benjimen, C. & Oliver, B. (2013) 'A critical analysis of workforce development research use in the transformation of children's services', *Journal of Social Work*. Published online before print April 3, 2013, doi: 10.1177/1468017313477977.

CWDC, NCSL and TDA, (2008) *2020 Children and young people's workforce strategy: Evidence & knowledge management* (Leeds: Department for Children, Schools and Families).

Danaher, G., Schirato, T. & Webb, J. (2000) *Understanding Foucault* (London and Thousand Oaks, CA: Sage Publications).

Davis, J.M. (2000) 'Disability studies as ethnographic research and text: Research strategies and roles for promoting social change?', *Disability and Society*, 15, 2, 191–206.

Davis, J.M. & Hogan, J. (2004) Research with children: Ethnography, participation, disability and self empowerment, in C. Barnes & G. Mercer (eds), *Implementing the social model of disability: Theory and research*, (Leeds: The Disability Press), pp. 172–191.

Davis, J.M. & Watson, N. (2001) 'Where are the children's experiences? Analysing social and cultural exclusion in "special" and "mainstream" schools', *Disability and Society*, 16, 5, 671–687.

Department for Education and Skills (2003) *Every Child Matters: Change for children* (London: Stationery Office).

Department of Health (1991) *Children Act 1989: Guidance and regulations* (London: HMSO).

Dreyfus, H.L. (2012) Heidegger and Foucault on the subject, agency and practices [Homepage of University of California, Berkeley]. http://socrates.berkeley.edu [accessed 28 July 2012].

Elden, S. (2006) 'Discipline, health, and madness: Foucault's *Le Pouvoir psychiatrique*', *History of Human Sciences*, 19, 1, 39–66.

Ennew, J. & Swart-Kruger, J. (2003) 'Introduction: Homes, places and spaces in the construction of street children and street youth', *Children, Youth and Environments*, 13, 1. http://www.colorado.edu/journals/cye/13_1/Vol13_1Articles/CYE_CurrentIssue_ArticleIntro_Kruger_Ennew.htm edn, [accessed 28 July 2012].

Faubion, J.D. (ed.) (1998) *The essential works of Michel Foucault 1954–1984*, Vol. 2: *Aesthetics, method, and epistemology* (London: Allen Lane).

Flynn, R. (2002) *Short breaks: Providing better access and more choice for Black disabled children and their parents* (Bristol: Policy Press).

Fook, J. (2004) What professionals need from research: Beyond evidence-based practice, in D. Smith (ed.), *Social work and evidence-based practice*, Research Highlights in Social Work 45 (London and Philadelphia, PA: Jessica Kingsley Publishers).

Foucault, M. (1974) *The archaeology of knowledge* (London: Tavistock).

Foucault, M. (1982) The subject and power, in H.L. Dreyfus & P. Rabinow (eds), *Michel Foucault: Beyond structuralism and hermaneutics*, trans. L. Sawyer (London: Harvester Wheatsheaf), pp. 208–226.

Foucault, M. (2005) Power, right, truth, in R.E. Goodin & P. Pettit (eds), *Contemporary political philosophy: An anthology*, 2nd edn (Oxford: Blackwell), pp. 541–548.

Franklin, A. & Sloper, P. (2007) *Participation of disabled children and young people in decision-making relating to social care* (Social Policy Research Unit, University of York).

Garrett, P.M. (2009) *'Transforming' children's services? Social work, neoliberalism and the 'modern' world* (Maidenhead: Open University Press).

Goodinge, S. (1998) *Inspection of services to disabled children and their families* (London: Social Services Inspectorate, Department of Health).

Goodley, D. (2011) *Disability studies: An interdisciplinary introduction* (London and Thousand Oaks, CA: Sage).

Goodley, D. & Runswick-Cole, K. (2010) 'Emancipating play: Disabled children, development and deconstruction', *Disability and Society*, 25, 499–512.

Goodley, D. & Runswick-Cole, K. (2011) Cyborgs: Photovoice and Disabled Children. Presentation to ESRC Seminar Series: Researching the Lives of Disabled Children and Young People, with a Focus on Their Perspectives. Seminar 4: Recent Research, University of Bristol, 21 January. http://www.strath.ac.uk/humanities/schoolofappliedsocialsciences/socialwork/esrcseminarseries/ [accessed 28 July 2012].

Gould, N. & Baldwin, M. (2004) *Social work, critical reflection and the learning organisation* (Aldershot: Ashgate).

Hall, S. (2001) Foucault: Power, knowledge and discourse, in M. Wetherall, S. Yates, & S. Taylor (eds), *Discourse theory and practice: A reader* (London: Sage).

Howe, D. (2006) 'Disabled children, maltreatment and attachment', *British Journal of Social Work*, 36, 5, 743–760.

Kendall, G. & Wickham, G. (1999) *Using Foucault's methods* (London: Sage).

Marchant, R. (2001) Working with disabled children, in P. Foley, J. Roche & S. Tucker (eds), *Children in society: Contemporary theory, policy and practice* (Basingstoke: Palgrave in association with Open University Press), pp. 215–224.

Meekosha, H. (2008) Contextualising disability: Developing southern/global theory. Keynote presentation, Disability Studies Association, 4th conference, Lancaster, 2–4 September 2008.

Morris, J. (2001) 'Social exclusion and young disabled people with high levels of support needs', *Critical Social Policy*, 21, 2, 161–183.

Murray, M. & Osborne, C. (2009) *Safeguarding disabled children practice guidance.* (Nottingham: Department for Children, Schools and Families, and Children's Society).

Nutley, S., Walter, I., & Davies, H.T.O. (2009) 'Promoting evidence-based: practice: Models and mechanisms from cross sector review'. *Research on Social Work Practice*, 19, 552 originally published online May 27, 2009.

Oliver, M. (1990) *The politics of disablement* (Basingstoke: Macmillan).

Oliver, M. & Barnes, C. (2012) *The new politics of disablement* (Basingstoke and New York: Palgrave Macmillan).

Oliver, M. & Sapey, B. (1999) *Social work with disabled people*, 2nd edn (Houndsmills: Macmillan).

Philp, M. (1979) 'Notes on the form of knowledge in social work', *Sociological Review*, 27, 1, 83–111.

Philp, M. & Duckworth, D. (1982) *Children with disabilities and their families* (Windsor: NFER-Nelson).

Priestley, M. (1999) Discourse and identity: Disabled children in mainstream high schools, in M. Corker & S. French (eds), *Disability discourse* (Buckingham: Open University Press), pp. 92–102.

Priestley, M. (2003) *Disability: A life course approach* (Cambridge: Polity Press).

Rabinow, P. (ed.) (1997) *The essential works of Michel Foucault 1954–1984*, Vol. 1: *Ethics, subjectivity and truth* (London: Allen Lane).

Read, J., Clements, L.J. & Ruebain, D. (2006) *Disabled children and the law: Research and good practice*, 2nd edn (London and Philadelphia, PA: Jessica Kingsley Publishing).

Rose, N. & Miller, P. (2010) 'Political power beyond the state: Problematics of government', *British Journal of Sociology.* http://www.bjsshapingsociology.com/view/0/index.html [accessed 28 July 2012].

Rossiter, A. (2001) 'Innocence lost and suspicion found: Do we educate for or against social work?', *Critical Social Work.* http://www.criticalsocialwork.com/CSW_2001_1.html [accessed 6 June 2001].

Roulstone, S. & McLeod, S. (eds) (2011) *Listening to children and young people with speech, language and communication needs* (Guildford: J & K).

Runswick-Cole, K. (2010) 'Living with dying and disablism: Death and disabled children', *Disability and Society*, 25, 7, 813–826.

Runswick-Cole, K. & Goodley, D. (2012) *Resilience in the lives of disabled people across the life course* (Manchester: Scope and Manchester Metropolitan University).

Schwan, A. & Shapiro, S. (2011) *Foucault's 'Discipline and Punish'* (London: Pluto Press).

Shah, S. (2007) 'Special or mainstream? The views of disabled students', *Research Papers in Education*, 22, 4, 425–442.

Shah, S. & Priestley, M. (2009) 'Home and away: The impact of educational policies on disabled children's experiences of family and friendship', *Research Papers in Education*, 25, 2, 155–174.

Shakespeare, T. (2000) *Help* (Birmingham: Venture Press).

Shakespeare, T., Barnes, C., Priestley, M., Cunningham-Burley, S., Davis, J. & Watson, N. (1999) *Life as a disabled child: A qualitative study of young people's experiences and perspectives* (Disability Research Unit, University of Leeds).

Simmons, B. (2011) The PMLD ambiguity: Articulating the life worlds of children with profound and multiple learning difficulties, Conference Paper, NNDR 2011.

Sloper, P., Rabiee, P. & Beresford, B. (2007) *Outcomes for disabled children* (Social Policy Unit, University of York).

Stalker, K. (2012) 'Editorial: Researching the lives of disabled children and young people', *Children and Society*, 26, 173–178.

Stalker, K., Green Lister, P., Lerpiniere, J. & McArthur, K. (2010) *Child protection and the needs and rights of disabled children and young people: A scoping study*, University of Strathclyde.. http://strathprints.strath.ac.uk/27036 [accessed 28 July 2010].

Todd, L. (2006) Enabling practice for professionals: The need for practical post structural theory, in D. Goodley & R. Lawthom (eds), *Disability and psychology*, (Basingstoke & New York: Palgrave Macmillan), pp. 141–155.

Tremain, S. (2001) 'On the government of disability', *Social Theory and Practice*, 27, 4, 617–636.

Tremain, S.L. (2005) Foucault, governmentality and critical disability theory: An introduction, in S.L. Tremain (ed.), *Foucault and the government of disability* (Michigan: University of Michigan Press), pp. 1–24.

Tremain, S. (2006) On the government of disability: Foucault, power, and the subject of impairment, in L.J. Davis (ed.), *The Disability Studies reader*, 2nd edn (New York and Abingdon: Taylor & Francis), pp. 185–197.

Walter, I., Nutley, S., Percy-Smith, J., McNeish, D. & Frost, S. (2004) *Improving the use of research in social care*, Practice Knowledge Review 7 (London: Social Care Institute for Excellence, and Policy Press).

Watson, N. (2012) 'Theorising the lives of disabled children: How can disability theory help?', *Children and Society*, 26, 192–202.

Wells, K. (2009) *Childhood in global perspective* (Cambridge: Polity Press).

Wickenden, M. (2011) 'Give me time and I'll tell you': Using ethnography to investigate aspects of identity with teenagers who use alternative and augmentative methods of communication, in S. Roulstone & S. McLeod (eds), *Listening to children and young people with speech, language and communication needs*, (Guildford: J&R Press), pp. 167–179.

Woodcock, J. & Tregaskis, C. (2006) 'Understanding structural communication barriers to ordinary family life for families with disabled children: A combined social work and social model of disability analysis', *British Journal of Social Work*, 1, 1–17.

11

The Oppressive Power of Normalcy in the Lives of Disabled Children: Deploying History to Denaturalize the Notion of the 'Normal Child'

Harriet Cooper

Introduction

> [T]he 'problem' is not the person with disabilities; the problem is the way that normalcy is constructed to create the 'problem' of the disabled person. (Davis, 1995: 24)

This chapter draws on Lennard Davis' influential work on the historical specificity of the notion of normalcy (1995), to denaturalise the contemporary Anglo-American notion of the 'normal child' (see also Foucault, 1991 [1977]). Following Davis, I argue that in order to comprehend the specificity of the contemporary disabled child's experience of oppression, we require an understanding of the contemporary hegemonic notion of the 'normal child'. In the context of race, Ruth Frankenberg (1993: 6) has observed that '[t]o speak of whiteness is [...] to assign *everyone* a place in the relations of racism'. To problematize normalcy is thus to reframe ableism as an issue that concerns everyone.

I begin the chapter with a brief rationale of my decision to historicize the notion of the 'normal child'. My argument is then developed through four distinct sections. In the first section, I reveal the hegemonic power of the notion of the 'normal child' in contemporary Anglo-American culture through a discussion of the British documentary series *Born to be Different*. The second section locates the rise of a notion of the 'normal child' in scientific literature on child development from the late nineteenth century. I then turn my attention to five childcare manuals published between 1839 and 1924: I demonstrate that there is a gradual shift of emphasis in the manuals from concerns about sickness to anxieties about normalcy. I seek to understand this shift both in terms of a rise of a notion of the 'normal child' in scientific discourse and in terms of a coeval separation of the maternal and the medical spheres. In my final section I suggest, however, that childcare manuals do not simply popularize scientific notions about the child. Rather, I contend, drawing on Foucault's (2003: 42) concept of ' "abnormal individuals" ', that the notion of the 'abnormal child' is a 'hybrid object' of medical and maternal discourse. This 'hybrid object' emerges out of the uncomfortable coexistence of these two discourses in the childcare manual.

Methodology: *'[D]iagnosing* the present'

It is precisely because the concept of normalcy is both so pervasive in Anglo-American culture and yet so abstract, so difficult to characterize and yet so hegemonic in terms of its operations, that it needs to be viewed in such a way as to defamiliarize it. This can be achieved by cross-cultural comparison: Clare Barker, for example, notes that 'normalcy is culturally contingent' in the context of her study of figure of the disabled child in postcolonial literature (2011: 4). Identifying the trope of the 'disabled child-nation', Barker argues for a postcolonial literary analysis that takes account of the 'materiality' of disability (2011: 3, 19). Although it is beyond the scope of my chapter to engage at length with the role of non-Western cultural contexts in denaturalizing Anglo-American notions of normalcy, in this piece I foreground the act of historicizing as a similarly potent tool in this process. The historical view allows the very normalcy of the notion of 'the normal' to be thrown into question. In Foucault's terms, it allows us to see that the present is 'just as strange as the past' rather than assuming that the present is necessarily more progressive than the past (Kendall & Wickham, 1999: 4). As Michael Donnelly notes, it is in this way that Foucault employs history as a 'weapon' against 'histories constructed (apparently) in the service of the present' – Foucault's historical writing works to 'represent the past otherwise, if not "as it really was", then nonetheless in such a way as to reveal the distortions or illusions introduced or sustained by conventional histories' (1986: 17).

A conventional view of history might see contemporary constructions of the disabled child as more progressive than those of the Victorian era, and might regard advances in medical knowledge as having a key role in enabling such changes. According to this 'common-sense' view, the physical emancipation that may, for some disabled people, have followed from the advancement of medical knowledge is conflated with overall emancipation. In this conventional view of history, aspects of the impact of advancing medical knowledge are obscured, producing the 'distortions' to which Donnelly refers. A Foucauldian approach to history seeks to bring such distortions to light, on the understanding that 'the history of a concept is not wholly and entirely that of its progressive refinement, its continuously increasing rationality' (Foucault, 2002: 5). I suggest that a conventional view of history fails to account for the oppressive impact of medical discourse's construction of normalcy on the disabled child.

In this chapter, I use historical objects as a means of *'diagnosing* the present' (Kendall & Wickham, 1999: 4). This focus on the present inevitably impacts on my choice of historical objects. In selecting childcare manuals, I have been guided by historian Christina Hardyment, who helpfully indicates the popularity of the volumes she discusses (Hardyment, 1983). I general I have chosen to examine popular manuals. However, my selection process is also unavoidably influenced by own *'situatedness'* as a researcher (Domanska, 2008: 20). My desire to unmask the hegemonic grip of normalcy on the present-day experience of the disabled child will have impacted on my reading and my research. This is not to say that I have ignored material that contradicts my thesis, for the material I found supported my argument. It is, however, to say that the process of 'finding' is not in itself an innocent activity, but rather is one undertaken by a particular researcher, whose 'feelings, biography and task impact on what and how s/he hears' (Elliott et al., 2012: 435). For Hayden White, the process of '[r]evealing one's ideological biases does not necessarily allow one to transcend them', but '[t]he important point is whether you feel that your location is congenial and whether your situation is uncomfortable or not' (Domanska, 2008: 21). Furthermore, if all historical discourse *'constructs* its subject matter in the very process of *speaking about it'* to some extent, to speak of historical objects is also to offer an interpretation (White, 1989: 22).

Location is thus inescapable: what matters is to be clear about the advantages and limitations of one's own location. For me, this means stating that I am not a historian by training, although I am a scholar of cultural studies; more importantly, I feel, it means stating that I have personal experience of growing up with a disability. If my location is 'congenial', it is so not *in spite of* the personal experience that makes me partial in particular ways, but *because* of it. As Tom Shakespeare puts it, discussing methods in disability research, 'independent research is [...] a fiction, and my own engagement gives me insights which can be useful in the research, and enable me to get closer to the people and experiences which I try to analyse' (Shakespeare, 1996: 117). In the next section, I begin my situated analysis of the present-day notion of the 'normal child' by exploring how it functions in a contemporary cultural object, that is, the British documentary series *Born to be Different*.

Born to be Different, made to be 'normal'?

Born to be Different is a documentary following the lives of six children who were born with impairments. The documentary has had eight series and was first aired on Channel 4 in 2003, finishing in June 2011. It follows the children during the first decade of their lives. What are the ethics of discussing a real child's life in a chapter such as this, without involving that child? As someone whose childhood was marked by intrusive adult gazes, I am conscious firstly that the television camera holds the potential to be experienced in this way by the children, especially since it must be assumed that the children themselves have not given consent to be filmed – they are filmed from birth. Secondly, I am aware that my own critique of the programme runs the risk of reproducing the camera's invasion. Given that my analysis of the documentary seeks to be emancipatory in its exposure of oppressive dominant ideologies, it would be a bitter irony if my own gaze were experienced as either intrusive or as critical of particular individuals. For this reason, and in particular because the documentary features children, I have chosen to preserve the anonymity of the individuals to whom I refer. While readers who have seen the documentary may recognize individuals from the discussion and the quotations, the decision to avoid using names will afford some protection for the children. Moreover, it will also, I hope, be read as a clear indication that the object of my critique is contemporary culture as represented by the documentary, rather than individuals and their life choices.

According to the programme website, *Born to be Different* provides a 'candid and unsentimental' portrayal of the lives of the six disabled children (Channel 4, 2011). Yet in apparently offering a 'commonsense' narrative about these lives, the documentary fails to challenge hegemonic notions of disability. The programme constructs the six children it focuses on in opposition to an imagined 'normal child'. The children's lives are constructed as narratives of success or failure to mimic the 'norm' of able-bodiedness, to use Robert McRuer's reconceptualization of the Butlerian notion of the performance of gender (McRuer, 2006; see also Butler, 1990). The programme subtly posits the children's life stories in these binary terms in the opening voiceover, which states that 'while some [children] have reached the milestones of every childhood [...] others have battled just to stay alive'

(Series 7, Episode 3). The noun 'milestones' suggests a normative route, and works to produce a notion of a 'normal child' who follows a particular, predetermined path through life. It echoes the language used in early twentieth-century childcare manuals, as I shall show. The adjective 'every' has connotations of inclusion, but here it acts to exclude those children whose childhoods do not follow the normative route.

The documentary mainly adopts the medical model of disability, in which disability is seen as a tragedy for the individual and for the family concerned, which must be medicated, mitigated or corrected if possible (Oliver, 1990). This view is epitomized by a surgeon featured in the series, who states, in his discussion of one of the children: 'I think there are surgeons who would say [?] "there is nothing we could do [...] this is your disability, get on with it", but I think there is something you can do, and I think there is a way to make [...] [this child] function better' (Series 7, Episode 2). Although, undoubtedly, medical intervention can and does bring huge benefits to such children's lives, the documentary would benefit from reflecting on alternative models of disability, such as the social model, in which the social barriers to inclusion are problematized, rather than the impaired body itself. Moreover, the medical model does not consider the child's own feelings about her body. In a paper exploring the ethics of 'non-directive' counselling for parents of babies with intersex conditions, Ellen Feder quotes a doctor who observes that '"there's nothing ambiguous about [...] [the] child's genitalia from the child's standpoint"' (2011: 1, 16). Similarly, for a child born with a physical impairment, there is nothing abnormal about her body as she perceives it. It is only in the encounter with the other who perceives her body as abnormal that she may begin to perceive her body as disabled.

The notion that this child might wish to preserve the embodiment in which she was born, instead of choosing to become more like the imagined 'normal child', is counter-hegemonic. Again, Feder's paper sheds light on what is at stake here. Feder argues that the decision to opt for surgery for children with intersex conditions is framed as 'do[ing] something' while the decision not to go ahead with surgery is regarded as 'do[ing] nothing' (2011: 15). The very framing of the choice may be unethical, Feder suggests (2011: 15). In the case of surgery for individuals with physical impairments, the benefits of medical intervention are usually highly visible, whereas any benefits of not intervening are less tangible and more difficult to quantify, and may be framed as – in Feder's terms – 'do[ing] nothing'. Interestingly, the surgeon refers to the operation in exactly these terms: 'there's no guarantee of success; it's trying to do something when doing nothing means severe disability' (Series 7, Episode 3).

Born to be Different fails to challenge the perceived normalcy of normalizing medical procedures for disabled children. However, the notion of the norm has not always structured our perception of the disabled child. Lennard Davis traces the rise of a notion of the 'norm' in Anglophone culture in the nineteenth century and observes that '[t]he word "normal" as "constituting, conforming to, not deviating or differing from, the common type or standard, regular, usual" only enters the English language around 1840' (1995: 24). Davis proposes that modern ideas about the normal body gradually replaced the classical notion of an 'ideal body' in nineteenth century culture as statistics developed as a branch of knowledge (1995: 24–26). The classical 'ideal body' had been regarded as a perfect body which could not be emulated, whereas the statistical 'ideal body' – the 'average' body – was, in theory, achievable (Davis, 1995: 24-28). In the next part of the chapter I consider the contribution of the rise of the scientific study of child development in late nineteenth-century Anglo-American culture to the cultural production of a notion of the 'normal body' and, more specifically, a notion of the 'normal child'.

The child study movement and the 'normal child'

In *The Mind of the Child: Child Development in Literature, Science and Medicine, 1840–1900*, Sally Shuttleworth states that the study of child development as a science began in

> the late 1870s, when the publication of Charles Darwin's article, 'A Biographical Sketch of an Infant' heralded the emergence, across Europe and America, of a new scientific domain of observation and experimentation which took as its subject the young child. (Shuttleworth, 2010: 7)

Although, as Shuttleworth indicates, it would be 'misleading' to think that before this point there was no such thing as a 'science of childhood', the publication of Darwin's 'Sketch' in 1877 marked the beginning of a new wave of interest in the scientific study of the child. (Shuttleworth, 2010: 8). From the late 1870s, child study expanded in both Europe and America, with Child Study Associations and journals such as *The Paidologist* being set up during this period (Hardyment, 1983: 105).

The child study movement contributes to the cultural production of the notion of the normal child in that, in the words of one its leading figures, James Sully, it seeks to 'know what happens in these first all-decisive two or three years of human life, *by what steps exactly* the wee amorphous thing *takes shape'* (my italics) (Sully, 1895: 4). By referring to the 'wee amorphous thing' in the singular, Sully makes one individual stand for all children, gesturing towards the idea of a 'normal child'. In seeking to know 'by what steps exactly' the child develops, Sully hints at an underlying belief in the uniformity of these 'steps' for all children. The reference to 'tak[ing] shape' again suggests a singular, normative trajectory for child development. The project of child study involves making the child an object of scrutiny, as well as recording and mapping findings about the child (in relation to these ideas, see Foucault 1991 [1977]: 189–190). Thus it is hardly surprising that the notion of the 'normal child' is inscribed at its heart.

Sully is also interested in the child's apparent malleability. He sees the infant as having a 'closer kinship to the natural world' than the adult human – he subscribes to the 'recapitulation theory', associated with Ernst Haeckel, which proposed that '[i]n the successive stages of foetal development' we can note 'the gradual unfolding of human lineaments out of a widely typical animal form' (Sully, 1895: 5; see also 'Haeckel, Ernst Heinrich' in Martin & Hine, 2008). Yet malleability is both a positive and a negative property of the child: as David Armstrong observes, the fact that the child 'underwent growth' meant that 'there was [...] a constant threat that proper stages might not be negotiated' (Armstrong, 1995: 396). '[G]rowth' was thus 'construed as inherently problematic, precariously normal' and as a result, development needed to be monitored closely (Armstrong, 1995: 396). Perhaps the emphasis in *Born to be Different* on the need for early medical intervention in the lives of impaired children can be understood in terms of the supposed malleability of the child's body.

The normal child is not only constructed in scientific discourse in this period, but also in instructional discourse – in the childcare manual. As I now show, in the early twentieth century, the figure of the 'abnormal child' came to replace the figure of the 'sick child' in the childcare manual. In the next section, I compare two mid-nineteenth-century childcare manuals with three later examples of the genre.

From the 'sick child' to the 'abnormal child'

Sickness is a theme that preoccupies the earlier manual writers to a great extent. Almost half of Thomas Bull's 1845 manual is devoted to dealing with sickness: almost 130 out of 309 pages. As he notes in the Preface, the book is divided into two parts, '[t]he first directs the mother how to manage the child in health; the second, in sickness' (Bull, 1845: vi). Similarly, Pye Henry Chavasse devotes long parts of his 1839 manual to discussing illness, as can be seen from the Contents pages (Chavasse, 1839: vi–xviii). By contrast, in Mabel Liddiard's *The Mothercraft Manual* (1924 [1923?]) – a popular early twentieth-century manual – only two chapters out of fourteen deal with sickness – a total of 34 pages out of 169. Meanwhile, another of the later manual writers, L. Emmett Holt, states in the 1904 edition of *The Care and Feeding of Children* that disease is not discussed in the book, since his aims are 'not to alarm the mother by acquainting her with all the possible diseases and accidents which may befall her infant, but to open her eyes to matters which are her direct and chief concern' (Holt, 1904: 2). For Holt, disease is a concern for the doctor, rather than the mother: 'no mother or nurse should depend upon any manual, but upon the advice of a physician' (Holt, 1904: 2). In Campbell's 1910 manual, is clear that decisions about the treatment of sickness must not be taken by the mother. She observes that the mother has, 'when in doubt but one chief, her doctor, in whom when once entrusted with the health of her child, she must trust wholly, and to whom she cannot be too loyal' (Campbell, 1910: 262). There is thus a shift in the instructional literature for mothers. Mid-nineteenth-century manuals include sickness as a key theme and advocate maternal treatment of the sick child. Later manuals exclude sickness, or are wary of its inclusion, and indicate that mothers can help by knowing symptoms, but should never try to prescribe for or treat their children.

This shift mirrors the late twentieth-century alteration of the ideology of 'scientific motherhood' charted by Rima D. Apple (1995: 161). As Apple notes, the early version of the ideology, which predominates in the mid-nineteenth century, empowers mothers to make decisions about children's sickness (1995: 162). Later, mothers are cast as simultaneously responsible for the health of their children and unqualified in the diagnosis and treatment of childhood sickness (1995: 162). This difference is illustrated with reference to two advertisements for baby food products. The 1885 advertisement 'attempts to sell with gentle persuasion' whereas the 1938 advertisement 'urges readers to "Ask your doctor"' (Apple, 1995: 162, 164). Yet although the spheres of the medical and the maternal have become separate by 1938 – and by this time a mother is expected to defer to medical professionals on questions of health – a mother must nevertheless be watchful enough to know when to '"[a]sk [her] doctor"'. It is thus not surprising that the early twentieth-century manuals display ambivalence about the maternal role in dealing with sick or 'abnormal' children.

It could be argued that the separation of the spheres of maternity and medicine takes sickness out of the domestic sphere, in an example of what sociologist Anthony Giddens terms the *'sequestration of experience'* (1991: 149). For Giddens, modernity is characterized by the removal of certain experiences, such as sickness and death, from view: a degree of 'ontological security' is 'purchased' through this process, although this sense of security is actually an illusion (1991: 156). Does the sequestration of sickness into hospitals leave mothers with less to worry about? If sickness is no longer a concern, does this leave families with more time to enjoy life?

We might expect to see less focus on the monitoring of babies in twentieth-century childcare manuals as a result of the sequestration of experience, yet the opposite seems to be true: it is simply that the subject of anxiety shifts from sickness to normalcy. In contrast with the earlier manuals, *The Care and Feeding of Children* adopts the terms 'normal' and 'abnormal' as descriptors for a wide range of babyhood behaviours – both crying and habits are discussed in relation to their normalcy (Holt, 1904: 123, 146–9). Liddiard's manual devotes a chapter to 'The Normal Infant and Management' (1924 [1923?]: 102–9). It opens with the following quotation from Holt: '"[b]y familiarity with what is normal, detection of the abnormal soon becomes easy"' (quoted in Liddiard, 1924 [1923?]: 102). Although Liddiard acknowledges that '[e]very child is an individual and develops along different lines', she states that 'it is well for the mother [...] to know the average so that they may recognise any large departure and be able to get proper advice' (1924 [1923?]: 102). In the 1948 edition of *The Mothercraft Manual*, Liddiard highlights the contemporaneity of a focus on normalcy, stating that '[t]his eleventh edition has been brought up-to-date and includes an additional chapter on the normal infant, giving hints as to routine and feeding, which I hope will be useful' (1948: v). Liddiard also includes a chart entitled 'Milestones' in this edition, which shows the expected progress of the 'normal child' using a sculpted milestone as a visual icon to illustrate this notion in very literal terms (1948, insert after p. 48). As Hardyment notes, Liddiard's notion of 'arbitrary "Milestones" of development added the spectre of the norm to parents' anxieties about their children' (1983: 162).

David Armstrong argues that this focus on normalcy is part of the rise of 'Surveillance Medicine', which 'requires the dissolution of the distinct clinical categories of healthy and ill as it attempts to bring everyone within its network of visibility' (1995: 395). More and more babies are at risk of being found to be 'abnormal' in a world in which the science of the child has determined the parameters of the normal in an increasing number of areas. Armstrong regards this new monitoring of the child's development as 'a new way of seeing a potentially hazardous normal childhood' (1995: 396). More 'abnormalities' can be defined than ever before, hence there is more surveillance to be done, to guard against the onset of these. As Georges Canguilhem puts it, '[o]nce the etiology and pathology of an anomaly are known, the anomalous becomes pathological': what was once diversity is now pathology (1991: 139). Towards the middle of the twentieth century, a childcare manual writer reflects that the new 'doctrine' around health has had the effect of 'concentrating the thought of parents and children alike not on health as something positive to be cultivated, used and enjoyed, but on disease, as something to be constantly feared, watched for and actively prevented' (Batten, 1939: 184). The notion of 'sequestration of experience' is again relevant, in that here we see that once serious illness has been mastered by medicine, and sequestered into hospitals, away from the public eye, the 'normal child' becomes the focus of attention.

Thus 'the abnormal' replaces sickness in childcare manuals for a variety of reasons. As I have argued, the separation of the maternal and medical spheres removes sickness from the maternal remit. With this shift, sickness becomes sequestered in hospitals where it is no longer visible as an everyday occurrence. Moreover, with the advent of techniques such as pasteurization, infant mortality rates decrease at the turn of the twentieth century, making fatal illness less of an immediate concern for parents (Hardyment, 1983: 99). During the same period, the child study movement produces a discursive notion of the 'normal child'. But what makes the 'abnormal child' such a suitable replacement for the sick child as the object of concern in the childcare manual? I will attempt to answer this question by reflecting on the disciplinary status of the discourse of a childcare manual in an age of separate maternal and medical spheres.

The childcare manual as disciplinary hybrid and the 'abnormal child' as hybrid object

The childcare manual is not a scientific paper, but it may reproduce information from scientific studies. It is not a medical manual, but it may provide medical information. It usually includes information about diet, about sleep, about play, about education, about siblings, about friends. It is, in short, a multi-disciplinary text that belongs to many disciplines and to none. The status of information offered by a single manual might be quite varied in terms of its claims to truth – medical information will be categorical and will make definitive truth-claims, information about play or education may only claim the status of advice and may co-exist with contradictory information. The childcare manual contains information directed towards the development of the healthy child, the happy child, the well-educated child. It is a hybrid.

However, the childcare manual can only be understood as a hybrid if it is produced in (or read by) a culture in which information about medical care is seen as having a different status from information about play and education. It is only a hybrid if the culture in which it is produced distinguishes between discourses, categorizing some types of discourse as 'scientific', some as 'political', some as 'pedagogic' and some as 'maternal'. It is only a hybrid in a culture in which there has been a separation of the spheres of medicine and maternity. I would therefore suggest that the twentieth-century childcare manual may be understood as a hybrid, but that it is anachronistic to see the manuals of Chavasse and Bull, published in the mid-nineteenth century, in these terms.

We might compare the hybrid discourse of the twentieth-century child-care manual to another hybrid discourse that Foucault identifies in the *Abnormal* lectures. This is the notion of 'medico-legal opinion', which, Foucault suggests, is an adulteration of both psychiatry and justice, the disciplines from which it is formed (2003: 41). Like the other discourses discussed here, the discourse of 'medico-legal opinion' begins to dominate towards the end of the nineteenth century, according to Foucault (2003: 39). As a hybrid of the fields of psychiatry and justice, Foucault suggests, '[e]xpert medico-legal opinion does not address itself to delinquents or innocents or to those who are sick as opposed to those who are well' (2003: 41). Rather it directs itself towards '"abnormal individuals"' (2003: 42). We might see the discourse of the childcare manual in the early twentieth century as a similar amalgamation of two ways of looking at the child – the combination of a 'medical' gaze and a 'maternal' gaze. Whereas – in the terms of the early twentieth century – the medical gaze sees either the sick child or the well child and the maternal gaze sees the happy child or the unhappy child, the hybrid gaze sees instead the normal or abnormal child. The early twentieth-century childcare manual is a vehicle for the reproduction of this hybrid gaze, in that it seeks to teach mothers how to see what is wrong with their children, whether this be in relation to health, to education, to socialization or happiness. It teaches them about looking for signs and about knowing the limits of their own knowledge.

From a twenty-first-century perspective – in which Armstrong's notion of 'Surveillance Medicine' has become the dominant model of medical practice – it might seem that the 'abnormal child' *is* the object of medical discourse, and hence that this object is not a true hybrid in the sense described above. However, as I have shown, the notion of the abnormal child emerged out of the scientific discourse of the child study movement. Thus it was the sick child, rather than the abnormal child, that was the 'natural' object of medical discourse in the nineteenth century and this changed only very gradually.

An article in the periodical *Babyhood* from 1888 provides evidence of the discursive construction of the hybrid 'medico-maternal' gaze in this period. Written by a medical professional, it is entitled 'A Physician's Hints to Observing Mothers' and informs mothers that:

> The faculty of ready observation is a rare and precious possession. The power to lay clearly and briefly before another the facts that have been observed is equally rare [...]. Together, their value to the young mother is incalculable. (Wood, 1888: 375)

The capacity to observe, advocated so strongly in this article, is conceived partly as an activity that produces medical information – it enables the mother to be 'the Doctor's Assistant' (Wood, 1888: 375). However, intriguingly, this doctor does not see observation exclusively in medical terms. Rather it is as an activity that is (or should be) integral to the maternal role – for example, it enables the mother of twins to 'seize upon differing characteristics' that distinguish her offspring and in this way to ensure that 'individual needs shall be fully met' (1888: 376). In this way, observation is characterized as an activity which, while being a technique of medicine, is also relevant to the mother's general care of her child. We thus might see it as a technique that enables the perception of the sick child but, more radically, makes it possible to perceive (and conceive of) the abnormal child, given that observation is being described here as relevant to all aspects of childcare. Indeed, the abnormal child might, like Foucault's abnormal individual, emerge in relation to a range of different frames of reference, medical or otherwise.

For Foucault, the production of '"abnormal individuals"' through the use of 'expert psychiatric opinion' in the courts leads to a generalization of the crime under discussion (2003: 42, 16). Whereas previously, the court would have been discussing a specific offence, the introduction of 'expert psychiatric opinion' pathologizes a whole 'way of being' – a type of 'conduct' as opposed to a particular 'action' (2003: 16). In a similar way, the categories sick/healthy, contented/discontented imply specific, distinct external referents, and the child can easily be placed in one category or the other. By contrast, the category normal/abnormal is more problematic in that it does not refer to a single external refer-ent but rather to a wide range of possible criteria and also, potentially, to a far more generalized 'way of being'. The concept of normalcy is thus all-encompassing and makes the task of monitoring and detection never-ending.

Conclusion

I have argued in this chapter that an abstract, notional 'normal child' structures our perception of the figure of the disabled child. I suggested that contemporary culture conflates the physical emancipation brought about by new scientific and medical knowledge with an overall eman-cipation, whereas, in fact, the notion of the 'normal child' – which is, in many ways, a product of medical knowledge – may have an oppres-sive impact on the everyday experience of disabled children. I sought to historicize the notion of the 'normal child', suggesting that it was produced by new scientific discourses about the child in the late nine-teenth century. However, it is not simply that the child study move-ment constructed a notion of the normal/abnormal child, which was then popularized in the childcare manual, although this was certainly the case and is part of the story I have told. In addition, I proposed that the 'abnormal child' is a hybrid object, which corresponds neither to medical discourse nor to maternal discourse, but has meaning only when the two discourses seek to find a mutually satisfactory object. In suggesting that the 'abnormal child' is firstly a cultural production and secondly a hybrid object, I have highlighted both its cultural specificity and its instrumentality in enabling the now separate discourses of the medical and the maternal to operate together while maintaining their distinct identities. The term 'abnormal child' thus has no real referent in the external world but is rather a signifier borne of the marriage of convenience of two discourses.

I shall conclude by exploring the relevance of the notion of the '(ab)normal child' as hybrid object in the context of the documentary *Born to be Different*. The documentary mobilizes the notion of the '(ab)normal child' as a tangible, rather than as a conceptual, object, as though it were the 'natural' principle that organizes experience. For example, the opening voiceover to the first episode of Series 4 notes that some of the children will 'succeed at [...] keeping up with their friends, [while] oth-ers will have to struggle just to stay alive'. The term 'keeping up' posits the existence of a tangible normative trajectory (which is constructed as inherently desirable) while simultaneously remaining vague about what 'keeping up' actually means. It is a term that could signify in the context of both medical and parental discourses, suggesting that we are in the domain of hybridity. In Foucault's terms, it pathologizes a whole 'way of being' as opposed to a specific attribute (2003: 16).

Although, as I have argued, *Born to be Different* reproduces hegemonic discourses about normalcy, there are, nevertheless, moments of resistance in the series. The mother of a child with severe physical and intellectual impairments is less concerned about her child's approximation of the norm than about being with her child and enjoying the present moment, since her child's life is likely to be short. Other parents might be understood as operating within a paradigm of 'reproductive futurism' – to use a term coined by Lee Edelman, who argues that 'politics [...] remains [...] conservative insofar as it works to [...] *authenticate* social order, which it then intends to transmit to the future in the form of its inner Child' (Edelman, 2004: 2–3). According to this model, the dominant social order, seeking to perpetuate and reproduce itself, invests in the child as a symbol of futurity. But what of children who do not have certain futures? Anna Mollow has argued that in the case of the disabled child, the hegemonic position can be reframed as '"rehabilitative futurism"': this is the notion that disabled children must be rehabilitated (normalized), in order to offer them the chance of a future (Mollow, 2012: 288). Yet this future is always one that has been imagined not by the child, but by another, imposed from the outside. While it is beyond the scope of this chapter to develop these ideas, it is interesting to note, in the context of *Born to be Different*, that resistance to futurist ideology is paired with resistance to normalizing discourses. The mother in the documentary who seeks not to make her child like others, but rather accepts that child for herself, also resists valuing her daughter in terms of what that daughter might be, or might represent, in the future.

Addendum

After completing this chapter I discovered that the history of the notion of the 'normal child' has been explored by Nikolas Rose in *Governing the Soul: The Shaping of the Private Self* (London: Free Association Books, 1999, 2nd edition, 1st edition 1989) and by Erica Burman in *Deconstructing Developmental Psychology* (Hove, East Sussex: Routledge, 2008, 2nd edition). These are important authors for those of us in the field and are referred to in other chapters in this book. Their scholarship will be discussed in detail in my PhD thesis.

References

Apple, R.D. (1995) 'Constructing mothers: Scientific motherhood in the nineteenth and twentieth centuries', *Social History of Medicine*, 8, 2, 161–178.

Armstrong, D. (1995) 'The rise of surveillance medicine', *Sociology of Health & Illness*, 17, 3, 393–404.

Barker, C. (2011) *Postcolonial fiction and disability: Exceptional children, metaphor and materiality* (Basingstoke: Palgrave Macmillan).

Batten, L.W. (1939) *The single-handed mother* (London: George Allen & Unwin).

Born to be Different 2009. Dir. by Anna Stickland. Series 4, Episode 1. More4. 13 May 2009, 10pm.

Born to be Different 2011. Dir. by Anna Stickland. Series 7, Episode 2. Channel 4. 16 June 2011, 9pm.

Born to be Different 2011. Dir. by Anna Stickland. Series 7, Episode 3. Channel 4, 23 June 2011, 9pm.

Bull, T. (1845) *The maternal management of children, in health and disease*, 2nd edn [first edn 1840] (London: Longman, Brown, Green & Longmans).

Butler, J. (1990) *Gender Trouble: Feminism and the Subversion of Identity* (London: Routledge).

Campbell, H. (1910) *Practical motherhood* (London: Longmans, Green & Co.).

Canguilhem, G. (1991) *The normal and the pathological*, translated by C.R. Fawcett (New York: Zone Books).

Channel 4 2011. http://www.channel4.com/programmes/born-to-be-different, [accessed 15 July 2011].

Chavasse, P.H. (1839) *Advice to mothers on the management of their offspring* (London: Longman, Orme, Brown, Green & Longmans).

Davis, L.J. (1995) *Enforcing normalcy: Disability, deafness and the body* (London: Verso).

Domanska, E. (2008) A conversation with Hayden White, *Rethinking History: The Journal of Theory and Practice*, 12, 1, 3–21.

Donnelly, M. (1986) Foucault's genealogy of the human sciences, in M. Gane (ed.), *Towards a critique of Foucault* (London: Routledge), pp. 15–32.

Edelman, L. (2004) *No future: Queer theory and the death drive* (Durham, NC and London: Duke University Press).

Elliott, H., Ryan, J. & Hollway, W. (2012) 'Research encounters, reflexivity and supervision', *International Journal of Social Research Methodology*, 15, 5, 433–444.

Feder, E.K. (2011) Neutralizing morality: Non-directive counseling of parents of children with intersex conditions. Conference paper at The Language of Illness and Pain, Birkbeck, University of London, 2–3 July.

Foucault, M. (1991 [1977]) *Discipline and Punish: The Birth of the Prison*, translated by A. Sheridan (London: Penguin).

Foucault, M. (2002) [first English edn 1972]. *The archaeology of knowledge*, translated by A.M. Sheridan Smith (London and New York: Routledge).

Foucault, M. (2003) *Abnormal: Lectures at the Collège de France 1974–1975*, translated by G. Burchell (London: Verso).

Frankenberg, R. (1993) *White women, race matters: The Social construction of whiteness* (Minneapolis, MN: University of Minnesota Press).

Giddens, A. (1991) *Modernity and self-identity: Self & society in the late modern age* (Cambridge: Polity).

Hardyment, C. (1983) *Dream babies: Childcare from Locke to Spock* (Oxford: Oxford University Press).

Holt, L.E. (1904) *The Care and Feeding of Children* 3rd edn [1st edn 1894], (London: Sidney Appleton).

Kendall, G. & Wickham, G. (1999) *Using Foucault's methods* (London: Sage).

Liddiard, M. (1924) *The mothercraft manual*, 2nd edn (London: J. & A. Churchill).

Liddiard, M. (1948) *The mothercraft manual*, 11th edn (London: J. & A. Churchill).

Martin, E. & Hine, R. (2008) *A dictionary of biology* (Oxford: Oxford University Press).

McRuer, R. (2006) Compulsory able-bodiedness and queer/disabled existence, in L.J. Davis (ed.), *The disability studies reader*, 2nd edn (Abingdon: Routledge), pp. 301–308.

Mollow, A. (2012). Is sex disability? Queer theory and the disability drive, in R. McRuer & A. Mollow (eds), *Sex and disability* (Durham, NC and London: Duke University Press), pp. 285–312.

Oliver, M. (1990) *The politics of disablement* (London: Macmillan).

Shakespeare, T. (1996) 'Rules of engagement: Doing disability research', *Disability & Society*, 11, 1, 115–121.

Shuttleworth, S. (2010) *The Mind of the Child: Child Development in Literature, Science and Medicine, 1840–1900* (Oxford: Oxford University Press).

Sully, J. (1895) *Studies of Childhood* (London: Longmans, Green & Co).

White, H. (1989) 'Figuring the nature of the times deceased': Literary theory and historical writing, in R. Cohen (ed.), *The future of literary theory* (Routledge: London and New York), pp. 19–43.

Wood, H.L. (1888) 'A physician's hints to observing mothers', *Babyhood*, 4, 48, 375–377.

12

Considerations of an African Childhood Disability Studies

Tsitsi Chataika and Judy McKenzie

Introduction

In this chapter, we explore how childhood disability studies can be theorized within 'African' ways of being and thinking, drawing on a socio-cultural and postcolonial paradigm. We recognize the dominance of theories imported from the global North, and note that the global South indigenous knowledge systems (particularly African communities) have been undermined. We begin our discussion by examining the changing structure of families in Africa and the impact that this has on disabled children. We then move towards conceptualizing disability as a social construct, which is not readily accounted for by the uncritical importation of models and theories into the African context. We recognize the impact of poverty on disabled children in particular and place this in the context of African notions of a collective well-being as expressed in *ubuntu*. We are mindful of the dangers of overgeneralizing for the entire continent and draw primarily, but not exclusively, on specific examples from South Africa and Zimbabwe, in our quest to explore the culturally complex and multi-dimensional daily African experiences of disabled children. We reflect on the literature and our experiences, and make some considerations for an 'African' childhood disability studies, mainly on the basis of issues resonating from these two countries. We promote the use of indigenous knowledge systems. In particular, we appreciate the concept of *ubuntu*, and how it can construct an African Childhood Disability Studies as opposed to the human rights-based approach, which is alien to Africa.

The African child in the family: Intersection with disability

The family is a very strong cultural institution in most African countries, with responsibilities between family members taken seriously. The bond that brings them together is manifested in such activities as having meals together and also holding consultations on various issues affecting the family. Children are members of a broad extended family, and arrangements for their care and upbringing are the concern of not just their biological parents, but also an extensive network of relatives (Nyambedha, Wandibba & Aagaard-Hansen, 2003). A family comprises of biological parents, children, paternal and maternal grandparents, uncles, aunts, nephews, nieces, cousins, and sons and daughters in-law (Nyamukapa & Gregson, 2005). Therefore, members of the extended family automatically become part of the immediate family members. The nuclear family is a foreign concept that came to Africa with colonization and apartheid (Peters & Chimedza, 2000). Any family member can pledge their willingness to take care of any of the wider family relations. Thus, responsibilities would include but are not limited to, providing shelter, clothing, food and tuition fees (Nyamukapa & Gregson, 2005).

In coping with both transient and chronic poverty, the extended family is an important factor in social security in Africa. The extended family system is usually the first point of reference when a problem arises (Nyamukapa & Gregson, 2005). Hospitality and mutual aid towards one's relatives, even quite distant ones, are important cultural values for African ethno-cultural groups (Mararike, 1999), and beneficiaries, in most cases appreciate the assistance, as indicated below:

> I grew up being looked after by my aunt. Though my parents were alive, financially, they were dead. I did not miss my parents that much because my aunt was like a father and mother to me. She was really, really good to me. She never treated me differently from her kids. I owe my aunt everything I have today. (Chataika, 2003: 35)

In South Africa and Zimbabwe, as in many other African countries, communities comprise of a cluster of families or clans. It is also the responsibility of those communities to ensure that children follow community values, norms and beliefs religiously. The understanding here is that it takes the whole village to raise a child. Thus, an individual has little latitude outside the context of the traditional African family and community (Mbiti, 1992).

The idea of the family as a social unit that takes the responsibility of its disabled members is an old one in Africa (Peters & Chimedza, 2000). Under pressures exerted by urbanization and changing patterns of production and employment, however, the institution of the family has weakened substantially. In colonial and apartheid Africa, the consolidated extended family began to break down and was gradually replaced by the nuclear family system with a very loose extended family base (African Rehabilitation Institute, 1991).

The disabled person slowly became the responsibility of the nuclear family (Sait, Lorenzo, Steyn & van Zyl, 2009). Owing to this limited family support and because family members had to work for colonial masters in their fields and factories, disabled people began to be locked away in houses, chained to trees and generally ill-treated, and began to be seen as a 'burden' (African Rehabilitation Institute, 1991).

Although the introduction of education for disabled people by the missionaries in the 1920s was a noble idea, it was however seen as a release from a burden by families of disabled children who managed to be enrolled in special schools (Peters & Chimedza, 2000). Thus, disabled children were institutionalized away from home, and most families valued these institutions more as custodial or respite homes rather than as educational centres. As a result, the majority of children were literally 'dumped' in these institutions, and they were never taken back home by their families. Consequently, from early childhood, young disabled children seemed to get the message that they were unclean, inferior and unworthy. This is against the background that the growing disabled child needs family love and a sense of belonging, just like any other non-disabled child.

The changing nature of families and child rearing is reflected in a study of childcare practices in the informal settlements surrounding Cape Town. Bray and Brandt (2007) established that there are many role players in child-caring in this setting. The notion of a single most responsible caregiver does not fit well in this migratory community. At the same time, they found that children tend to contribute to family care from a young age. However, this might not be the case for disabled children, as reports exist of the extreme loneliness and isolation of disabled children. Parents seem to find it difficult to let their disabled children be cared for by other relations because of fear of sexual and other forms of abuse or neglect (Sait et al., 2009).

Important to note is that families are often torn apart by the birth of a disabled child, although this is slowly changing (Charowa, 2005). While divorce is common among families of disabled children elsewhere, in Africa it is more pronounced and a common practice for the man's relatives to blame a woman who has given birth to a disabled child (Charowa, 2005). For instance, Gara (2007) reported that the absence of a father is a pervasive feature in most South African's families with a disabled child. In Zimbabwe also, a mother of a disabled child shared her experiences:

> I separated from my husband who could not come to terms with the disability of our child and was under pressure from his relatives. (Charowa, 2005: 2)

The United Nations Children's Educational Fund (UNICEF) conducted a study and found out that most of the relatives of the husband's side blamed the disability on the wives (UNICEF, 2006). The caregivers in the focus group related stories of sour relationships between mothers-in-law and their daughters-in-law with disabled children. Most mothers-in-law were said to be angry with a daughter-in-law who 'brought' disabled children into the family, and in most cases, they ended up in broken marriages (UNICEF, 2006).

Parents may even believe the child to be a curse, so they may hide the child as a way of coping with the affliction and retaining social equilibrium. The United Nations Educational, Scientific and Cultural Organization (UNESCO) established that:

> Often these children are excluded from society. They might be hidden away at home if they look different because of fear and superstition. ... Often their needs are not recognised and they are thought to have little to contribute to their community. But this exclusion reduces children's opportunities to learn, grow and develop. (UNESCO, 2001: 10)

One of the authors from Zimbabwe was involved in outreach programmes that identified disabled children, and found out that disabled children were hidden away. In some cases, the family would deny that they had a disabled child in the family. It was only when efforts to locate such children were made through the intervention of local chiefs that disabled children could be identified, for instance, hidden in granaries. However, when one examines the cultural context in the following section, this notion of hiding and rejection is more complex than is apparent from the above discussion.

Cultural conceptions of disability

One of the widely documented conceptions of disability in African contexts is that disabled children are a curse, and therefore should be hidden away (UNESCO, 2001). The reason given for this is that the mothers are being punished for wrongdoing, and that the child is living proof of her error. We believe that this conception is far more complex and relates to the way in which disability is strongly associated with spiritual values. Thus, on the one hand, there are negative beliefs about the role of the mother in giving birth to a disabled child. On the other hand, there is an understanding that a disabled child is a 'gift' from God (McKenzie & Swartz, 2011). This 'gift' is presented as a challenge in which God will support the family and give them the strength to cope. The disabled child is then given an opportunity to live through the will of God, making an important contribution to the life of the caregivers. This highly spiritual understanding of the nature of disability colours the nature of disabled childhood in South Africa.

In a study on resilience and spirituality of Xhosa-speaking families in the Western Cape Province of South Africa, family and the love that they share are seen as a gift from God (Greeff & Loubser, 2008). Thus, parents and caregivers often express the importance of 'love', as exemplified by a mother of a disabled child below:

> I have a child; the only thing that makes me strong is love, accepting him, not to be ashamed of him. To be able to have love makes things easier. (McKenzie & Swartz, 2011)

Muderedzi and Ingstad (2011) also reported positive experiences in Binga (Zimbabwe), where families within the Tonga community did not find it problematic to accept their disabled children. In their study, there were no signs that Tonga families are purposely hiding their disabled children. Although there were historical traces showing that disabled children used to be left to die or were hidden away in rural areas, this is no longer practised. Despite the Tonga people being among the most economically deprived ethnic groups in Zimbabwe, they showed love to their disabled children (Muderedzi & Ingstad, 2011). Thus, parents of disabled children were more concerned about whether or not the child would survive, rather than having a visible impairment. The paradigm shift on the attitudes towards disabled children was attributed to the high mortality of children among the Tonga. Interviewed mothers felt that they had to be grateful to have a surviving child rather than a dead one. Similar findings have been reported among the Tswana people of Botswana (Ingstad, 1997).

Extended dialogues with people in a variety of contexts in Botswana indicated that positive attitudes toward disability may relate to the belief that all abilities, as well as disabilities, contribute to each person's individuality (Geiger, 2010). Inclusion and participation are not universal notions but need to be considered in specific contexts (Turmusani, Vreede & Wirz, 2002). Geiger (2010) provides a case study where a disabled boy, Boiki, could not attend school, along with his siblings, as they lived more than ten kilometres from the closest school. In this context, therefore, school attendance was not significant as an indicator of social inclusion and participation. Boiki was, however, fully included in the daily lives of the neighbourhood in terms of typical play activities that engage multiple age and ability levels simultaneously (Geiger & Alant 2005). Therefore, to say that Africans do not accept their disabled children may be an overstatement, when we take the above findings into account. Consequently, it becomes vital to use a postcolonial lens, when designing an African Childhood Disability Studies. Hence, the focus on care rather than formal education, and belonging rather than independence, have a significant place in the African context.

Disabled children in poverty

A discussion of childhood in Africa needs to take into account the impact of poverty, especially as there is an inextricable relationship between poverty and disability. Malnutrition and limited access to healthcare may cause disability and lead to further poverty in the family unit. This relationship leads to a vicious cycle of increasing poverty and disability. Moreover, disabled family members frequently have higher needs for which resources need to be found (Palmer, 2011). In a study of disabled children in Africa, the African Child Policy forum found that up to 88 per cent of caregivers were unable to meet the basic needs of their children with disabilities. These families found the provision of medical care, assistive devices and transport particularly onerous. Yeo (2003) notes that where the family is struggling for survival the disabled child can be seen as less deserving of medical care and education as they are perceived as a poor investment for the family. However, this picture needs to be tempered with an understanding of traditional ways of coping with limited resources through relying on the collective, embodied in the concept of *ubuntu*.

Ubuntu in African cultures

A distinctive feature of many of the different cultures of Africa is the emphasis on the philosophy of '*unhu*' (Shona), '*ubuntu*' (Ndebele/Nguni) or 'beingness' (Mbiti, 1992). The concept is synonymous with valuing human dignity. Participation within the family and community is valued more than individual differences or other human attributes. Thus, the notion of *unhu/ubuntu* challenges the more individualistic orientation of the global North. In terms of our discussion of childhood disability, the ideas of autonomy, independence and self-determination take on a different aspect in African culture. *Ubuntu* challenges the notion that the individual should be the focus of attention (Mbiti, 1992).

The Shona concept of '*ukama*' (being related to other people) also places inclusiveness at the core of humanness. Through totems and marriages, most Africans are related to each other, and can therefore assist each other in various forms. *Ukama* conveys a sense of wholeness of human situatedness with the 'human world [individual], the natural world [accepted or expected], and the spiritual world [religious or sacred]' (Gonese, 1999: 38). For example, through *ukama*, one can be linked to present and past relatives. Similarly, the Shona dictum, '*munhu wese ihama yako*' (everyone is your relative) is the backbone of Africanhood. Thus, individualism has little latitude in the African context.

For instance, from the *ubuntu* perspective, the idea of disability grants may not be successful if they focus more on the individual, instead of family needs (Nhlapo, Watermayer & Schneider, 2006). In South Africa the income from the care dependency grant is intended to cover the care of a disabled child. However, in situations of poverty, the disabled individual's needs become inextricable from those of the whole family. Thus, disabled children or adults become breadwinners of the family, thus embracing the concept of *ubuntu* (Nhlapo, Watermayer & Schneider, 2006). Consequently, disability grants become the major source of income, instead of being used to address disability-specific needs. This is because Mbiti noted how an individual has little latitude outside the context of the African family and community:

> Whatever happens to the individual happens to the whole group, and whatever happens to the whole group happens to the individual. The individual can only say: 'I am, because we are; and since we are, therefore I am'. (Mbiti, 1992: 109)

Ubuntu can be perceived as a cardinal point in the understanding of the African view of humanity. This implies that various approaches to disability that may work well in the Western world may not apply in an African setting. The *ubuntu* perspective on disability stands in opposition to a discourse of autonomy and human rights as it foregrounds care and interdependency and restricts individual agency. We would like to suggest that care is a central element of disability in the African context. This is so because opportunities are even less available to the child with a disability than to their able-bodied siblings, and the only future that can be imagined is one where the child is well cared for. Furthermore in the absence of rehabilitation and education the child's dependency becomes entrenched. The central question that disability poses in situations of poverty is how disabled children can be supported as they grow up into adulthood. Notions of care and belonging are important. Hence, access to health, education and rehabilitation services becomes a complex issue. Where, then, does this view of focusing solely on assisting the disabled person fit, under the concept of *ubuntu* where individualism has little latitude?

Considerations for an African Childhood Disability Studies

Childhood Studies takes views of childhood and youth as a focus of critical enquiry, by considering a range of perspectives and ideas held by parents, professionals and young people that impact on children's lives and the cultures in which they live. The discipline encourages us to consider the potential of young people to actively contribute to society (Watson, 2012).

In this chapter, we make a connection between childhood studies and disability studies. These approaches are both based in a postmodernist understanding of both disability and childhood being socially constructed; and both question the way in which traditional conceptions of disability and childhood render the disabled person and the child passive, a recipient rather than an agent (Davis, 2006; James, 2010). Children themselves are rarely asked about their lives. Instead, researchers ask parents, teachers or staff of institutions. Similarly, disabled activists have long fought for their voices to be heard above those of medical professionals who have adopted the expert position in relation to disability (Oliver, 1996).

However, the majority of childhood studies literature is located within the Western imagination. Thus the motif of the child, with its conventional abstraction from culture and society, obscures the position of the child by overlooking the many global South children, particularly those from Africa (Ennew, 2003; James, 2010). While the United Nations Convention on the Rights of the Child has become an increasingly powerful legal instrument in protecting the rights of children, the same cannot be said of disabled children. It becomes more important for African childhood researchers and practitioners, as well as disability studies researchers, to reconsider the position of disabled children in the wake of such an influential legal framework. A postcolonial analysis of the emerging Childhood Disability Studies is useful in this regard.

Postcolonial analysis

The articulation of intersecting identities is a significant though ignored area in most disciplines; and the emerging Childhood Disability Studies is no exception. In cases where there are intersections, most of the time, they are defined by the global North and its epistemologies (Chataika, 2012). For instance, disability and childhood studies in Africa have largely been spearheaded by global North scholars. In many cases, the challenge is that the dominant discourse of these disciplines struggles to be framed in the language of African epistemology, but in the Eurocentric pedagogy. The consequences are that African challenges are not solved by African solutions that are likely to be relevant and sustainable. In turn, such a situation changes the way we would engage in 'African Childhood Disability Studies', thus perpetuating alien belief systems that are irrelevant to the African discourses.

One now questions the extent to which global North stakeholders bring along their beliefs and values into the global South space when engaging in childhood disability studies (Chataika, 2012). Sadly, this reproduces the social hierarchies that have always prevailed between global South and global North under colonialism. Unfortunately, the African indigenous knowledge systems and cultural dynamics are undermined. It becomes crucial to adopt a postcolonial understanding and reflect the colonial past, and discover a new way of creating and promoting an African childhood disability studies understanding (Chataika, 2012; Said, 2004). Thus, the use of postcolonial analysis in this chapter helps to explore the indigenous knowledge systems and how that might link to the colonial socioeconomic history and its present relations of inequality (Chataika, 2012).

Concluding remarks

In this chapter, we have argued that concepts from the global North in most cases do not reflect African thought and day-to-day realities. Specifically we have highlighted the notions of family, cultural conceptions of disability, poverty and the importance of *ubuntu* as a value system focused on the collective rather than the individual. The implications of each of these issues are considered in our conclusion.

Western research has moved on from viewing the disabled child as a 'burden' and the impact of disability on the family (Watson, 2012). Current research makes much of encouraging participation and presenting children as social agents who mediate the impact of adult's actions on their lives. African research needs to consider the role of the family carefully because of its different structure and meaning in the African context. The extended family provides a substantially different milieu for the disabled child, and the deep significance of what it means to be part of a whole needs to be highlighted.

The family assumes even greater significance in situations of poverty where the survival of all is in the balance. Where there are no services, where resources are extremely limited and where there is little state-sponsored support, families have to find a way to care for all their family members. This difficult task is one that is deserving of support and should not be undermined by notions of children's agency that place adult and child with different interests.

The significance of *ubuntu* has been discussed at length above. What needs to be emphasized is the possible clash between the individualistic values of a human rights perspective as embodied in the UN Convention on the Rights of People with Disabilities and the collective values of belonging and caring within a hierarchical system that is evident in *ubuntu*. We argue that the African conception of human rights should be embedded in the spirit of *ubuntu* – an aspect of African humanism sustained by the principle of accountability to the ancestral shades.

While Northern research might focus more on children's participation, the importance of protection and provision is abundantly clear in many African contexts (James, 2010). Assumptions about the role of the nuclear family and what constitutes children's and adults' spaces need to be reconsidered in the light of traditional culture, cultures in transition and the unequal effects of globalization on African families. Similarly, the over-regulation of disabled children and their families by medical and care services (McLaughlin & Goodley, 2008) might be viewed very differently by families of disabled people in the global South, who get little or no support in coping with disability in the home.

Having noted these divergences from a Northern perspective, it would not be helpful to shut down the dialogue between North and South in its entirety. The valuable recognition of the voice of disabled children and the acknowledgement of their need to participate in decisions that affect them directly should be incorporated within an African Childhood Disability Studies. Watson (2012) argues for adopting different levels of analysis that can highlight the complex interaction between the disabled person and their environment. Similarly, James (2010) proposes a research agenda within childhood studies that integrates the study of the agency of the child within the larger structural framework within which the child lives. This would imply paying careful attention to all of the issues noted above but would not preclude listening to the voices of children as active agents in their own right.

We might then consider questions such as the following: When we overshadow care by autonomy, is it appropriate in Africa? Are we not contradicting the *ubuntu* concept? How can self-advocacy be seen as something positive in the African context? What would be the role of parents' organizations? To what extent should we avoid encroaching into the African indigenous knowledge systems and engage in a post-colonial analysis? To what extent should we amplify the voices of children, and in particular, disabled children? How can we use the *ubuntu* spirit to raise the voices of disabled children so that they are heard? These and many other questions need to be taken into account when developing an African Childhood Disability Studies.

References

African Rehabilitation Institute (1991) *A report on the needs of the person with disabilities and their families in the rural area* (Harare: Jongwe Press).

Bray, R. & Brandt, R. (2007) 'Childcare and poverty in South Africa' *Journal of Children & Poverty*, 13, 1, 1–19.

Charowa, G. (2005) *Poverty and Gender. Body Blows New International Magazine.* http://www.newintlorg/issues384/body-blows.htmPoverty and Gender NI 384 [accessed 12 February 2012].

Chataika, T. (2003) Policy and provision for disabled students in higher educational institutions in Zimbabwe, Unpublished MEd Dissertation (University of Leeds: Leeds).

Chataika, T. (2012) Postcolonialism, disability and development, in D. Goodley, & B. Hughes (eds), *Social theories of disability: New developments and directions* (London: Routledge), pp. 252–269.

Davis, J.M. (2006) Disability, childhood studies and the construction of medical discourses: Questioning attention deficit hyperactivity disorder: A theoretical perspective, in G. Lloyd, J. Stead & D. Cohen (eds), *Critical new perspectives on ADHD* (London: Taylor and Francis), pp. 45–65.

Ennew, J. (2003) 'Difficult circumstances: Some reflections on "street children" in Africa'. *Children, Youth and Environments* 13, 1. http://cye.colorado.edu [accessed 12 February 2012].

Gara, N. (2007) Effects of caring on mothers of intellectually disabled children in Alice, Eastern Cape, South Africa, Unpublished MPhil Dissertation (University of Cape Town: Cape Town).

Geiger, M. & Alant, E. (2005) 'Child-rearing practices and children's communicative interactions in a village in Botswana', *Early Years*, 25, 83–19.

Geiger, M. (2010) 'Using cultural resources to build an inclusive environment for children with severe communication disabilities: A case study from Botswana', *Children's Geographies*, 8, 1, 51–63.

Gonese, C. (1999) Culture and cosmovision of traditional institutions in Zimbabwe, in B. Haverkort & W. Hiemstra (eds), *Food for thought: Ancient visions and new experiments of rural people* (London: Zed Books), pp. 237–248.

Greeff, A.P. & Loubser, K. (2008) 'Spirituality as a resiliency quality in Xhosa-speaking families in South Africa', *Journal of Religion & Health*, 47, 3, 288–301.

Ingstad, B. (1997) *The myth of the hidden disabled: Studies in African Health and medicine* (New York: Mellen, Lewiston).

James, A.L. (2010) 'Competition or integration? The next step in Childhood Studies?', *Childhood*, 17, 4, 485–499.

Mararike, C.G. (1999) *Survival strategies in rural Zimbabwe* (Harare: Mond Books).

Mbiti, J.S. (1992) *African religions and philosophy* (Nairobi: Heinemann).

McKenzie, J. & Swartz, L. (2011) 'The shaping of sexuality in children with disabilities: A methodological study', *Sexuality and Disability*, 29, 4, 363–376.

McLaughlin, J. & Goodley, D. (2008) 'Seeking and rejecting certainty: Exposing the sophisticated lifeworlds of parents of disabled babies', *Sociology*, 42, 3, 317–335.

Muderedzi, J. & Ingstad, B. (2011) Disability and social suffering in Zimbabwe, in: A.H. Edie & B. Ingstad (eds), *Disability and poverty: A global challenge* (Bristol: Policy Press), pp. 171–188.

Nhlapo, C.M., Watermeyer, B. & Schneider, M. (2006) Disability and human rights: The South African Human Rights Commission, in B. Watermeyer, L. Swartz, T. Lorenzo, M. Schneider & M. Priestley (eds), *Disability and social change: A South African agenda* (Cape Town: Humanities Sciences Research Council Press), pp. 97–107.

Nyambedha, E.O., Wandibba, S. & Aagaard-Hansen, J. (2003) 'Changing patterns of orphan care due to the HIV Epidemic in Western Kenya', *Social Science & Medicine*, 57, 301–311.

Nyamukapa, C. & Gregson, S. (2005) 'Extended family's and women's roles in safeguarding orphans' education in AIDS-afflicted rural Zimbabwe', *Social Science & Medicine*, 60, 2155–2167.

Oliver, M. (1996) Defining impairment and disability: Issues at stake, in C. Barnes & G. Mercer (eds), *Exploring the divide* (Leeds: The Disability Press), pp. 29–54.

Palmer, M. (2011) 'Disability and poverty: A conceptual review', *Journal of Disability Policy Studies*, 200–210.

Peters, S. & Chimedza, R. (2000) 'Conscientization and the cultural politics of education: A radical minority perspective', *Comparative Education Review*, 44, 3, 245–270.

Priestley, M. (1998) 'Childhood disability and disabled childhoods: Agendas for research', *Childhood*, 5, 207–223.

Said, E.W. (2004) *Humanism and democratic criticism* (New York: Columbia University Press).

Sait, W., Lorenzo, T., Steyn, M. & van Zyl, M. (2009) Nurturing the sexuality of disabled girls: The challenges of parenting for mothers, in M. Steyn & M. van Zyl (eds), *The prize and the price shaping sexualities in South Africa* (Pretoria: Human Sciences Research Council), pp. 192–219.

Turmusani, M. Vreede, A. & Wirz, S. (2002) 'Some ethical issues in CBR in developing countries', *Disability and Rehabilitation*, 24, 10, 558–564.

UNESCO (2001) *Overcoming exclusion through inclusive approaches in education: A challenge and a vision* (Paris: UNESCO).

UNICEF (2006) *State of the world's children* (New York: UNICEF).

Watson, N. (2012) 'Theorising the lives of disabled children: How can disability theory help?', *Children & Society*, 26, 192–202.

Yeo, R. (2003) 'Including disabled people in poverty reduction work: Nothing about us without us', *World Development*, 31, 3, 571–590.

13

The Disavowal of Uncanny Disabled Children: Why Non-Disabled People Are So Messed Up Around Childhood Disability

Dan Goodley and Rebecca Lawthom

Introduction – The 'non-disabled'

We know from recent research that disabled children, their families and other allies are subjected to a whole host of responses from people, organizations and systems in society. What we perhaps know less about are the reasons why 'the non-disabled' or 'normative' imaginary responds to disability in terms of the often contradictory processes of fear/fascination; attraction/repulsion; recognition/extermination. Genetics, medicine and clinical psychology formally capture this ambivalent response to childhood disability – recruiting bodies and minds into the psycho-biological register in order to recognize them as disorders while, simultaneously, threatening to erase these bodies/minds as deficient kinds of humanity. Just as important are those informal moments that disabled people experience every day, in mundane and recurring encounters with what we might call the normative imaginary. In this chapter we want to explore this imaginary through the stories of disabled people. Adopting a social psychoanalytic account, we will consider the ways in which disability becomes wrapped up in responses of the non-disabled. We will make, employ and evaluate the concepts of the 'uncanny' and 'disavowal', and consider them in light of stories shared with one of us (Dan). Finally, we will conclude with some thoughts on cure, rehabilitation and therapy for the non-disabled – those poor souls caught up in the normative imaginary – albeit with tongue in cheek.

It is important for us to first acknowledge that not all non-disabled people engage exactly in the same ways to disability. Many of the 'non-disabled' are advocates, friends, supporters, family, parents and partners of disabled people. Some of these people even craft disability studies articles, carry out disability research and write book chapters in texts on childhood disability. Each of us – whether we are disabled or not – is marked by differences associated with class, gender, age, sexuality and ethnicity. Nevertheless, we can say that the 'non-disabled' category exists not as a simple fixed position of humanity but as a register, a subject position, a preferred way of living life and a phenomenon of ableist cultures. Being non-disabled is the preferential ontological state. Remaining non-disabled is a somatic preoccupation of contemporary life. Borrowing from Fanon (1993): the non-disabled is a preferred moral category of contemporary life. And the non-disabled describes a dominant social group, a comfortable space, the White Anglo Saxon Protestant (WASP) heartland of Western liberation (Hughes, 1999: 158). For our purposes, then, the non-disabled is chosen over other synonyms such as the able-bodied (Wendell, 1989), normalcy (Davis, 1995), the normate (Garland Thomson, 2005) or ableist normativity (Campbell, 2009). By deploying the concept 'non-disabled' we are permitted to emphasize the cultural, relational and psychological processes involved in distancing the non-disabled self from the disabled other. The term also acknowledges the tensions and defence mechanisms – in the broadest socio-cultural senses – to be found in a dominant culture that struggles with the precarious nature of trying to be what it often is not. In challenging this comfortable space we can, in some small way, build on feminist disability scholarship from authors and activists such as Garland Thomson (1996; 1997; 2005; 2006), Reeve (2005; 2008), Thomas (1999; 2007) and Wendell (1989; 1996). This ground-breaking work demands – according to Wendell (1996) – social and political theories of disability and, simultaneously, deep understandings of disability that include thinking about the ethical, psychological and epistemic issues of living with disability.

An email

In October and November 2011, one of us (Dan) sent an email request to the Disability Research distribution list (DISABILITY-RESEARCH@ JISCMAIL.AC.UK) hosted by the Centre for Disability Studies at the University of Leeds.

Comrades
I am writing a slightly tongue in cheek (as you can tell by the working title) but also, I hope, serious, article exploring non-disabled people's reaction to disability. I would like to collect stories from list members about non-disabled people's verbal or other responses

to disability that you have witnessed. In writing the article I will be making clear that not all non-disabled people engage in such responses, that many non-disabled people are allies, friends, supporters and parents of disabled people and that we are all marked by differences associated with class, gender, age, sexuality, ethnicity, etc. Moreover, of course, what counts as non/disabled is open to debate. However, I do want the article to expose, hopefully explain and also challenge some of the common reactions of non-disabled society to disability. I have already collected a number of stories from existing disability studies texts, research and my own personal accounts. Some of these include:

'You get that all the time people stare, people comment, or people. ... I would rather people said to me, "What's wrong?" rather than just stare. Then you can hear them as soon as you walk past [whisper sounds].' (Jemma, mother of a disabled child, reported in McLaughlin et al., 2008)

When people comment on my impaired experience I am shocked, amused and angered all at once. (Hewitt, 2004: 13)

A lifetime with psychic armour as sure as skin ... where thousands of daily encounters are layered with danger, disgust or distress. (Lurie, 2004: 85)

'Your child's the naughty boy in my child's class, isn't he?' (A parent's question to the mother of a child with the label of ADHD)

'I never think of you as disabled.' (A common 'positive' comment from friends of the disabled writer Michalko, 2002)

'At least he's not too disabled.' (A health visitor's comments to the mother of a new-born baby)

'Did you read on the web that 52 per cent of the American public would prefer to be dead than disabled?' (Bar chat on a November night)

'You are just so brave, I don't know how you cope.' (A mother's comment to another mother of a disabled child in the playground)

'I don't know how you can work with those people. ... It must be so rewarding to work with those people.' (Contradictory comments from a friend to a key worker for people with learning difficulties)

'I've had coins dropped in my lap by strangers in the street.' (Hewitt, 2004)

'Don't worry about paying, love, we don't charge for retards.'

If you would be willing to share some similar (or not!) stories then please could you email them to d.goodley@mmu.ac.uk. Any reference to these stories in the article would recognize the source

(e.g., personal communication) but, of course, if you would prefer to keep these anonymous then that would be totally fine too.
Thanks for reading
Dan Goodley

What we managed to gather were stories and, in many cases, analytical accounts by the respondents of those stories. This approach to narrative inquiry – which positions the storyteller as commentator and critic – adds a distinct ethico-political weight to the stories collected (for an overview, see Goodley & Clough, 2004). Twenty-five respondents provided stories. Most of the accounts were from disabled people. Non-disabled allies offered a few. No attempt was made to record impairment labels, though stories included experiences of people with physical, sensory and cognitive impairments from countries including Australia, Britain, Canada, Norway, North America, Portugal, Turkey and Zimbabwe. Inevitably, many of the stories reflected on disabled childhoods. The accounts represented here either name respondents or anonymize them, in keeping with the requests of respondents.

Social psychoanalytic encounters

In recent writing (Goodley, 2011a, 2011b) one of us has argued that a social psychoanalytic approach to the study of disablism might permit us to grapple with the complex relationships between culture, society and the psyche. This approach fits well with Hook's (2004: 115) vision of psychopolitics – that is, the explicit politicization of the psychological – which occurs through the placing of a series of ostensibly psychological concerns and concepts within the register of the political. Exteriority rather than interiority. A psychopathological study of the non-disabled excavates the discourses, institutional practices and cultural norms that converge around disability and service the constitution of what is known as 'the non-disabled' or 'normative' imaginary. It seeks to address what Hughes (1999: 164–5) terms as 'the perceptual pathology of non-disablement'. We can add to Hughes' observations that pathology is not simply about negation: disability evokes competing, contradictory and ambivalent responses ranging from hate–love; care–control; charity–extermination; use–refusal. On the same day last year we read the disturbing account of a disability hate crime in the local paper in the morning and by the evening were being stopped outside the supermarket to give generously to a charity raising money for a disabled children's charity: from hate to charity in six hours. What is needed, to paraphrase (Marks, 2002), is a more sophisticated understanding of the meanings and experiences of disability as analytic dynamic, encounters, with a particular focus on non-disabled people's investments and an investigation of the social, cultural and political formations that feed such investments.

The exponential rise in impairment labels we know is a growing common feature of childhood. In the sprawling global medicalization of difference and distress and the pharmaceutical monopolization of unhappiness, disability remains a favoured referent point for the novel and the movie. Disability is something that both haunts and produces humanity. When an ideal life, a functioning body and being sound of mind is understood it can only ever be done so in relation to apparent opposites: the monstrous lives of the poor, broken bodies and lacking intellect (Campbell, 2009; Reeve, 2008). Just as blackness and femininity remain key cultural touchstones of the occidental or patriarchal gaze, disability provides an opportunity to gaze at the exotic and the unexplained (Michalko, 2002). This is the particularly the case in childhood when deviations from the norm risk being made Other.

Neurosis, for Freud, was the sine qua non of a civilized society. Humanity is *necessarily* neurotic in order to struggle, contain and display desires and maintain a bounded sense of self and autonomy. Consequently, certain perceived human differences promote neurotic responses such as phobia, hysteria, fear and compulsive fascination. One of these differences is 'race' in which people of colour are subjected to and objectified by neurotic reactions of non-black others within a broader racist socio-historical landscape (see Fanon, 1976, 1993; Hook, 2004). Another of these differences is disability; promulgating neurotic responses on the part of non-disabled people galvanized by a contemporary disablist society that economically, culturally, socially and psychically excluded disabled people (Thomas, 2007; Goodley, 2011a, 2011b). Interestingly, a pop-psychology website on phobias lists a number of phobias specifically related to impaired body parts, including apotemnophobia (fear of persons with amputations), scotomaphobia (fear of blindness in visual field) and psellismophobia (fear of stuttering) (http://phobialist.com/). Fanon (1993: 141) describes 'the negro' [sic] as a phobogenic object, a concept we can easily apply to disabled children. Phobias are neuroses characterised by fear of an object in which the object is endowed with negative intensions (Fanon, 1993: 142). Where there is fear there is also fascination. Campbell (2009: 128) categorizes a number of non-disabled people's desires for disabled bodies into *devotees* who are attracted to people with a physical disability and their prostheses; *pretenders* who simulate having impaired bodies through mimicry or the use of assistive devices like calipers; and *transableists* who have an overpowering desire to become physically or sensorially impaired. While it is important that we address these perhaps extreme corollaries our analysis must also address the mundane and everyday elements of (disabling) social life.

Neurotic responses – particularly on the part of non-disabled people – say much about wider disabling practices and more personalized reactions to embodied difference. We should seek to deploy psychoanalytic terms to political effect without becoming too reliant on them (Hook, 2004). The first, **the uncanny**, is a term developed by Freudian psychoanalysis and refers to something that is 'undoubtedly related to what is frightening – to what arouses dread and horror ... that class of frightening which leads back to what is known of old and long familiar' (Freud, 1919: 219, cited in Allison, 2004: 277). The uncanny is often offered to explain specific mild forms of anxiety, relating to strange and sinister phenomena in real life and to certain motives (Masschelein, 2003: np). Yet, the uncanny is also a typically ambivalent and contradictory psychoanalytic concept. The first sense is the most literal: domestic, familiar and intimate. The second meaning departs from the positive, literal sense to the more negative metaphorical sense of hidden, secret, clandestine, furtive. What appears unfamiliar and unhomely is actually familiar and homely. Uncanny things are simultaneously familiar and unfamiliar, strange and terrifying, fearful and fascinating (Carlin, 2008). The uncanny extends beyond fear to encompass fascination; we can feel the 'faintly paradoxical emotional tenor of the uncanny' (Seppenan, 2011: 203). When faced with the uncanny we may ask 'why does this strange thing seem so familiar?' 'Why is the uncanny thing provoking such feelings of fear but also fascination?' So, how do we deal with the uncanny? We engage with its contradictory nature through contradiction: we bring it home and expel it; look at and look away; see the familiar and augment the strange.

Wider society – the normative imaginary – has a number of reactions to the uncanny presence of disability ranging from hatred, to benign curiosity, to desire of disability. These reactions might be broadly termed **disavowal**: the simultaneous contradictory and ambivalent response to the uncanny. Drawing on the psychoanalytic writings of Lacan, in recent work Goodley (2012) and Goodley and Runswick-Cole (2012) have suggested that disabled bodies (and minds) expose the ontological insecurities of the non-disabled psyche, body and culture. While all bodies/minds fail to match up to the 'autonomous', whole, speaking subject demanded by the imaginary and symbolic aspects of culture, the non-disabled deal with such failings by finding failings in others.

Disabled people are cast out as the true other: 'You are lacking, not I.' Often, we find children subjected to forms of disavowal from adults, for example, in the case of children's good and responsible behaviour found to be lacking when many adults fail to reach these behavioural standards. Simultaneously, and paradoxically, people mourn the loss of dependence and narcissism associated with their early lives where they were nothing more than a psychic scrambled egg, a desiring body in flux, nurtured by the love of the primary (m) other. Disability – as one of the key cultural markers of dependence – disability *and* child-hood both appear as a reminder of dependence that is so often desired though repressed. Disability is a curious, familiar thing: 'what must it mean to be disabled?' These reactions to disability need to be understood in the emerging socio-cultural and economic context of modernity. Hughes (1999) observes that the oppression of disabled people is umbili-cally linked to the constitution of impairment in modernity. For Dolar (1991: 7) the uncanny came to occupy a place of fear and fascination post-enlightenment: 'Ghosts, vampires, monsters, the undead dead, etc., flourish in an era when you might expect them to be dead and buried, without a place ... [but] they are something brought about by modernity itself.' One might, therefore, suggest that disabled people are the quintes-sential uncanny gothic subject and disavowed object of modern society: precisely because people with labels of physical, sensory or cognitive impairments appear to embody the undead dead – or social death – of modernity's obsession with bodily integrity and rational thought.

The uncanny resides in the space between strange/familiar, alive/dead and animate/inanimate. The only thing we can be certain about is that the non-disabled disavow the uncanny event of disability, with a multi-plicity of potential impacts on the self-worth and identities of disabled people. Disavowal captures those moments of cultural catharsis, projec-tion, anxiety, paranoia, uncertainty and ambivalence on the collective part of the non-disabled towards the phenomenon of disability.

Stories

Our narrative project revealed a number of disavowing reactions to the uncanny presence of disability. We only have space here in this chapter for three points of analysis. These evoke memories from disabled child-hoods and responses to disabled children. The significance of relational exchanges between non-disabled selves and disabled others, and vice versa, are illuminated throughout in each of these accounts. Consequently, the stories bring other key actors into the frame to join disabled children, including adults, professionals, strangers and other community members.

(1) Charitable donations: Giving with one hand and taking with the other

Perhaps one of the most obvious examples of disavowal is found in those clumsy attempts to relate to disability that seeks recognition while combining this with negation:

> My friends with the ASD child get comments like 'We love [your son] regardless of what he has.' Something I would find incredibly offensive. (Anonymous)

Disavowal is encapsulated by the admittedly implicitly ableist saying 'giving with one hand and taking with the other', perfectly captured in the act of charity:

> One time I was in a lift and an old lady wanted to give me money and I told her 'Madam, I don't need it, I work' and she kept saying 'But take it' and I got the money, it was a coin, one euro. She was very insistent and I had to take it otherwise she would be upset. So then she was happy and for me it was fine. She could've given me more money, right? (John, wheelchair user interviewed by Ema Loja)

The normative imaginary charitably responds to the disabled child through looking at her and then looking away. Children are aware of this disavowal and in one case used it to fit their own requirements:

> Memories: My older sister taking me (in my clearly displayed leg splints) to ice cream vans and her explaining that her poor sister is disabled so we would both get free ice cream. (This always worked, ingenious of her, really.) I also used to do this, as awful as it sounds. ... I have one memory of being in Harrods' Food Hall aged about 7 yrs and going round and asking for free stuff because I was aware that being a disabled child was a powerful thing, particularly to adult women. I ended up with a massive cardboard tub full of free Harrods' cakes and nibbles. ... I also, aged around 8/9 (this is really bad), would write to celebrities telling them about my disability (the 'woe is me' story) and they would send me free stuff. ... I had obviously caught on to the fact that it was very easy to evoke people's pity, and that this could be productive. (Anonymous)

The choice of the term 'productive' is insightful here: in which the uncanny of disability is utilized as a means to access one end of the axes of disavowal: the giving.

(2) Ontological invalidation: Putting the 'dis' in disability

When disabled people are reacted to as an 'inexplicable oddity' (Malec, 1993: 23) they risk becoming objects frozen in the vision of the non-disabled (Hughes, 1999):

> If you are 'other' to me, I see you primarily as symbolic of something else – usually, but not always, something I reject and fear and that I project onto you. (Wendell, 1996: 250)

Wendell argues that we live in a world structured for people who have no weaknesses, in a socio-cultural context that values the activities of labour and commodity exchange, the physically strong and the ideally shaped. Disavowing that which sits/stands outside of the normative imaginary threatens the very ontological status of disabled people: fear brings with it distrust and dismissal:

> So, briefly, I was raised in a home where being different was just not acceptable. We pretended I could see better than I did, and never, never, talked about it. There was a complete no talk zone, and Mom particularly would tear out someone's throat if they ever mentioned it. ... Remarkably narcissistic if you think about it. (Anonymous)

The second account draws on psychoanalytic discourse – accounting for the invalidation on the part of the non-disabled as a clear example of narcissism – lending support to the argument that, whether we like it or not, we live in a psychoanalytic culture (Parker, 1997). Such language fills institutions of work, education and family:

> I'm talking to a cousin who I think of as one of the healthier members of the extended family. While discussing types of literature, she drops the sentence 'I just can't handle the physical manifestation of difference'. There it was, 9 words that sum up my family and much of my experience dealing with people in the world. As my brother has said on more than one occasion, 'it's just hard to watch'. (Anonymous)

Therapeutic discourse around the pathological potentiality of disabled people may shape anticipations and expectations:

> By the time I had the accident I had lots of visits at the hospital. And the nurses said to my mother 'People are all very nice at the beginning but be prepared because she is going to be alone, people will disappear.' (Mary, wheelchair user interviewed by Ema Loja)

Indeed, measures of ontological validation moved to considerations of the (de)valuing of specific impairments:

> Also a number of non-disabled people have said to me 'I would rather be deaf than blind' ... now this one really confuses me as I am assuming that they have never been either deaf or blind and why would anyone say that to someone that is registered blind as I am and I think the fact that they don't seem to see anything offensive in saying this to me is what really amazes and at times amuses me. I am still trying to figure that one out! (Patricia Mary McCarthy)

Ontological invalidation is not solely a case of misrecognition or denial. In some cases recognition of embodied difference led to mimicry and mockery:

> I have walked all my life visibly different from non-disabled people. People tend to comment on my walking style or ask questions. Children sometimes try to mimic my slightly asymmetrical walking style: 'Amazing that you can walk that way!' (This was said by a teenager who tried to mimic my walking style but did not succeed.) (Karen Mogendorff)

Attempts to redress invalidation might coalesce around some clumsy form of disavowal:

> I sometimes have this strange thing, seeing a disabled person, that I obstinately do not want to stare, and then on top of that, that I think that the disabled person sees this, sees me not looking; and then I sometimes do look, to restore the balance! (Anonymous)

For Malec (1993: 22) many 'persons with disabilities are made into the "other" by many, if not most, non-disabled people'. Disability is a key mark of difference – of the other – distinct from the non-disabled self. This difference 'seems to at once attract and repel' (Malec, 1993: 22). For Malec disability is something to be imagined by the non-disabled self, which risks turning the uncanny disabled other into an object of curiosity, thus overshadowing the complex humanity and personhood of the disabled other:

> It is seldom comfortable to know that one is on display, on stage, as it were. ... In public places, whether alone or with friends, I'm

constantly aware of remarks made by others in my hearing. ... When I am alone, I know that I am being watched as I walk down the sidewalk or through buildings. I am told that people in cars will turn their heads as they pass me in order to continue staring. (Malec, 1993: 22)

For Dolar (1991) uncanny figures represent the limits of enlightenment and, therefore, the limits of the self. Uncanny figures come to occupy a contradictory place: they exist as romantic figures seemingly outside of the realm of modernity but also as frightening/fascinating targets for invalidation.

(3) Disability kitsch and common parlance: Consuming and fetishizing disability

One of the strongest contributions of a social psychoanalytic account of disablism is the significance it attaches to the fetishization of difference. The psychopathology of the non-disabled also appears to reside in the practices of consuming disability and imbuing these cultural disability artifacts with certain values (McGuire, 2011; Mallett & Runswick-Cole, 2012). If kitsch is a form of art that is considered to be a worthless imitation of art of recognized value then popular cultural images of disability are appropriated and fetishized by the artless non-disabled in their depictions of disabled people. One respondent informed us;

> Quite a few stories about how non-disabled people react towards people with dwarfism. A lot of the comments made by people relate to dwarf stereotypes such as Snow White and Willy Wonka. Here are a few things that have been said to me:
> Where's Snow White?
> Where's the yellow brick road?
> Do you get your clothes specially made?
> Are your parents small?
> You're the right size for a blowjob.
> I know a dwarf from Scotland, do you know him?
> Also like the quote below: a Doctor once asked my Mam if I had thought about joining the circus.

While the social history of people with restricted growth or 'Dwarfism' has been marked by a move from oppressive curiosity/exoticism to disability politics and activism (Adelson, 2005), the account above would suggest that people with restricted growth are still reacted to as uncanny

exotic creatures fuelled by kitsch views of the small person as panto-
mime actor. Similarly, one respondent wrote of the response of another:
'He's autistic? [She said] Well, all the celebrities have them, don't they?
It's like a Gucci handbag or Jimmy Choos.'. Following Snyder and
Mitchell (2006) different disability discourses have served specific tem-
poral and spatial requirements of non-disabled culture:

> This happened many, many years ago – 1970s – when I was at a local
> football match. The local team was playing badly and a man behind
> me started shouting: 'Come on, you're playing like a bunch of spastics!'
> After the third repeat, I turned around and yelled: 'Do me a favour
> mate, I wouldn't have that lot in MY bloody team!' At half time he
> came and apologized and promised never to say it again. (Anonymized)

The reiteration of disability slang such as 'spastic' says much about the
insecurities of the non-disabled. Hook's (2004: 132–3) appropriation of
Fanon is useful here when he asks of the racist:

> Why, one is tempted to ask the racist, is it necessary continually to
> reaffirm, to reiterate and act out one's own racial superiority to con-
> tinually point out the Other's supposed inferiority if this is simply a
> known fact? Why does one continually need to reassert this fact of
> one's own superiority and the Other's inferiority if you are so confi-
> dent of it?

Similar questions could be leveled at the non-disabled to ask them why
so much time is being spent painting monstrous, kitsch representations
of disability.

Conclusions

So what tactics can we identify in troubling the cultural disavowal of
the uncanny presence of disability? Hughes (1999: 162) suggests that
resistance is the refusal to be seen as one is supposed to be seen by the
eye of power. Wendell (1998: 253) sites potential in sitting outside of
the normative imaginary:

> Not only do physically disabled people have experiences, which are
> not available to the able-bodied, they are in a better position to tran-
> scend cultural mythologies about the body, because they *cannot* do
> things that the able-bodied feel they *must* do in order to be happy,
> 'normal' and sane. (Wendell, 1998: 253)

Clearly, the politics of disability and disabled people's politics must continue to be supported and celebrated as direct methods and means for challenging the psychopathological tendencies of the non-disabled. This work should be extended to include disabled children whose early years are often subjected to such psychopathological responses. One wonders if these same activists could engage themselves in cure and rehabilitation services aimed at the non-disabled. Perhaps new forms of therapy – undergirded by disability studies theories and activism – would proliferate in ways. Could we set up self-help groups, drop-in centres and neighbourhood visits run by disabled activists in which we tackle the psychopathologies of the non-disabled? Perhaps we could produce documents that tackle the inadequacies, the social incompetencies and maladaptive functioning of the normative imaginary? The United Spinal Association, for example, has produced a booklet *Disability Etiquette: Tips on interacting with people with disabilities*. There are many very useful suggestions here for the non-disabled to engage with disabled people in respectful, considerate and thoughtful ways. This is a good start, but one wonders if the deeper issues of the non-disabled can be sufficiently challenged through a set of fairly normative and common-sensical rehabilitative procedures.

Rather than reinvigorating the arenas of psychology, therapy and rehabilitation we might better see our task as targeting the deeply insidious nature of normality and ableism endemic within our culture. This task is, of course, more complex but fits well with the primary challenge of critical disability studies. On one level this means reconfiguring those aspects of humanity that we value. Jim Overboe's work is helpful here as he demands us to rethink how we understand humanity and its reliance upon normative shadows: a normativity that threatens to impose a 'wholesome, ideal, flavorless, odorless, colorless, and non-threatening identity upon me' (Malec, 1993: 23). Respondents to Dan's original email request were good enough to share resources including websites which publicize encounters with the non-disabled, and in some cases amusingly turn the tables to pathologize 'the normals' among us:

www.holeyvision.blogspot.com

http://www.touretteshero.com/

http://isnt.autistics.org/dsn-npd.html_– Institute for the Study of the Neurologically Typical Project Cleigh: http://www.raggededgemagazine.com/cgi-bin/mt/mt-comments

In embracing these counter-cultural narratives one would hope that we continue to challenge the representational frames of disabling society against which normative discourses are framed and registered.

References

Adelson, B.M. (2005) *Lives of dwarfs: Their journey from public curiosity toward social liberation* (Piscataway, NJ: Rutgers University Press).

Allison, L. (2004) 'Reading the Uncanny', Review of *The Uncanny* by Nicholas Royle. (Manchester: Manchester University Press, 2005), *The Cambridge Quarterly*, 33, 3, 277–281.

Campbell, F.K. (2009) *Contours of ableism: Territories, objects, disability and desire* (London: Palgrave Macmillan).

Carlin, N. (2008) 'The uncanny hospital ro:m: Psychoanalytic observations and recommendations for pastors and chaplains', *The Year 2008 Proceedings of the Association for the Scientific Study of Religion, South West*, pp. 68–80.

Davis, L.J. (1995) *Enforcing normalcy: Disability, deafness, and the body* (New York: Verso).

Dolar, M. (1991) '"I shall be with you on your wedding-night": Lacan and the uncanny', *October*, 58: *Rendering the Real*, pp. 5–23.

Fanon, F. (1976) *The wretched of the Earth*, trans. Constance Farrington (London: Penguin).

Fanon, F. (1993) *Black skins, white masks*, 3rd edn (London: Pluto Press).

Freud, S. (1919) The uncanny, in J. Strachey (ed.), *The standard edition of the complete psychological works of Sigmund Freud*, Vol. xvii (London, 1919), pp. 219–252.

Garland Thomson, R. (ed.) (1996) *Freakery: Cultural spectacles of the extraordinary body* (New York: New York University Press).

Garland Thomson, R. (1997) *Extraordinary bodies: Figuring physical disability in American literature and culture* (New York: Columbia University Press).

Garland Thomson, R. (2005) 'Feminist disability studies', *Signs: Journal of Women in Culture and Society*, 30, 2, 1557–1587.

Garland-Thomson, R. (2006) 'Ways of staring', *Journal of Visual Culture*, 5, 2, 173–192.

Goodley, D. (2011a) *Disability Studies: An interdisciplinary introduction* (London: Sage).

Goodley, D. (2011b) 'Social psychoanalytic disability studies', *Disability and Society*, 26, 6, 715–728.

Goodley, D. (2012) Paul Hunt + Lacan = Psychoanalytic disability studies, in D. Goodley, B. Hughes & L.J. Davis (eds), *Disability and social theory* (London: Palgrave Macmillan), pp. 179–194.

Goodley, D. & Clough, P. (2004) 'Community projects and excluded young people: Reflections on a participatory narrative research approach', *International Journal of Inclusive Education*, 8, 4, 331–351.

Goodley, D. & Runswick-Cole, K. (2012) 'The body as disability and possability: Theorising the "leaking, lacking and excessive" bodies of disabled children', *Scandinavian Journal of Disability Research*, 15, 1, 1–19.

Hewitt, S, (2004) Sticks and stones in a boy, in B. Guter & J. Killacky (eds), *Queer crips: Disabled gay men and their stories* (New York: Haworth Press), pp. 117–120.

Hook, D. (2004) Fanon and the psychoanalysis of racism, in D. Hook (ed.), *Critical psychology* (Lansdowne, South Africa: Juta Academic Publishing), pp. 114–137.

Hughes, B. (1999) 'The constitution of impairment: Modernity and the aesthetic of oppression', *Disability & Society*, 14, 2, 155–172.

Lurie, S. (2004) Loving you, loving me, in B. Guter & J. Killacky (eds), *Queer crips: Disabled gay men and their stories* (New York: Haworth Press), pp. 83–86.

Malec, C. (1993). 'The double objectification of disability and gender', *Canadian Woman Studies*, 13, 4, 22–23.

Mallett, R. & Runswick-Cole, K. (2012) Commodifying autism: The cultural contexts of 'Disability' in the academy, in D. Goodley, B. Hughes & L.J. Davis (eds), *Disability and social theory* (Basingstoke: Palgrave Macmillan), pp. 33–41.

Marks, D. (2002) 'Some concluding notes – healing the split between psyche and social: Constructions and experiences of disability', *Disability Studies Quarterly*, 22, 3, 46–62.

McGuire, A. (2011) Representing autism: A critical examination of autism advocacy in the neoliberal West, Unpublished PhD thesis, University of Toronto.

McLaughlin, J., Goodley, D., Clavering, E. & Fisher, P. (2008) *Families raising disabled children: Enabling care and social justice* (London: Palgrave).

Masschelein, A. (2003) A homeless concept: Shapes of the uncanny in twentieth-century theory and culture, Issue 5, *Image and Narrative*, Online Magazine of the Visual Narrative. http://www.imageandnarrative.be/inarchive/uncanny/anneleenmasschelein.htm [accessed 2 December 2012].

Michalko, R. (2002) *The difference that disability makes* (Philadelphia, PA: Temple University Press).

Mitchell, D. & Snyder, S. (2006) Narrative prosthesis and the materiality of metaphor, in L. Davis (ed.), *The Disability Studies reader*, 2nd edn (New York: Routledge).

Parker, I. (1997) *Psychoanalytic culture* (London: Sage).

Reeve, D. (2005) Towards a psychology of disability: The emotional effects of living in a disabling society, in D. Goodley & R. Lawthom (eds), *Disability and psychology: Critical introductions and reflections* (London: Palgrave), pp. 94–108.

Reeve, D. (2008) Negotiating disability in everyday life: The experience of psycho-emotional disablism, Unpublished PhD thesis, University of Lancaster.

Seppanen, J. (2011) 'Lost at sea: The Freudian uncanny and representing ecological degradation', *Psychoanalysis, Culture & Society*, 16, 2, 196–208.

Snyder, S.L. and Mitchell, D.T. (2006). *Cultural locations of disability*. Chicago: University of Chicago Press.

Thomas, C. (1999) *Female forms: Experiencing and understanding disability* (Buckingham: The Open University Press).

Thomas, C. (2007) *Sociologies of disability, 'impairment', and chronic illness: Ideas in disability studies and medical sociology* (London: Palgrave).

United Spinal Association (2008) Disability etiquette: Tips on interacting with people with disabilities, United Spinal Association, 75–20 Astoria Boulevard, Jackson Heights, NY, 11370–1177. http//:www.unitedspinal.org [accessed 3 December 2012].

Wendell, S. (1989) 'Toward a feminist theory of disability', *Hypatia*, Special Issue: *Feminist Ethics and Medicine*, 4, 2, 104–124.

Wendell, S. (1996) *The rejected body: Feminist philosophical reflections on disability* (New York: Routledge).

14
Research with Dis/abled Youth: Taking a Critical Disability, 'Critically Young' Positionality

Jenny Slater

Introduction

> The need to listen carefully, or to find a way to take seriously the words of youth depends not only on methodological issues but on theoretical ones as well (Biklen, 2004, 722).

Disability is too often side-lined, returned to, added on, or omitted altogether from research surrounding youth. In this chapter I want to argue for the productive potential of appreciating disability and disabled youth, not as entities to be considered separately from other research concerning young people, but as places to begin wider anti-oppressive theorizations of youth.

I begin by outlining how youth has been conceptualized as a post-war socio-cultural category in a UK context, and the consequences this has for research with disabled youth. Looking first at the emergence of 'the teenager', I contrast service-driven approaches to youth research with research coming from the discipline of youth subcultural studies, highlighting how different research approaches position youth differently. In the former youth are largely considered passive within service-based transitions, whereas in the latter young people are considered to be actively resisting and subverting the cultural commodity (Priestley, 2003). I ask where disability fits in. I find disabled youth have been excluded from youth subcultural research, and that present-day research continues to take a service-based approach considering young disabled people's 'transitions to adulthood'. Service-based research focuses on disabled youth's future endeavours, as, it is hoped, 'normative adults'. I worry that such research can fail to: (1) appreciate here-and-now experiences of being young; and (2) expand notions of 'activity' to incorporate and celebrate endeavours of dis/abled youth outside of service-provision. Furthermore, such approaches leave the ableism that surrounds normative adulthood dangerously intact, and therefore do not aid in a theoretical repositioning of youth. I argue that broadening research around disabled youth challenges approaches to research and can alter, how we think about and with all young people.

Drawing on Butler's notion of 'critically queer' (1993) and McRuer's (2006) 'severely disabled', I therefore lay down my methodological gauntlet: to develop cultures of critical youth within research. These are cultures that are conscious of and vigilant to adulthood normativity. I outline four requirements for cultures of critical youth: (1) researcher reflexivity; (2) intersectionality; (3) transdisciplinary engagement; and (4) questioning an inside/outside academia divide. I use the term dis/abled youth to highlight that and argue that broadening our research around youth, including Critical Disability Studies (Goodley, 2011) perspectives, can help us find less oppressive and exclusionary ways of thinking through, and with, the lives of *all* young people. In this chapter, therefore, I argue for the productive potential of appreciating disability and disabled youth as places to begin wider anti-oppressive theorizations of youth. I turn first to consider how post-war youth research has positioned young people.

Post-war conceptions of youth in research

Youth as a cultural category is a post-war concept (France, 2007). Whereas youth research previously resided within studies of child development (and questions of what is 'a/typical'; Berk, 2010), the emergence of 'the teenager' brought with it new socio-cultural studies of youth. A desire to make a world 'fit for heroic young soldiers', aided by greater Western affluence and the development of the welfare state resulted in new services aimed at young people. Youth research developed in relation to these services: considering young people's transitions to adulthood within service-provision (France, 2007). Young people's positioning within this research was as pawns being passively passed from one institution to another (France, 2007; Priestley, 2003).

During the same period, young people as a group were for the first time in possession of disposable incomes. Therefore, youth consumer markets developed alongside state-funded services. Hence, the rise of 'subcultures' – teddy boys, mods, rockers, and so on (Hodkinson, 2008). 'Moral panic' at the influx of subcultures (France, 2007) positioned young people paradoxically. Young people were deemed to be passively appropriated by markets. However, subcultural activity was seen as a dangerously over*active* response to market appropriation (Hall & Jefferson, 2006b). Young people were demonized as deviant, disruptive and dangerous. As a new academic discipline, youth subcultural studies aimed to counter this. It challenged the idea that young people were passively appropriated by markets, arguing that relationships between young people and markets were dialectic. Ethnographic subcultural research conceptualized 'deviant behaviour' as metaphorical of wider social change: simultaneously acting within, reflecting and challenging political landscapes (Hall & Jefferson, 2006a).

Yet, there was little engagement between youth subcultural and service-based research. The latter continued to rest upon notions of young people's passivity (France, 2007). The anxiety evoked by the new status of 'teenager' in fact legitimized further service-provision. Youth services would ensure young people were 'on track' to become the new adult generation post-war Britain desired (France, 2007). We see from the above that different approaches to research position young people differently (Biklen, 2004). Whereas service-based research conceptualizes youth as passive (Priestley, 2003), youth subcultural studies challenges young people's 'deviant' behaviour: telling stories of active young people (Hall & Jefferson, 2006a). Yet, in the late 1970s and 1980s criticisms emerged that youth subcultural theorists focused solely on public, spectacular accounts of white, male youth – ignoring often more private accounts of young women (see, for example, McRobbie, 1980, 1982, 1990, 2000; McRobbie & Garber, 2000). Since the 1980s, missing accounts of gender, and to a lesser extent race and sexuality, have been considered (Rattansi & Phoenix, 2005). Perhaps unsurprisingly, disability is rarely mentioned (R. Butler, 1998). McRobbie and Garber (2000) highlight that youth subcultural researchers were drawing on what were new theories of deviance, which considered so-called deviant activity within wider societal and cultural practices. They argue that, with the possible exception of sexual deviance, girls and women were not considered excitingly deviant *enough* to be celebrated within these frameworks: could we say the same for disabled youth, with its connotations of paternalism and passivity? To bring these arguments up to date, I turn to consider current depictions of disabled and young people in welfare-cutting neoliberal Britain.

Media depictions of young and disabled people

Consultation done for the government strategy *Positive for Youth* (Department for Education, 2011: 6–7) reported that young people feel negatively stereotyped by the media, with 'boys feel portrayed as "drug taking antisocial criminals" and girls as "sexually promiscuous fashionistas"'. Although unhelpful, this narrative of activity is far from depictions we are offered of disability. The same year a survey commissioned by *Scope* reported that disabled people had experienced increased hostility, discrimination and physical attacks, and attributed this to ministers 'portraying people with disabilities as scroungers as they seek to cut the number of people on disability benefits' (Boffey, 2011). Disabled youth are not considered the dangerous, disruptive hoodies and hooligans often portrayed in the media (Slater, 2012b). An overarching discourse of disability links it with passivity. Consequentially, disabled young people are routinely positioned as 'passive youth' (Slater, 2013, f.c.).

This does not, however, mean that the demonization of disabled young people is any less. Neoliberalism is, to deliberately use an ableist idiom, about 'standing on your own two feet'. Thus, passivity acts as a threat to the desired neoliberal subject (Giroux, 2009; Kelly, 2006). Discourses surrounding those construed as passive therefore soon slip from the paternalistic (victims/charity cases), to the demonizing (burdensome/a drain on society), resulting in what Garthwaite (2011) calls a 'language of shirkers and scroungers' surrounding disability. Rhetoric of passivity is used to justify service cuts, with the violent consequences as reported by *Scope* above. The absurdity of such representations is illustrated when it is taken into account that the cuts slash funding to the very tools disabled people use to lead 'independent', 'productive' lives. Changes from *Disability Living Allowance* to *Personal Independence Payments* in the UK, for example, leaving disabled people unable to afford vehicles, personal assistants and so on, which allow them to work (P. Butler, 2012).

Goodley and Runswick-Cole (2012) ask us to consider our readings and writings of disabled children. When youth subcultural researchers argued that young people are not passively appropriated by markets, but actively engaged within and shaping them (Hall & Jefferson, 2006a; McRobbie, 2005), they attempted to tell different stories about young people. From the above we see the importance, as both allies to dis/ abled youth, and disability and youth researchers, of telling different stories from the ones generally depicted in the media about dis/abled youth. Today, youth subcultural research has largely subsided, thought unsuitable for an interconnected, postmodern world (Muggleton & Weinzierl, 2003). Service-based approaches to researching youth have also declined, considered more appropriate in immediate post-war years with clearer coming-of-age signifiers, such as marriage, and more distinct boundaries between education and work (Blatterer, 2010). That is, unless the focus is on disabled youth (Priestley, 2003). Not only has disability not entered the world of youth subcultural studies (in its heyday, or since), but much research surrounding disabled youth continues to be affiliated with service-provision and disabled young people's 'transitions to adulthood' (see, for example, Beresford, 2004; Caton & Kagan, 2007; Hudson, 2006; Morris, 1999, 2002; Smith, 2010; Winn & Hay, 2009). My concern is that the stories shared about disabled young people do not adequately reposition disabled youth. I turn now to expand upon these concerns.

Disabled youth and research: Portrayals and concerns

Messages from service-based research around disabled youth often tell us that disabled youth are no different from their non-disabled peers. We are told that young disabled and non-disabled people have the same aspirations, but material and attitudinal barriers make it harder for disabled youth to meet these aspirations. One way of removing barriers is through services that young people themselves should be in control of (Hendey & Pascall, 2002; Morris, 1999, 2002; Rabiee, Priestley & Knowles, 2001). Morris (2002: 10) notes that service providers should 'recognise that transition is a process, rather than a series of assessments and reviews; and that disabled young people's transition to adulthood may well take longer – because of the barriers they face – than that of their non-disabled peers'. Hendry and Pascall (2002: 273) argue that disabled young people aspire to 'achieve adulthood through employment, to gain resources for independent living in their own choice of housing, wider social networks, escape from poverty, and a sense of contributing to society'. Morris (2002: 7) is not alone when she highlights that 'sex and sexuality figure as important issues in the transition to adulthood for non-disabled young people but adults do not always recognise that disabled young people will have the same sexual feelings as others of their age'.

I do not dispute these arguments, which indeed hold strategic political legitimacy. Disabled youth are more likely to be accessing services than their non-disabled peers, and research is necessary to review and revise these services. Murray (2002: 3) voices two disabled young people's comments that a segregated leisure scheme in their area 'saved their lives' as it allowed them to make friends with other disabled young people and realize that the isolation they were feeling in mainstream school was also being experienced by their peers. Research has to make clear the potentially devastating impact of removing service-provision for disabled youth and their families. Furthermore, we have already seen that along with a loss of services comes an onslaught of media demonization and misrepresentation. Portraying disabled youth as having the same aspirations of independence and financial self-sufficiency as their non-disabled peers (Hendey & Pascall, 2002) can help debunk stereotypes of dependency and unproductiveness that surround disability. However, although I see a time and place for the arguments presented above, their dominance of research around disabled youth poses concerns for me. I stress these below, before turning to propose the development of critically young methodologies.

1. Research that focuses on future adulthood endeavours fails to appreciate different here-and-nows of being 'young' and 'disabled'

That there is a need to assert that the aspirations of disabled young people are similar to those of their non-disabled peers is telling. It speaks of the general assumption that to be disabled is to be different – should we be surprised that disabled and non-disabled young people have similar hopes and dreams? Non-disabled and disabled young people are, after all, living in the same society, which prioritizes the attributes of 'adulthood' (I outline these further below, and in Slater, 2013, f.c.). Arguably, messages of what it is to be 'adult' are delivered louder and stronger to disabled young people and others that it is worried are less likely to meet convention (Kelly, 2006). Scholars have noted that although young people's priorities tend to be 'here-and-now' experiences of fun and friendships, even *leisure* services for disabled youth focus on 'learning life skills, increasing independence and/or self-esteem' (Murray, 2002: 2) and preparing for a 'meaningful life without work' (Priestley, 2003: 93). Add to this an 'overcoming' or 'supercrip' narrative of disability (Barnes, 1992; Deal, 2003), and we understand that disabled young people may feel the pressure to meet up to adulthood expectation more than their non-disabled peers in order to 'prove themselves'. My worry is that this denies them to time and space to (1) 'be young people' (in whatever form this may take); and (2) be/come as disabled people (Ferguson & Ferguson, 2001).

2. Service-based approaches to research fail to expand notions of 'activity'

We have already seen how disabled people, including disabled youth, are portrayed as passive. We should learn from history the dangers of such a depiction. The rhetoric of 'the burden to society' has been used before with devastating consequences during the Holocaust (Hughes, 2001). The British government and media are today painting similar pictures (Garthwaite, 2011). It is therefore vital that any research with disabled youth rightly positions them as valued, active and politically engaged citizens. To do this, we need to expand conceptions of the 'active citizen'.

According to the UK policy document *Positive for Youth* (Department for Education, 2011) young people should actively engage 'in all decisions that affect their lives'. When young people engage in politics outside of adult and government-mediated consultation, however, the response is less-than favourable. Those involved in the UK 'riots' of 2011, for example, were not considered in relation to a wider politics of inequality and alienating political systems, but pathologized through an entourage of racist media rhetoric aimed at black and working-class youth (Brand, 2011). For disabled young people, anger and frustration is often individualized as challenging behaviour. The 'good' 'active' neoliberal subject is one who is economically active, yet politically docile (Barber, 2007). Although passivity acts as a threat to the neoliberal subject, we do not want our young people to be too active, as we do not consider youth as rational. To be rational, one must be adult (Burman, 2008b). Therefore, active youth without adult mediation leads to depictions of criminal, unstable and, in terms of politics, naively idealist young people (Giroux, 2009; Kelly, 2003, 2006).

Despite the criticisms relayed above, youth subcultural studies has been given the rare accolade of delivering positive messages of active young people (Hodkinson, 2008). Rather than routine demonization, youth subcultural researchers considered so-called 'deviant' activity within wider societal and cultural practices. Could method/ologies such as those utilized by youth subcultural researchers help us reframe young dis/abled people as active outside of adult mediated consultation? I come back to the need for transdisciplinary conversations below.

3. Ableist adulthood normativity remains intact

We have seen that young people do not make up a homogeneous group. How they are positioned depends upon a host of intersectional identities. I have synthesized just a few of the contradictory messages we are delivered about young people. Whereas black boys and working-class youth, for example, may be considered over-active and demonized as hoodies and hooligans (Giroux, 2009), disabled youth's positioning simultaneously works from and supports notions of passivity and paternalism that surround disability (see Slater, 2013, f.c. for a fuller account). The linking factor is that all these young people evoke anxiety as they are deemed 'off track' to meet normative signifiers of adulthood; they challenge the pedestalled 'neoliberal man'. They are, therefore, 'youth at risk', and subject to a host of professional interventions (Kelly, 2003). That 'certain types' of young people continually fail in embodying adulthood normativity of course says more about the priorities of Western neoliberal society than it does about the individuals in question. One of our jobs as youth researchers, whatever axis of identity we approach it from (be it disability, gender, race, class, or so on), is to question these hallmarks. Rather than challenge, the service-based literature I cited above 'emphasises independence, achieved through separation from parents, financial self-sufficiency and establishment of heterosexual relations' (Gordon & Lahelma, 2002: 2); thus confirming normative constructions of adulthood.

Davis (2002) warns us that taking a purely rights-based approach to disability activism can result in attempts to mirror the already established rights of the normative (non-disabled, white, heterosexual male) subject, rather than striving for a society accepting of different ways of living. Some have within CDS have attempted to counter this, turning the gaze from disabled bodies to consider concepts of 'ableism'. Campbell explains ableism as:

> A network of beliefs, processes and practices that produces a particular kind of self and body (the corporeal standard) that is projected as the perfect, species-typical and therefore essential and fully human. Disability then is cast as a diminished state of being human. (Campbell, 2009: 44)

My above review of literature surrounding disabled youth highlights that the concept of ableism is rarely utilized in studies concerning disabled youth. Instead the portrayal we are offered is that disabled youth are 'just like anybody else', striving for normative, and I stress ableist, adulthood (Slater, 2013, f.c.).

To expand my argument, let me consider one of the major markers of adulthood: independence (Gordon & Lahelma, 2002). Youth is seen as a time that bridges childhood dependency and adulthood autonomy (Burman, 2008b). As Hughes (2001) highlights, fighting for and troubling our conceptions of independency has been at the crux of disability activism. Under neoliberal agendas, rather than considered as socially constituted, autonomy has been fetishized into some biologically inherent: something you either do or do not have. Those not deemed to be in 'possession' of 'autonomy' are excluded from numerous endeavours.

As young people move towards 'adulthood', it is expected they become 'autonomous', 'independent' beings: it is a notion that fails to incorporate the often interconnected lives of disabled youth (Shildrick, 2009; Ware, 2005). Current political times make those taunting signifiers of adulthood ever more illusionary, not just for disabled youth, but for all young people. Adulthood independence is merely a façade some of us manage to hide behind (Shildrick, 2009). All youth researchers, therefore, can learn by turning the gaze away from dis/abled youth to consider the ableism and other axes of normativity inherent to undertheorized and implicit conceptions of adulthood (Slater, 2013, f.c.).

Developing critically young methodologies

I therefore call for new approaches to thinking about and researching with youth, which are inclusive to the experiences of all young people. To do this we must challenge normative developmental assumptions around what it is to be 'adult'. There are examples within critical psychology (Burman, 2008a, 2008b), youth studies (Wyn & White, 1997) and the new sociology of childhood (James, 2007) that question traditional developmental discourse, and the devalued, incomplete-adult status of children and young people. Yet, these tend to neglect experiences of disability. Furthermore, CDS texts questioning normative assumptions surrounding 'neoliberal man' (Campbell, 2009; Davis, 2002; McRuer, 2006), alongside the organic intellectuals of disability movements (Hughes, 2001), have done much of our questioning-ableist-adulthood work for us. Yet, within these, adulthood is not a phenomenon critically engaged with, but the unspoken assumption (Slater, 2013, f.c.), and therefore CDS arguments are rarely included in studies of youth. Reaching out and engaging between disciplines, by taking CDS approaches alongside more 'liberatory' method/ologies emerging from disciplines such as youth subcultural studies, could help us not only in research with disabled youth, but to find less oppressive ways of conceptualizing and conducting research with all young people. For me, this approach involves developing cultures and methodologies in which to be 'critically young'.

I opened this chapter by quoting Biklen (2004). She told us that listening to young people requires theoretical, as well as methodological repositionings. We have seen the different ways young people are conceptualized, dependent on the approach taken to research. A critically young method/ology, therefore, begins with a theoretical repositioning of dis/abled youth, through a critique of adulthood normativity. Butler (1993) distinguishes between being virtually queer, 'which would be experienced by anyone who failed to perform heterosexuality without contradiction and incoherence (i.e., everyone)', and critically queer, which would mean 'working to the weakness in the norm', using the inevitable failure to meet up to this 'ideal' as a way of mobilizing (cited in McRuer, 2006: 30). McRuer draws on this to distinguish between being virtually disabled and what he terms 'severely disabled':

> Everyone is virtually disabled, both in the sense that able-bodied norms are 'intrinsically impossible to embody' fully and in the sense that able-bodied status is always temporary. [...] What we might call a critically disabled position, however, would differ from such a virtually disabled position; it would call attention to the ways in which the disability rights movement and disability studies have resisted the demands of compulsory able-bodiedness and have demanded access to a newly imagined and newly configured public sphere where full participation is not continent on an able body. (McRuer, 2006: 30)

Just as McRuer (2006) argues in reference to disability, I argue the impossibility of embodying adulthood. None of us are the independent and financially self-sufficient autonomous body neoliberal rhetoric would like us to believe (Shildrick, 2009). We are all, therefore, some hybrid form of child and adult, and can all be critically young.

To be critically young requires us to be vigilant to and consciously work against adulthood normativity; to use our inevitable failure to meet up to adulthood normativity as a way of mobilizing. Adulthood is an ableist and heteronormative concept (Slater, 2013, f.c.). Being critically young therefore requires us to be simultaneously critically queer and severely disabled. Being critically young opens up the possibility of 'a newly imagined and newly configured public sphere where full participation is not contingent on an able body' (McRuer, 2006: 30), nor on the embodiment of adulthood ideals. I argue below that there may be times when we need to strategically argue disabled youth into normative adulthood, for the sake of survival. However, developing cultures of critical youth allows us to begin celebrating the non-conformists of youth and disability, *for*, rather than *despite* their differences to adulthood. I go one step further than those in the new sociology of childhood, therefore: not only approaching young disabled people as social actors with views to share, but arguing that their marginal position is an advantage to 'imagining adulthood otherwise' (Shildrick, 2004). I believe cultures of critical youth can be beneficial to all young, and not-so-young, people. To all of those who fail to embody adulthood normativity; i.e. everyone (McRuer, 2006).

I turn to outline briefly four requirements I believe necessary for youth and disability researchers to begin embracing cultures of critical youth.

1. Reflexivity

Drawing on Butler (1993), a critically young methodology uses the inevitable failure to meet up to adulthood normativity as a way of mobilizing. Like the 'able-body', adulthood norms are strongly engrained into Western culture and convention. To be critically young, therefore, requires conscious researcher reflexivity in order to recognize and shout about our own failures to embody adulthood normativity. 'Adulthood' needs to be interrogated alongside and over 'youth', to enable us to cross-examine our own devaluing of children and young people as less-than-adult.

2. Intersectionality

It is obvious, yet depressingly routinely denied, that dis/abled young people are also gendered, sexed, raced, classed beings (Goodley, 2011; Priestley, 2003). Our identity positionings help us to navigate the world (Woodward, 1997). In my PhD research (Slater, 2012a) I found young disabled people fighting to be recognized not just through narratives of disability, but through their aged identities, gendered identities, raced identities, sexual identities, and so on. To not take an intersectional approach to research undermines young disabled people's own efforts to assert their multiplicities of intersecting identities. Furthermore, we have seen in this chapter how intersectional identities position young people differently. The expectations put upon different young people are similarly dependent on a host of intersectional identities. Garland-Thompson's (2002: 24) term 'paradoxical liberties' is useful to us. Although sometimes the different expectations put on young people may seem oppositional, it is too simple to say that one side is 'liberated' while the other is 'oppressed'. Feeling constrained by and excluded from certain discourses, such as those of normative femininity and sexuality, can be similarly angst-inducing (Slater, Ágústsdóttir & Haraldsdóttir, 2012) – harking to the importance of questioning normative expectation at whatever angle it comes at us.

3. Transdisciplinary engagement

Intersectional approaches to research therefore *demand* transdisciplinary engagement. Telling different stories of disabled youth must happen not only within CDS, but across (and outside) academic disciplines. I have argued that disability is rarely considered in more critical studies of youth. Disability needs to enter the imaginations of those outside disability studies. Furthermore, disability researchers can learn from other disciplines, such as youth subcultural studies, the new sociology of childhood and critical psychology. In this chapter I have touched upon youth subcultural studies, as a discipline that has told positive accounts of active young people (Hodkinson, 2008), yet failed to engage with disability (R. Butler, 1998). 'Plundering' (Hughes, Goodley & Davis, 2012) theories and methodologies from other academic disciplines can help us in our own (different) story-telling projects.

4. Questioning an inside/outside academia divide

Moreover, the repositioning of disabled youth must not remain within academia. Hughes (2001) writes of how organic intellectuals of disabled people's movements have reconceptualized independence. Spending time with disabled youth through my PhD research showed me that challenging dis/ability, youth and adulthood,is already going on through day-to-day interactions of disabled youth (Slater, 2012a). Our job as disability researchers is to support and enhance those challenges to normativity. We need to help share these stories so they are cast not as devalued difference, but productive places we can all learn from. One way we can do this is by challenging an inside/outside of academia divide. The 'opening up' of academia provided by this book, sharing the stories of disabled children, young people and their families alongside more 'traditionally academic' texts, exemplifies the kinds of academic queering a critically young methodology demands.

Conclusion

At the end of this chapter it is important to assert that I am not calling for an end to service-based research around disabled youth. Neither do I feel we are at a point in time where it is never important to argue disabled youth into normative becoming-adult discourse. For the wider war of critical youth to occur without casualty, it will involve different battles, dependent upon time and place. For families, friends, practitioners, researchers and other allies of disabled youth, there may be times when supporting disabled youth means asserting them as normative becoming-adults. On the other hand, when and where it is safe to do so, one can be a critically young ally to disabled youth by questioning adulthood normativity.

What I am calling for, therefore, is for youth and disability research-ers to learn from one another, in order to broaden their methodological thinking. Importantly, a critically young culture must extend beyond academic arenas. It is about influencing service-provision; writing publicly through both research channels and the social media; valuing first-hand experiences of youth and disability alongside, on a par with and above academic texts; but also reflexively noticing our everyday mundane interactions. For those of us already able to assert ourselves within normative adulthood discourse, and/or are speaking from a prioritized position that allows us safely to do so, the task is to take up a critically young positionality in all aspects of our lives. When we feel ourselves 'slotting into' what may be oppressive or exclusionary to our comrades, we need to resist it, and shout about our difference from whatever idealized form it may take. Our task is to unhook youth from adulthood expectation, and relieve dis/abled young and not-so-young people of the pressures of trying to be the mythical adulthood norm. Only then will we be part of a critically young culture within which we celebrate the multiplicity of ways dis/abled people 'do' disability, youth and adulthood.

References

Barber, B.R. (2007) *Consumed: How markets corrupt children, infantilize adults, and swallow citizens whole* (New York: W.W. Norton).

Barnes, C. (1992) *Disabling imagery and the media: An exploration of the principles for media representations of disabled people.* http://www.leeds.ac.uk/disability-studies/archiveuk/Barnes/disabling%20imagery.pdf [accessed 2 December 2012].

Beresford, B. (2004) 'On the road to nowhere? Young disabled people and transi-tion', *Child: Care, health and development*, 30, 6, 581–587.

Berk, L.E. (2010) *Development through the lifespan*, 5th edn (Boston, MA: Pearson Education).

Biklen, S.K. (2004) 'Trouble on memory lane: Adults and self-retrospection in researching youth', *Qualitative Inquiry*, 10, 5, 715–730.

Blatterer, H. (2010) 'The changing semantics of youth and adulthood', *Cultural Sociology*, 4, 1, 63.

Boffey, D. (2011) 'Disabled people face abuse and threats of violence after fraud crackdown', *The Observer*. http://www.guardian.co.uk/society/2011/may/15/disability-living-allowance-scope-cuts [accessed 2 December 2012].

Brand, R. (2011) 'Big Brother isn't watching you', *The Guardian*, p. 4. Retrieved from http://www.guardian.co.uk/uk/2011/aug/11/london-riots-davidcameron [accessed 2 December 2012].

Burman, E. (2008a) *Deconstructing developmental psychology* (Hove: Routledge).

Burman, E. (2008b) *Developments: Child, image, nation* (Hove: Routledge).

Butler, J. (1993) *Critically queer: Bodies that matter* (London: Routledge), pp. 223–242.

Butler, P. (2012) 'Disability cuts: Thousands of us will become prisoners in our own homes', *The Guardian*. http://www.guardian.co.uk/global/patrick-butler-cuts-blog/2012/jun/26/disability-benefit-cuts-will-damage-motability-carundustry [accessed 2 December 2012].

Butler, R. (1998) Rehabilitating the images of disabled youth, in T. Skelton & G. Valentine (eds), *Cool places: Geographies of youth cultures* (London: Routledge), pp. 83–100.

Campbell, F.K. (2009) *Contours of ableism: The production of disability and abledness* (Basingstoke: Palgrave Macmillan).

Caton, S. & Kagan, C. (2007) 'Comparing transition expectations of young people with moderate learning disabilities with other vulnerable youth and with their non-disabled counterparts', *Disability & Society*, 22, 5, 473–488.

Davis, L.J. (2002) *Bending over backwards: Disability, dismodernism, and other difficult positions* (New York and London: New York University Press).

Deal, M. (2003) 'Disabled people's attitudes toward other impairment groups: A hierarchy of impairments', *Disability & Society*, 18, 7, 897–910.

Department for Education (2011) *Positive for Youth: A new approach to cross-government policy for young people aged 13 to 19* (London: HMSO).

Ferguson, P.M. & Ferguson, D.L. (2001) 'Winks, blinks, squints and twitches: Looking for disability, culture and self-determination through our son's left eye', *Scandinavian Journal of Disability Research*, 3, 2, 71–90.

France, A. (2007) *Understanding youth in late modernity* (Maidenhead: Open University Press).

Garland-Thomson, R. (2002) 'Integrating disability, transforming feminist theory', *NWSA Journal*, 14, 3, 1–32.

Garthwaite, K. (2011) '"The language of shirkers and scroungers?" Talking about illness, disability and coalition welfare reform', *Disability & Society*, 26, 3, 369–372.

Giroux, H. (2009) *Youth in a suspect society: Democracy or disposability?* (New York: Palgrave Macmillan).

Goodley, D. (2011) *Disability Studies: An interdisciplinary introduction* (London: Sage Publications Ltd).

Goodley, D. & Runswick-Cole, K. (2012) 'Reading Rosie: The postmodern disabled child', *Education and Child Psychology*, 29, 2, 53–66.

Gordon, T. & Lahelma, E. (2002) 'Becoming an adult: Possibilities and limitations – dreams and fears', *Young*, 10, 2, 2–18.

Hall, S. & Jefferson, T. (2006a) Once more around: Resistance through rituals, in S. Hall & T. Jefferson (eds), *Resistance through rituals: Youth subcultures in post-war Britain*, 2nd edn (Oxon: Routledge), pp. vii–xxxii.

Hall, S. & Jefferson, T. (eds) (2006b) *Resistance through rituals: Youth subcultures in post-war Britain*, 2nd edn (Oxon: Routledge).

Hendey, N. & Pascall, G. (2002) *Becoming adult: Young disabled people speak* (York: Joseph Rowntree Foundation).

Hodkinson, P. (2008). Youth cultures: A critical outline of key debates, in P. Hodkinson & W. Deicke (eds), *Youth cultures: Scences, subcultures and tribes* (Oxon: Routledge).

Hudson, B. (2006) 'Making and missing connections: Learning disability services and the transition from adolescence to adulthood', *Disability & Society*, 21, 1, 47–60.

Hughes, B. (2001) Disability and the constitution of dependency, in L. Barton (ed.), *Disability, politics and the struggle for change* (London: David Fulton Publishers), pp. 33–34.

Hughes, B., Goodley, D. & Davis, L.J. (2012) Conclusion: Disability and social theory, in D. Goodley, B. Hughes & L.J. Davis (eds), *Disability and social theory: New development and directions* (Basingstoke: Palgrave Macmillan), pp. 308–318.

James, A. (2007). 'Giving voice to children's voices: Practices and problems, pitfalls and potentials', *American Anthropologist*, 109, 2, 261–272.

Kelly, P. (2003). 'Growing up as risky business? Risks, surveillance and the institutionalized mistrust of youth', *Journal of Youth Studies*, 6, 2, 165–180.

Kelly, P. (2006) 'The entrepreneurial self and "youth at-risk": Exploring the horizons of identity in the twenty-first century', *Journal of Youth Studies*, 9,1, 17–32.

McRobbie, A. (1980) 'Settling accounts with subcultures: A feminist critique', *Screen Education*, 34, Spring, 37–49.

McRobbie, A. (1982) *Jackie*: An ideology of adolescent femininity, in B. Waites, T. Bennett & G. Martin (eds), *Popular culture, past and present: A reader* (Kent: The Open University), pp. 263–283.

McRobbie, A. (1990) *Feminism and youth culture* (London: Routledge).

McRobbie, A. (2000) The culture of working class girls, in A. McRobbie (ed.), *Feminism and youth culture*, 2nd edn (London: Macmillan Press), pp. 44–66. http://www.gold.ac.uk/media/working-class-girls.pdf [accessed 2 December 2012].

McRobbie, A. (2005) *The uses of cultural studies: A textbook* (London: Sage).

McRobbie, A. & Garber, J. (2000) Girls and subcultures, in A. McRobbie (ed.), *Feminism and youth culture*, 2nd edn (London: Macmillan Press), pp. 12–25.

McRuer, R. (2006) *Crip theory* (New York: New York University Press).

Morris, J. (1999) *Move on up: Supporting young disabled people in their transition to adulthood* (Essex: Barnardo's).

Morris, J. (2002) *Young disabled people moving into adulthood foundations: Analysis informing change* (York: Joseph Rowntree Foundation).

Muggleton, D. & Weinzierl, R. (2003) What is 'Post-subcultural Studies' anyway?, in D. Muggleton & R. Weinzierl (eds), *The Post-subcultures reader* (Oxford: Berg), pp. 3–23.

Murray, P. (2002) *Hello! Are you listening? Disabled teenagers' experiences of access to inclusive leisure* (York: Joseph Rowntree Foundation).

Priestley, M. (2003) *Disability: A life course approach* (Cambridge: Bridge Press).

Rabiee, P., Priestley, M. & Knowles, J. (2001) *Whatever next? Young disabled people leaving care* (Leeds: First Key).

Rattansi, A. & Phoenix, A. (2005) 'Rethinking youth identities: Modernist and postmodernist frameworks', *Identity*, 5, 2, 97–123.

Shildrick, M. (2004). 'Performativity: Disability after Deleuze', *Scan: Journal of media arts culture*, 1 3. http://www.scan.net.au/scan/journal/display.php?journal_id=36 [accessed 2 December 2012].

Shildrick, M. (2009) *Dangerous discourses of disability, subjectivity and sexuality* (New York: Palgrave Macmillan).

Slater, J. (2012a) Constructions, perceptions and expectations of being young: A critical disability perspective, Unpublished PhD thesis, Manchester Metropolitan University.

Slater, J. (2012b) 'Stepping outside normative neoliberal discourse: Youth and disability meet – the case of Jody McIntyre', *Disability & Society*, 27, 5, 723–727.

Slater, J. (2013, f.c.) Playing grown-up: Using critical disability perspectives to rethink youth, in A. Azzopardi (ed.), *Youth: Responding to lives – An international handbook* (Rotterdam: Sense Publications).

Slater, J., Ágústsdóttir, E. & Haraldsdóttir, F. (2012) Queering adulthood: Three stories of growing up, Paper presented at the Child, Youth, Family and Disability Conference, Manchester Metropolitan University.

Smith, P. (2010) 'Transition failure: The cultural bias of self-determination and the journey to adulthood for people with disabilities', *Disability Studies Quarterly*, 30, 1. http://dsq-sds.org/article/view/1012/1224 [accessed 2 December 2012].

Ware, L. (2005) Many possible futures, many different directions: Merging Critical Special Education and Disability Studies, in S. Gabel (ed.), *Disability Studies in education: Readings in theory and method* (New York: Peter Lang Publishing), pp. 103–124.

Winn, S. & Hay, I. (2009) 'Transition from school for youths with a disability: Issues and challenges', *Disability & Society*, 24, 1, 103–115.

Woodward, K.M. (1997) *Identity and difference* (London: Sage Publications).

Wyn, J. & White, R. (1997) *Rethinking Youth* (London: Sage).

15
Concluding Thoughts and Future Directions

Katherine Runswick-Cole and Tillie Curran

In this concluding chapter, we revisit aims of the book and touch on some of the key messages and themes highlighted throughout the text. We draw out the authors' agenda for future directions, we revisit the aims of the book and touch on some of the key messages and themes highlighted throughout.

The first aim of this text was to discuss and develop the future agenda for disabled children's childhood studies. First-hand accounts were presented as Part I, 'Voices for Creative Theory, Policy and Practice'. In their reflections on their childhoods, disabled children and adults and their family members revealed their experiences and their aspirations. What emerged strongly from the voices in the first section was that disabled children want people to listen to them. This is, of course, nothing new and yet, despite the UN Convention on the Rights of the Child (UNICEF, 1989) and the explicit call to adults to listen to the views and aspirations of all children, including disabled children, disabled children and young people tell us that this is still not happening in their lives.

In Part I, Stevie and Billie Tyrie tell us that disabled children are both the 'same' and 'different' from other children. Disabled children have hopes and dreams like other children, but they also tell us that these aspirations are not recognized or supported by those around them. Friendship emerges as an important issue for disabled children as it is for many non-disabled children. Jo Skitteral (Chapter 4) talks about the value of peer support, but Billie Tyrie (Chapter 2) tells us that friendships are often made difficult for disabled children, especially when those around them are unaccepting of difference.

The complexities of listening to disabled children in research, especially when adult gate-keepers are present, is closely linked to the roles that families play for disabled children, but they also tell us of supportive, accepting and enabling families (Chapters 1, 2, 5 and 9). Their families have actively resisted discriminatory practices in many ways and they show how hard they work to raise the expectations of the 'public', professionals and wider family. The anger and emotional labour this often entails for disabled children, their mothers, families and communities is highlighted by all the authors in Part I and is the focus of Katherine Runswick-Cole (Chapter 9). The accounts of disabled children and historical accounts of disabled people's childhood make the impact of policy in everyday life very clear and, as Sonali Shah suggests (Chapter 7), 'new understandings of the past can frame the future'. It seems that the future agenda for disabled children's childhood studies should focus on listening to disabled children in ways that recognize that their hopes and aspirations. As Grech (Chapter 8) and Shah (Chapter 7) stress, listening to disabled children gets away from individualized views towards understanding experiences within specific situations and socio-economic policy practices.

The second aim is to show how disabled children are involved in research and to raise the ethical issues that emerge when carrying out research with disabled children. We know that disabled children feel that no one is listening to them but, at the same time, we know that they are under constant scrutiny and surveillance by 'professionals' (Chapters 11 and 14) who measure their behaviour and development in reference to the 'norm'. The complexities of ethical research with children are examined in detail in Chapter 1 and Chapter 6, and they remind us that this is and should be an ongoing concern for disabled children's childhood studies.

Several chapters take a narrative approach to research with disabled children (Chapter 6, 7 and 9), but they stress that stories are never just about the lives of individuals, and rather they reveal personal narratives that speak of and to society and culture. It is also through stories that disabled children can resist and challenge the discourses that circulate about them. All the chapters presenting research studies show how key ethical considerations and judgements are made throughout the research process. David Abbott (Chapter 6) calls for honesty in research and its publication, and Shaun Grech (Chapter 8) calls for a serious rethinking of research agendas and relations to end colonial practices. The use of research is also an important concern, and Tillie Curran (Chapter 10) encourages professionals to participate in research and education projects with disabled children and disabled adults to experience alternative relations of authority.

The authors in this text could be described as collectively using plunder as method (Chapter Hughes, Goodley and Davis, 2012) as they draw on a wide range of theories and theorists. On the other hand, they are meticulous in their decision-making about theory. None of the chapters depend on the child development and medical discourses that have dominated the literature pertaining to disabled children. As Tillie Curran (Chapter 10) points out, studies of disabled children's development or medical conditions are not studies of their childhoods. The authors draw on a wide range of theories and extend their application. Sonali Shah's work is firmly rooted in the social model of disability (Chapter 7) whereas Shaun Grech questions the use of social model theory in global South contexts. Jenny Slater takes an overtly Critical Disability Studies perspective in which she examines the interconnections between disability, youth and gender and the intersections between Disability Studies and Queer Theory. Dan Goodley and Rebecca Lawthom (Chapter 13) turn to psychoanalysis to interpret the 'normal', Katherine Runswick-Cole to the work of the sociologist Hochschild and Tillie Curran and Harriet Cooper (Chapter 11) to the work of Foucault in their accounts.

The issue of ableism emerges throughout the book. Most chapters show how children's lives are overshadowed by ableist assumptions and expectations (Chapters 9 and 14). Jo Skitteral (Chapter 4) begins by questioning the very idea that there is such a thing as 'good' or 'bad' bodies, a theme Harriet Cooper (Chapter 11) returns to in her sustained questioning of the 'normal child'. We know from Linda Derbyshire (Chapter 5) that when bodies are described negatively and then labelled, this has an impact on disabled children's future choices and life chances.

The third aim of the book is to reflect on North/South global relations, the imposition of Western concepts of disability and childhood and developments that engage with postcolonial theory. Shaun Grech and Tsitsi Chataika and Judy McKenzie draw our attention away from the dominant global North accounts of disabled children's childhood studies and encourage us, instead, to consider how global North and global South accounts might be in dialogue with one another. Tsiti Chataika and Judy McKenzie (Chapter 12) remind us of the need to deconstruct 'Western' accounts while Shaun Grech (Chapter 8) calls for a move beyond a focus on the individual and a recognition of different family and community structures that goes beyond fetishizing and exoticizing the lives of disabled children in the global South to consider 'community rights'.

Each author locates their study, and some are clearly critical of the history of Western concepts and practices around childhood and disability that continue to underpin welfare approaches. The 'normal' constructions and statements from 'normal people' are the problem to be analyzed for Dan Goodley and Rebecca Lawthorn (Chapter 13), and Jenny Slater (Chapter 14) shows how the category of youth has limited understanding of young people's diverse experiences. This critique of the West is a starting point towards what Shaun Grech calls 'a genuinely global disabled children's childhood studies'. He opposes 'epistemic violence' – the practices that silence the global South, ignore and continue colonial history and impose models of 'development'. He advances engagement with the global South though recognition of specific complex issues and for intervention to support community-based action for poverty reduction. The connections between the global North and South are key to understanding poverty and its reduction.

The overall purpose of the book was to explore disabled children's lives without the child development, health and service development focus that tends to limit the scope of current policy and professional literature in the West. The chapters show the areas that professionals, policy-makers and research commissioners can engage with that is very much about every aspect of disabled children's well-being. The book highlights the violence and poverty experienced by disabled children and young people that is brought about by 'non-disabled' people's behaviour and inaction and the far-reaching impact of global North socio-economic policy. The authors focus on how different life can be when people are listened to and how much emotional and practical work goes into 'writing back' and resisting excluding behaviour and policies. The emerging agenda within the book includes suggestions about how to bring about change.

Perhaps, the hope from this book is that there will be moments when disabled children's childhood studies can, and should, retreat to make space for, as Freyja Haroldsdottir would say, 'simply' childhoods.

References

Hughes, B., Goodley, D. & Davis, L. (2012) Conclusion: Disability and social theory, in D. Goodley, B. Hughes & L. Davis (eds), *Disability and social theory* (Basingstoke: Palgrave Macmillan), pp. 308–318.

UNICEF (1989) *United Nations Convention on the Rights of the Child* (Geneva: Office of the High Commissioner for Human Rights).

Index

Made in the USA
Middletown, DE
11 January 2018